Idaho

John Gottberg
Photography by William H. Mullins

COMPASS AMERICAN GUIDES
An Imprint of Fodor's Travel Publications

Compass American Guides: Idaho

Editor: Shannon Kelly
Compass Senior Editor: Jennifer Paull
Design: Tigist Getachew, Chie Ushio
Creative Director: Fabrizio La Rocca
Photo Editor and Archival Researcher: Melanie Marin
Editorial Production: Evangelos Vasilakis
Map Design: Mark Stroud, Moon Street Cartography
Production Manager: Matthew Struble

Cover photo (Lost River Range in central Idaho): William H. Mullins

Third Edition
Copyright © 2009 Fodor's Travel, a division of Random House, Inc.
Maps Copyright © 2009 Fodor's Travel, a division of Random House, Inc.

ISBN 978–1–4000–0741–7

Compass American Guides, 1745 Broadway, New York, NY 10019
PRINTED IN CHINA
10 9 8 7 6 5 4 3 2 1

For Elaine, who inspired me to come to Idaho

C O N T E N T S

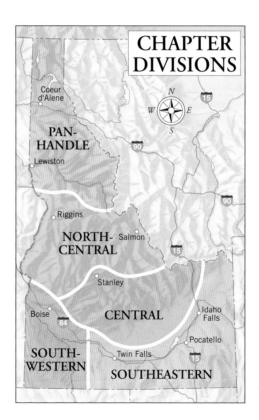

LITERARY EXTRACTS
& TOPICAL ESSAYS

IN EACH CHAPTER

MAPS

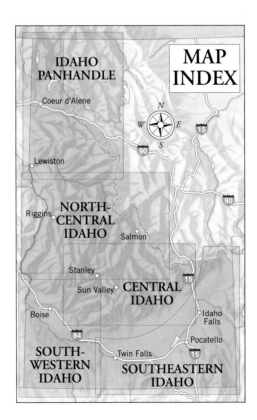

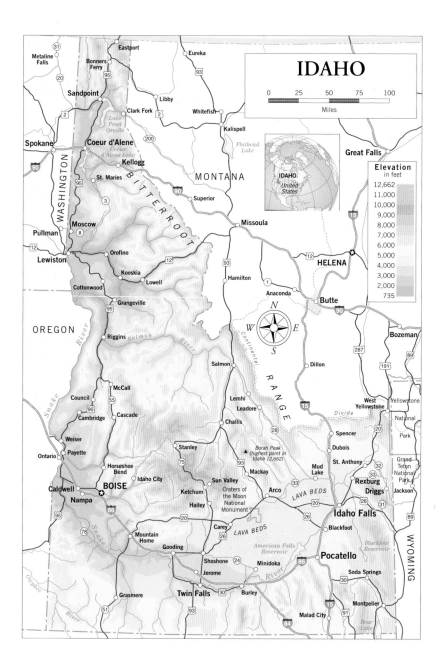

IDAHO

Miles
0 25 50 75 100

Elevation
in feet
12,662
11,000
10,000
9,000
8,000
7,000
6,000
5,000
4,000
3,000
2,000
735

IDAHO
United States

Metaline Falls
Eastport
Eureka
Bonners Ferry
Sandpoint
Libby
Clark Fork
Whitefish
Kalispell
Lake Pend Oreille
Spokane
Coeur d'Alene
Coeur d'Alene Lake
Kellogg
St. Maries
Great Falls
Flathead Lake

WASHINGTON
MONTANA

BITTERROOT
Superior
Moscow
Missoula
Pullman
HELENA
Lewiston
Orofino
Kooskia
Lowell
Hamilton
Cottonwood
Anaconda
Butte
Grangeville
N W E S
Bozeman
OREGON
Salmon River
Riggins
River
Salmon
Dillon
RANGE
Continental
McCall
Lemhi
Leadore
Council
Challis
West Yellowstone
Yellowstone
Cambridge
Divide
National
Weiser
Spencer
Park
Ontario
Payette
Stanley
Dubois
Grand Teton National Park
Horseshoe Bend
Borah Peak (highest point in Idaho 12,662)
St. Anthony
Jackson
Cascade
Mackay
Mud Lake
Rexburg
Driggs
Caldwell
BOISE
Idaho City
Sun Valley
Arco
LAVA BEDS
Nampa
Ketchum
Craters of the Moon National Monument
Idaho Falls
Hailey
Carey
LAVA BEDS
Blackfoot
Mountain Home
Blackfoot Reservoir
Gooding
American Falls Reservoir
Pocatello
Shoshone
Minidoka
Soda Springs
Jerome
River
Grasmere
Twin Falls
Burley
Montpelier
Owyhee River
Malad City
Bear Lake
WYOMING

INTRODUCTION

When I was a schoolboy in neighboring Oregon, the state of Idaho was an enigma to me. It didn't have a Disneyland, like California to the south, nor a Space Needle, like Seattle to the north. Yet there it was, propped like a bookend against our eastern border, a transition between the rain-soaked Pacific Northwest and the laid-back cowboy country of the northern Rocky Mountains.

I visited Idaho several times in high school and college, sometimes to ski at Sun Valley, a couple of times en route to Wyoming's Yellowstone and Grand Teton national parks, once (in 1964) as a delegate to the World Scout Jamboree on Lake Pend Oreille, in the northern Panhandle.

Yet it wasn't until I moved from Los Angeles to Boise in the spring of 1994—a return to my beloved Northwest after having lived and worked in seven other states and six foreign countries—that I truly began to appreciate this great state.

I recall my first drive north through Idaho from Boise to Coeur d'Alene, a 400-mile excursion via two-lane state and U.S. highways. I was astounded by the variety of terrain, from the rugged Salmon River country around Riggins to the rolling sweep of the Palouse farmlands to the evergreen forests near the Canadian border. Culturally, it was equally diverse, from historic mountain mining and logging towns to Native American communities to modern lakeshore resorts.

And this was just one portion of the state! In subsequent months I found a broad volcanic plain into which mountain rivers disappear only to burst from sheer canyon walls a hundred miles distant; sand dunes taller than those of Death Valley; a broad waterfall higher than Niagara Falls; a chasm half again as deep as the Grand Canyon. I discovered the greatest nesting population of raptors on the continent, walked in the footsteps of pioneers who crossed the state on the Oregon Trail 150 years ago, and savored the unique culture of Basque immigrants who have made Idaho their "home away from homeland." I even ran my fingers through the dirt of the vast potato fields that have given Idaho its greatest fame.

Most of all, I discovered Idaho's rivers.

Explorers Lewis and Clark followed the Clearwater and Snake river drainages through the northern part of modern Idaho after they crossed the Continental Divide in 1805. Decades later, the Oregon Trail pioneers traced hundreds of miles of the Snake River in their arduous journey west. Rivers like the Salmon (the largest stream to drain a single state outside of Alaska) and the Payette today

Relaxing on the shores of Mariam Lake in the Lost River Range near Idaho's tallest mountain, Borah Peak.

offer endless recreational opportunities to rafters, fishermen, and other lovers of the outdoors. And the component mountains of the Rockies—Idaho has been identified with 81 distinct ranges—make this a winter and summer paradise for skiers and hikers alike.

The Snake River dominates, cutting a swath across Idaho from east to west, through mountains and deserts and fertile plains. As it turns north along the Oregon border and heads for its confluence with the Columbia, it carves Hells Canyon, nearly a mile and a half deep. All but one of Idaho's 15 largest towns lie within 25 miles of the Snake, which is the lifeblood for the otherwise arid farmlands of the south.

Only one-and-a-quarter million people make their homes in Idaho, and that may be why the state's haughty individualism is so exalted. A politically paradoxical people, Idahoans run the gamut from Mormon conservatives to university liberals, from right-wing survivalists to environmental activists. Farmers, miners, and timber workers prize their small-town privacy; urbanites decry building booms and traffic woes but enjoy fine restaurants and cultural events.

By its very nature, this is a subjective book. It doesn't pretend to peer into every nook and cranny of this fascinating corner of America. Instead, it is an introduction to the state and its people.

The text reflects my personal enthusiasm for Idaho in years of crisscrossing the state from south to north, west to east. The photographs are the heartfelt work of native-son Bill Mullins, who has spent a lifetime exploring Idaho's rivers, mountains, and deserts. We only hope our work will pique the curiosity of other adventurers to find their own private Idahos.

HOW TO USE THIS BOOK

Our guide begins with background chapters on natural history and human history.

The regional chapters start with Boise, the state capital and largest city, and southwestern Idaho, then move on to the state's southeastern corner and continuing north all the way up the Panhandle. Within these regions, towns and attractions are organized geographically. Star icons highlight the places or experiences that we consider particularly outstanding. You'll also find our recommendations for the best places to eat and stay throughout the state.

At the end of the guide, you'll find resources such as the Practical Information chapter and suggestions for further reading.

"Stalking Goats" in the Idaho wilderness as depicted by
Harpers Weekly in 1878. (Library of Congress)

NATURAL HISTORY
GEOLOGY, GEOGRAPHY AND WILDLIFE

GEOLOGIC HISTORY

Hundreds of millions of years ago, perhaps more than a billion years ago, Idaho was the shoreline of an antediluvian continent. Geologists who read history in rocks tell us that beds of sediment three to five miles deep built up in parts of the state's northern Panhandle and in its southeastern corner.

In the Mesozoic Era, about 225 million years ago, these sedimentary layers began to be folded into mountain ranges by molten granite that pushed upward from deep within the earth. As the rock cooled, cracks and fractures filled with veins of silica, rich in gold, silver, zinc, lead, and other precious metals.

With the North American coastline rising beyond the mountainous wall of the Cascade and Sierra Nevada ranges, much of Idaho became an inland sea. The continuing uplift and tilt of the land, however, eventually drained the water westward through the course of the Columbia and other rivers, leaving behind a sedimentary plain.

The Miocene Epoch ushered in widespread volcanism about 25 million years ago. Successive intervals of lava flows, spreading sheets of basalt over the plain, alternated with spans of geological stability, perhaps 30 times in all. About nine million years ago, basalt plugged river outlets and created ancient Lake Idaho. For some seven million years, this body of water waxed and waned, covering most of what is today southwestern Idaho. Eventually, the meandering Snake River established itself, draining the lake.

Unlike the eastern slope of the northern Rockies or Utah's Morrison Formation, Idaho's rocks bear no records of the great dinosaurs. Fossil records leap from sea creatures of the Paleozoic Era, which ended about 250 million years ago, to mammals of the Pliocene Epoch, beginning about five million years ago, when Idaho's climate was subtropical. The marshy shoreline of Lake Idaho was inhabited by saber-toothed tigers, camels, and other mammals, including a zebra-like horse known as *Equus simplicidens*. Since the 1930s, when its bones were discovered by a team from the Smithsonian Institution at today's Hagerman Fossil Beds National Monument, 150 skeletons of this little horse have been recovered; the area is now considered Earth's richest deposit of terrestrial Upper Pliocene fossils.

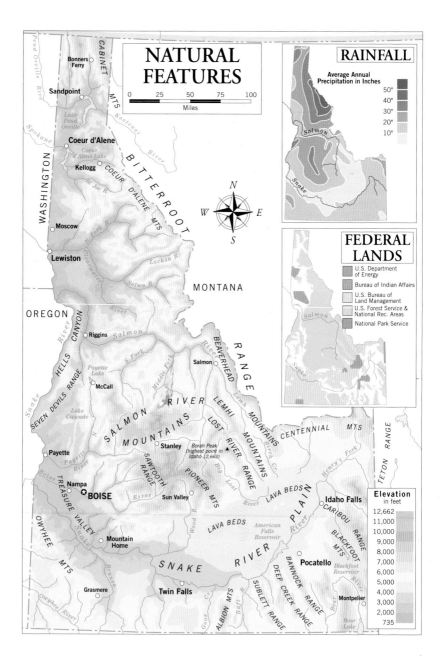

NATURAL FEATURES

Miles
0   25   50   75   100

RAINFALL

Average Annual
Precipitation in Inches

50"
40"
30"
20"
10"

FEDERAL LANDS

U.S. Department of Energy
Bureau of Indian Affairs
U.S. Bureau of Land Management
U.S. Forest Service & National Rec. Areas
National Park Service

Elevation
in feet

12,662
11,000
10,000
9,000
8,000
7,000
6,000
5,000
4,000
3,000
2,000
735

WASHINGTON
OREGON
MONTANA

Pend Oreille River
Bonners Ferry
Sandpoint
Spokane
Lake Pend Oreille
Kootenai River
CABINET MTS
Coeur d'Alene
Coeur d'Alene Lake
Kellogg
St. Joe R.
COEUR D'ALENE MTS
Moscow
N. Fork R.
BITTERROOT
Lochsa R.
Selway R.
Clearwater
Lewiston
Riggins
HELLS CANYON
Salmon River
S Fork
SEVEN DEVILS RANGE
Payette Lake
McCall
Lake Cascade
Snake R.
SALMON MOUNTAINS
RIVER
Payette R.
SAWTOOTH RANGE
Stanley
Borah Peak (highest point in Idaho 12,662)
PIONEER MTS
Salmon
BEAVERHEAD
RANGE
LEMHI MOUNTAINS
LOST RIVER RANGE
Birch Cr.
Big Lost River
CENTENNIAL MTS
Henry's Fork
TETON RANGE
Payette
Nampa
BOISE
Boise R.
Sun Valley
Wood R.
LAVA BEDS
LAVA BEDS
SNAKE
RIVER
PLAIN
American Falls Reservoir
Idaho Falls
CARIBOU RANGE
BLACKFOOT MTS
Blackfoot Reservoir
Pocatello
Montpelier
Bear Lake
TREASURE VALLEY
Mountain Home
Snake R.
OWYHEE MTS
Owyhee River
Bruneau R.
Grasmere
Twin Falls
Goose Cr.
Raft R.
ALBION MTS
SUBLETT RANGE
DEEP CREEK RANGE
BANNOCK RANGE
Salmon
Snake

N
W   E
S

Salmon
Snake

14 IDAHO

Two events must have led to the departure of *Equus* and its companions from Idaho: the ice ages and the Bonneville Flood.

Ice ages have visited the earth many times in the distant geologic past. The most recent, the Quaternary Ice Age, started about 2.5 million years ago, and passed through four distinct phases of expansion and retreat. Though most of the ice disappeared about 10,000 years ago, scientists cannot agree whether the Quaternary Ice Age has ended, or we are merely now in an interglacial epoch. At the height of the glacial epoch, the Selkirk and Cabinet mountains were covered with ice as much as a mile deep. Glaciation didn't extend into the southern part of the state, but the icy invasion certainly cooled the climate. Subtropical mammals migrated south or died out; the coarse-haired woolly mammoth thrived. The most observable legacies of the glaciers are the great lakes of Idaho's northern Panhandle.

Probably in the second interglacial period, about 1.5 million years ago, **Lake Bonneville** filled with glacial meltwater and rainfall, its level rising as the northerly glaciers receded. Another vast inland sea comparable in size to the Great Lakes, it covered most of western Utah, extending a short distance into Idaho. About 340 miles long and 140 miles wide, it reached a depth of more than 1,000 feet.

Lava flows created millennia ago track across the eastern Idaho landscape along the state's Great Rift Zone.

The Bruneau River, a tributary of the Snake, winds through a canyon in the Owyhee uplands of southwest Idaho.

Toward the end of the Pleistocene Epoch, about 15,000 years ago, lava flows south of modern Pocatello diverted the Bear River, which previously had flowed northward, into Lake Bonneville. The sudden rush of water caused the lake to overflow at Red Rock Pass. The shale-and-limestone passage quickly eroded as Lake Bonneville poured from its bed at 15 million cubic feet per second, more than three times the average flow of the Amazon, the world's largest river. Estimated to have been about 300 feet deep at its high-water mark, which may have lasted eight weeks, the Bonneville Flood took on Herculean qualities as it poured over the long-abandoned bed of ancient Lake Idaho, sculpting Shoshone Falls and Hells Canyon en route to the Pacific Ocean via the Columbia River Gorge. Utah's Great Salt Lake is a legacy of this flood.

About the time Lake Bonneville was overflowing its banks, a new wave of volcanic activity began just to its north, continuing until only about 2,000 years ago. A series of earthquakes and lava eruptions along the southern fringe of the Idaho Rockies created a 60-mile-long Great Rift Zone. Today, thousands of square miles of **Snake River Plain** east and west of the rift are cloaked in spatter cones

The state's rivers have long supplied an abundance of fresh fish. This photo from the late 19th century depicts a day's catch of salmon from the Snake River. (Idaho State Historical Society)

and fissure vents, lava-tube caverns and basaltic cinders. Craters of the Moon National Monument preserves some of the most spectacular of these.

Most geologists acknowledge a migrating "hot spot" just beneath the earth's crust as the cause of this activity. Fifteen million years ago, this gargantuan pool of magma lay beneath the **Owyhee Plateau** near the borders of Idaho, Oregon, and Nevada, where volcanic eruptions created many of the badlands formations. Over the millennia, the North American continental plate has drifted southwestward, so that today the hot spot lies beneath Wyoming's Yellowstone National Park, heating the water of the park's famous thermal features.

Scientists know that a new wave of volcanism or seismic activity could happen at any time in Idaho. Borah Peak—Idaho's tallest mountain at 12,662 feet—grew by two feet in the 7.3-magnitude earthquake of October 1983, while the valley floor along a 21-mile-long escarpment dropped by five feet. Hot springs and geysers in southeastern Idaho indicate that volcanism is far from dead there.

GEOGRAPHY

Geographically speaking, Idaho wears several different faces. Southern Idaho is dominated by the Snake River Plain, an arid region of lava beds that gives way in the west to an irrigated semi-desert. The center of the state, around Sun Valley, is primarily a rugged wilderness of high mountains and swift rivers. The far north has a markedly different topography of large and deep lakes surrounded by lush evergreen forests.

SNAKE RIVER BASIN

The single most distinguishing feature of Idaho geography is the Snake River. Rising on the Continental Divide near Yellowstone Park in Wyoming, it courses into Idaho south of the Teton Range, sketching a broad arc around the porous Snake River Plain before slicing north through Hells Canyon on the Idaho-Oregon border and eventually joining the Columbia in Washington—a total distance of 1,038 miles. Where it enters and departs from Idaho, the Snake is the delight of fishermen and white-water rafters. But it's also a life-support system for farmers, ranchers, and urbanites. Fourteen dams divert its waters for irrigation, turning desert into arable cropland, and providing hydroelectric energy for homes and industries.

The upper Snake, from Palisades Reservoir on the Wyoming border through its confluence with Henry's Fork, north of Idaho Falls, is one of the most ecologically important regions in the northern Rockies. The cottonwood forests that line the Snake through the Swan Valley are home to a wide range of wildlife. Fly fishermen acclaim Henry's Fork, which descends through pine forests from the crest of the Rockies on the Montana border, as one of the world's great trout streams.

The plains along the Snake River below Idaho Falls are naturally sagebrush country, but irrigation has converted them to rich farmland, especially famous for potatoes. The Middle Snake (as Idahoans call the river on its southern arc) around Twin Falls also revels in a wealth of irrigated croplands. More impressive are its riparian birch woodlands, and the extraordinary richness of geological and natural phenomena within the 105-mile **Snake River Canyon.** Shoshone Falls ("The Niagara of the West") and dozens of waterfalls at Thousand Springs put on an impressive water show. Paleontologists have discovered a number of Pliocene skeletons at Hagerman Fossil Beds National Monument. Farther downriver, the Snake bypasses the Bruneau Dunes, America's tallest, and wends through the

A stand of 500-year-old Western red cedar.

A brilliant sunrise lights up the Lower Salmon River.

canyon walls of the Snake River Birds of Prey National Conservation Area, with North America's largest concentration of nesting raptors.

Sagebrush, the signature Great Basin Desert plant, covers much of the land south of the river, where the age-old canyons of the Owyhee, Bruneau, and Jarbidge rivers feed the Snake by tortuous channels. (The only portion of Idaho that lies in the Great Basin proper is the tiny southeastern corner drained by the Bear River.)

At the Oregon border the Snake turns north, where it is joined by four of its major tributaries—the Boise, Payette, Owyhee, and Weiser rivers—whose combined waters have created the fertile **Treasure Valley.** This region is home to Boise, the state capital.

From the state border to Lewiston, the Snake flows more than 200 miles through a series of reservoirs (criticized by environmentalists for their effect on the once-prolific Snake River salmon run) and Hells Canyon. The Hells Canyon National Recreation Area and Wilderness surrounds the 1.5-mile-deep abyss of the continent's greatest gorge. At Lewiston, a seaport 470 miles from the Pacific Ocean, the Snake again turns west to join the Columbia.

ROCKY MOUNTAINS

East of Hells Canyon and north of the Snake River Plain soar the myriad ranges of the Rocky Mountains, climaxed in Idaho by the chiseled features of the **Sawtooth Range.** Encompassed by the Sawtooth National Recreation Area and Wilderness, this rugged region contains the headwaters of the Salmon, Wood, Payette, and Boise rivers, all famous for their white-water rafting. Sun Valley, western North America's first "destination" ski resort, is just south of the Sawtooths. The largest U.S. wilderness area outside of Alaska, the 6.2-million-acre Frank Church—River of No Return Wilderness, is just north.

The Salmon River—the longest river contained in any one American state (excluding Alaska)—effectively splits Idaho in two. Flowing northeasterly from its source in the Sawtooths, the river arcs sharply westward below the Bitterroot Range, joining the Snake south of Lewiston. This undammed "River of No Return" is so swift, and locked in such wilderness, that no one succeeded in navigating upstream until after World War II. The Salmon's westward sweep marks the southern limit of the state's Panhandle. Only one road connects the Snake plateau of the south with Idaho's forested north, breeding a sectionalism that has the Panhandle population looking more toward Spokane, Washington, than to Boise as its economic capital.

Vast evergreen woodlands speckled with alpine lakes mark the terrain of the Salmon River drainage and that of its sister to the north, the Clearwater River. The Clearwater enters the Snake at Lewiston, drawing a line between the Camas Prairie, a lush grazing district to its south, and the rolling Palouse Hills, a rich forage-crop farming area to its north.

Idaho's eastern boundary—from the Bear River north to the sliver of Yellowstone that falls within the state's boundary—also embraces a fair swath of Rocky Mountains. Among the biggest surprises for those familiar with the Jackson Hole side of the Grand Tetons is that the famous range is perfectly visible from the Idaho side.

THE PANHANDLE

Idaho's northern Panhandle is geographically distinct from the rest of Idaho. It is not a part of the Snake River drainage: the rivers that flow from its great lakes (Pend Oreille, Coeur d'Alene, Priest, and others), a bequest of the ice ages, enter the upper Columbia well above its confluence with the Snake. Farming is not as important to the economy here as it is elsewhere in Idaho. Logging and mining (silver, lead, and zinc) are the mainstays. The Silver Valley, east of

Coeur d'Alene, produced more silver than any other area in the world, thanks to Mesozoic Era deposits.

CLIMATE

Because Idaho lies on the west side of the Continental Divide, its climate is more affected by prevailing winds from the Pacific than by the continental fronts of the Great Plains. Summers are not as hot, nor winters as cold, as those of Wyoming or most of Montana. Still, daytime midsummer temperatures in the Snake River Plain average above 90 degrees Fahrenheit, and frequently are well over 100. In winter, daytime temperatures often drop below 20 degrees. In Stanley, at the foot of the Sawtooth Range on the Salmon River headwaters, it's not unusual to find temperatures of 25 degrees below zero. Average annual rainfall varies from about 40 inches, on the west slope of the Rockies near Coeur d'Alene, to 10 inches in the Snake River Plain.

WILDLIFE

Idaho's varied topography and climate—from the semiarid Snake River Plain to evergreen forests and alpine tundra—provide a diverse habitat for wildlife.

BIRDLIFE

The state's rich birdlife includes such resident avian species as the mountain blue-bird (the official state bird), and migratory birds like the wide-ranging Caspian tern, ducks and geese of many species, snowy egrets, and herons, including the great blue heron and the black-crowned night heron. A large year-round population of white pelicans has established itself in the Middle Snake since the mid-1980s, when a colony migrated north from the Great Salt Lake to the Minidoka National Wildlife Refuge.

Idaho's most significant waterbird may be the large, white trumpeter swan, which weighs 24 pounds on average and has a 10-foot wingspan. Once nearly extinct, it has made a remarkable recovery in the Henry's Fork area and the greater Yellowstone ecosystem. The swans' blaring call can be heard well before they fly into view.

Game birds are plentiful. They include five species of grouse, pheasant, and chukar, a type of partridge. Sage grouse are unique to the high plain—because they don't have gizzards to digest seeds or other hard foods, they feed on the leaves of sagebrush. These birds also have a distinctive mating ritual: each spring they return to ancestral courtship grounds, or leks, where the males strut and dance at dawn to establish covey hierarchies and rights to female grouse observing and awaiting the outcome.

Idaho's most noted birds are its raptors. Within an hour's drive of the state capital of Boise are the **Snake River Birds of Prey National Conservation Area**—a prime raptor habitat of nearly a half-million acres set aside by act of Congress—and the World Center for Birds of Prey, an unaffiliated breeding, research, and educational facility.

The conservation area, which surrounds a deep, wide canyon, is home to more than 800 nesting pairs of raptors of 15 species—the largest such concentration on earth. Eagles, hawks, falcons, and owls nest in crevices in the high basalt cliffs that flank the chasm, and ride updrafts to scout the surrounding plateau for jackrabbits and other burrowing rodents.

Foremost among the population are prairie falcons, which feed almost exclusively on the plateau's prolific population of Townsend's ground squirrels. The largest resident is the magnificent golden eagle, which has a built-in population-control mechanism: the first-hatched chick of its two eggs usually kills its younger sibling, ensuring itself all of its parents' food deliveries.

Other Snake River raptors include the turkey vulture, northern harrier, kestrel, three hawks (red-tailed, ferruginous, and Swainson's), and seven owls (among them the great horned, barn, and screech owls, and the burrowing owl, which nests in old badger or ground-squirrel holes). The peregrine falcon is one of nine migratory species.

Bald eagles and osprey visit occasionally, but they are more at home in the wooded, fast-flowing streams northeast of Idaho Falls—Henry's Fork, and the upper Snake through Swan Valley—and along the Payette and Boise river systems in the west, where they can spot trout and mountain whitefish from treetop aeries.

MAMMALS

Idaho's large-mammal population includes bear, elk, moose, white-tailed deer, mountain goats, and mountain lions (cougars). Pronghorn, mule deer, bighorn sheep, and coyotes can be seen on the Snake River Plain, but most other species prefer the less conspicuous surroundings of the forests or the high country.

No denizen of the sagebrush plains is better adapted to this environment than the pronghorn. Its remarkable eyesight and great speed (60 miles per hour in sprints, up to 50 over long distances), as well as a white patch of rump hair that flares to signal alarm, enable it to elude danger in the open country. The sole member of the family *Antilocapridae,* the pronghorn has short bony horns, the outer sheaths of which it sheds annually. In modern times, its range has been severely restricted by fencing: adapted to the open plains, the pronghorn is unable to leap anything higher than sagebrush.

Thousands of mule deer move freely between the plain and the forests of the foothills. Bighorn sheep, their populations once severely reduced by hunting and disease, have become reestablished in recent decades in several canyons on the Owyhee Plateau, where small herds of wild horses also roam. Coyotes are everywhere, from semiarid plain to dense woodland. These highly intelligent canines hunt in packs like wolves, and will eat anything from insects and berries to small rodents and young pronghorn.

Gray wolves are the state's most controversial animal. Absent from the Idaho Rockies since the early 20th century, victims of a rampant bounty campaign by stock ranchers, they were reintroduced in early 1995 to the backcountry of the Frank Church—River of No Return Wilderness and to Yellowstone National Park. Ranchers fear they will slaughter sheep and cattle, despite environmental-

Biologist Rich Howard and son observe a young ferruginous hawk (above) in the Snake River Birds of Prey Conservation Area.

A mountain goat ponders Heart Lake in the Mallard-Larkins Pioneer Area.

Pronghorn lope through a grain field in Camas County.

Gray wolves (top) have recently been reintroduced to the Idaho wilderness, much to the consternation of ranchers. Grizzly bears (below) usually stick to the Greater Yellowstone area.

ists' assurances they will not. There are some murmurs about reestablishing a central Idaho colony of grizzly bears as well; currently they are found mainly in the greater Yellowstone and Glacier park ecosystems.

Unlike grizzlies, black bears are common. Less aggressive than their more-feared cousins, they nevertheless grow to several hundred pounds in size. Their diet is mainly roots, berries, fish, and carrion; human attacks are rare unless the bears feel their cubs or food caches are being threatened.

Elk can be seen in higher-elevation woodlands and meadows. Moose are found in marshy areas near lakes and streams, especially near Henry's Fork and in the northern Panhandle. White-tailed deer are common in any forested location of northern Idaho, but are very rare south of the Salmon River. In winter, mountain snows drive the animals into river valleys. Their chief predators, other than man during hunting season, are cougars.

Consider yourself fortunate if you don't see a cougar. Reclusive rock dwellers, stealthy nocturnal hunters, these carnivores are great leapers and fleet runners, whose favorite food is mule deer. Though no record exists of their having attacked

Bonneville ciscos are found only in Bear Lake on the Utah border.

a human in Idaho, they have done so in California, and family pets have been taken in suburban Colorado.

The cougar's smaller feline relative, the short-tailed bobcat, is likewise a nocturnal carnivore, though its dietary requirements are less demanding: small rodents and birds suffice. Another cat—the lynx—is occasionally sighted in the forests of the Panhandle. Other Idaho meat-eaters include members of the weasel family, among them the voracious wolverine (mainly in remote wilderness), the burrowing badger (which competes with the prairie falcon to feed on ground squirrels), and the fierce forest weasel.

In high alpine regions such as the Sawtooths, the shaggy mountain goat is sometimes seen, along with small high-altitude rodents like the marmot and the pika.

Beavers, raccoons, otters, minks, and muskrats dwell in and around the state's many rivers. Beavers can even be spotted building lodges and gnawing tree trunks on the Boise River as it flows through the state capital. Common in woodlands are cottontail rabbits, red foxes, porcupines, skunks, squirrels, and chipmunks.

Rattlesnakes may be encountered anywhere but higher elevations: cold-blooded reptiles, they are effectively paralyzed by low temperatures, and are rarely found above 7,000 feet.

FISH

The fish population in many of Idaho's lakes, rivers, and streams has changed considerably in the last century, mainly because of dam construction. Great chinook salmon runs are apparently a thing of the past. Now the fish that once swam up the Snake and its tributaries as far as Shoshone Falls to spawn cannot get beyond the Hells Canyon dams, built without fish ladders between 1955 and 1968. Spawning salmon still run the Salmon and Clearwater rivers, but their numbers are barely one percent of what they were three decades ago.

The huge white sturgeon also once journeyed the Snake and Columbia rivers to the Pacific Ocean and back, but unlike the salmon, it does not require saltwater exposure to survive. Primitive creatures related to the shark, in that both have skeletons of cartilage rather than bone, sturgeon are bottom feeders that grow to be 12 feet long, several hundred pounds in weight, and more than 100 years old. The milky-gray fish are found today in some reservoirs (notably Brownlee on the Oregon border) and in the deeper pools of free-flowing rivers.

The most popular game fish in Idaho today is trout. Some, like the rainbow, cutthroat, and the rare red-band and bull trout, are native to the state's waters;

others, including brook trout, have been introduced. Fishermen rave about the steelhead, a larger, ocean-going rainbow trout whose annual autumn runs of the Salmon, Clearwater, and other rivers draw thousands of anglers.

Freshwater giants like the chinook and kokanee salmon, mackinaw (lake trout), northern pike, and tiger muskellunge live in the big lakes of the northern Panhandle. Several unique species make their home in Bear Lake, in Idaho's southeastern corner, among them the Bonneville cisco, a sardine-like whitefish that sparks a flurry of ice fishing during its winter run.

Other native Idaho cold-water game fish include whitefish and burbot. Among species introduced in the late 1800s and early 1900s were channel catfish, largemouth and smallmouth bass, yellow perch, black crappie, bluegill, and pumpkinseed sunfish.

Commercial, state and federal "fish farms" on the Middle Snake River, west from Twin Falls to Hagerman, produce catfish, tilapia, and more than two million rainbow trout a year, some 70 percent of all farmed trout in the United States.

An environmental controversy rages on the Middle Snake River over five tiny mollusks, including the Bruneau Hot Springs snail, a direct descendant of Ice-Age snails that may be threatened with extinction by pollutants and warming waters. But officially listing the mollusks as endangered species could compromise the livelihoods of farmers and power developers.

Two Nez Percé women pose for this portrait from the early 20th century. (Idaho State Historical Society)

H I S T O R Y

Two distinct groups of native peoples, the Shoshone-Bannocks and Nez Percé, inhabit Idaho, their cultures separated between north and south in much the same way as the rest of the state.

In the south, the Snake River Plain and adjacent river valleys and highlands are the traditional home of the Shoshone tribes, whose customs and Uto-Aztecan language classify them in the Great Basin native tradition. The **Shoshones** once dominated the high deserts from Oregon to Wyoming, but their only official homeland now is the Fort Hall Indian Reservation near Pocatello. They share this reservation with the **Bannocks,** a band of Northern Paiutes formerly from southeastern Oregon, who moved into eastern Idaho after obtaining the horse. The combined Shoshone-Bannock tribe is now referred to as "Sho-Bans." (The remote Duck Valley Indian Reservation, on the Idaho-Nevada border south of Boise, is home to western Shoshones and Paiutes, or "Sho-Pais.") Early trappers and settlers called these tribes collectively the "Snake Indians," a name derived from pictographic symbolism and also bestowed upon their principal river.

Idaho's Panhandle, north of the Salmon River, is the homeland of the Plateau tribes. Most widespread are the **Nez Percé,** who did not pierce their noses despite the name given them by French-Canadian trappers. Calling themselves Ne-Mee-Poo, "the people," they inhabited a territory extending from the Clearwater River drainage into northeastern Oregon and southeastern Washington. Their modern reservation is east of Lewiston.

The Nez Percé spoke a Sahaptian dialect, like the tribes of central Oregon; their cousins in the northern Panhandle spoke Salish tongues, akin to the tribes of the lower Pacific Northwest coast. These included the Coeur d'Alenes (Skitswish in their own language), who now operate the National Indian Lottery from their reservation south of the city of Coeur d'Alene; and the Pend d'Oreille (Kalispel) and Kutenai peoples, whose reservations are in Flathead, Montana, and Colville, Washington.

Despite their cultural differences, Great Basin and Plateau tribes prior to the arrival of the white man had similar lifestyles as semi-nomadic hunters and gatherers.

The first people to arrive in Idaho probably were Eurasian hunters who crossed the Bering land bridge from Siberia during the Ice Age. These early people may have witnessed the cataclysmic Bonneville Flood (*see* the Natural History chapter); they certainly observed volcanic upheaval on the Snake River Plain. A Shoshone legend even tells of the demise of a great snake that roasted in molten rock melted in the pressure of its coils.

The earliest archaeological evidence of habitation of the Snake River Plain is dated about 12,500 BC. Excavations at Wilson Butte Cave, east of the town of Shoshone, have revealed primitive hunting tools and remains of animals long extinct, including Camelops (a genus of camel) and bear-size ground sloths. At the time, Ice Age snow still blanketed the northern Idaho Rockies, but the Snake region, several hundred miles south, had a relatively hospitable climate. What is now desert steppe was likely covered by coniferous forest.

Over time, early humans in Idaho progressed from temporary to semi-permanent residence in caves and rock shelters; always dependent upon large game for subsistence, they gradually refined their weapons and added more plant foods to their diet. Domesticated dogs assisted in group hunts of such animals as bison and mastodons. By about 7,000 years ago, as southern Idaho's climate became warmer and drier in the wake of the final glacial recession, native peoples were using grinding stones to process seeds into flour.

Most big-game animals (except bison) found the climate disagreeable, and either died out or migrated. Footwear and basketry made their first appearance, as did digging and foraging tools and the atlatl, or spear-thrower, which provided speed, distance and accuracy in hunting such animals as the swift pronghorn. Decorative items, gaming pieces, and religious figurines from this period indicate the evolution of a more complex culture.

In the north, tribes moving inland from the coast found the forests and glacial lakes to their liking. They hunted deer, elk, and mountain sheep; dried and ground salmon into a nutritious foodstuff; and harvested the starchy camas bulb, bitterroot, and biscuit root for winter food.

Their semi-nomadic behavior was not much different from that of the more southerly Shoshones, who migrated seasonally between mountains and meadows, forests and river valleys. Salmon and firewood were plentiful along the Snake River, as were deer, rabbits, and ground birds. The Shoshones made base camps there, climbing in spring and early summer to subalpine meadows to reap green plants and roots. As summer turned to fall, they found berries, seeds, and fruits ready for harvest in small canyons. Then they returned to their winter camps along the Snake, where they used cache pits to store their dried meats, roots, and seeds they had ground into flour. When the late-fall salmon run began, they

Indian petroglyphs along the Middle Fork of the Salmon River.

snared fish with traps, weirs, and more conventional hook-and-line gear, then dried and smoked them on wooden racks.

About AD 1000, Idaho's tribes replaced the atlatl with the bow and arrow as their primary hunting tool and first began to make and use pottery. Both northern and southern tribes dwelt in winter in circular homes, 15 to 20 feet in diameter, built partially underground with hearths and earthen roofs; in summer, in the meadows, they used wickiup-style, thatch-covered pole lodges.

A rich tradition of rock art dates from this period. Petroglyphs have been carved into rock walls and boulders on the western Snake River Plain, particular at Wees Bar (beside the river in the Birds of Prey National Conservation Area) and in the Owyhee uplands. Pictographs painted on rock with natural pigments are often seen on the eastern plain. Their purposes probably ranged from practical (the marking of trails) to spiritual (communicating with the gods).

Southern and northern tribes alike shared a spiritual respect for nature as their provider. Hunting and gathering only what they needed for food, clothing, and shelter, the native peoples lived in harmony with nature for centuries.

HORSE CULTURE

Much of that changed sometime in the early 18th century, when the horse ushered in the first great revolution in the lifestyles of Idaho's Native Americans.

Long before they ever saw a European-American face, the Shoshones were racing across the plains on horseback. Introduced to the New World by Spanish conquistadors in the Southwest, horses spread north through trade with the Utes and Comanches, from whom the Shoshones probably obtained them. They subsequently were traded to the Nez Percé and other northern tribes.

With the horse, Idaho's Indians adopted a very different lifestyle. Suddenly they could travel great distances to hunt and trade. Shoshones pursued buffalo on the Wyoming plains, and Nez Percé did the same in Montana. Interaction with Great Plains tribes led to the adoption of fashions (feathered headdresses, beaded buckskin jackets, buffalo robes, leather saddles) and technologies (tepees, horseshoes, animal-hide containers, new food-preservation methods). Unfortunately, this interaction also increased the danger of disease, as in 1781, when a smallpox epidemic transmitted from the Great Plains (where it had been introduced from the East Coast) took a large toll among the Nez Percé and Coeur d'Alenes, but largely missed the Shoshones.

Tribal politics changed as well. The Nez Percé, for instance, had been divided into as many as 60 autonomous small bands, each with no more than a few dozen people who chose their leader by consensus rather than heredity. The greater tribe had a council to speak on behalf of all Nez Percé, but it had no head chief. With the horse, these formerly scattered bands began to formally organize as larger tribes, with chiefs to lead them on hunts and into battle.

Before long, the new equestrian culture dominated Idaho's northern tribes and the eastern bands of Shoshone, soon joined by the Bannocks. Some tribes, like the Nez Percé and the Lemhi Shoshone (at the foot of the Bitterroot Range), selectively bred horses. But such mountain bands as the Boise and Bruneau Shoshone continued their traditional lifestyles. Their homeland in the high meadows and deep valleys was best trodden by human foot; besides, horses competed for the grasses the Shoshone's usual prey (deer and pronghorn) craved.

For most natives throughout the Northwest, the horse made it easier to attend an annual intertribal rendezvous, held near modern Weiser at the north end of the riverine region now known as the Treasure Valley. Timed to coincide with the early-summer salmon run, it lasted for a month or two and included extensive trading, gambling, and ceremonial dancing. Nez Percé

A Nez Percé tribal powwow in 1904. (Idaho State Historical Society)

brought their Appaloosa ponies, Shoshones their dried meat and buffalo hides. Umatillas from the Columbia River carried shells from the Pacific coast. Paiutes from inland Oregon offered shiny obsidian arrowheads. Territorial skirmishes between tribes, especially between the Shoshones and Nez Percé in the Salmon River country, were put aside. This gathering was a precursor of the trapper rendezvous of the early 1800s, which in turn were replaced by permanent trading posts later in that century.

Although the Shoshones and Nez Percé were among the first tribes to use horses, they were late in obtaining rifles. This put them in an awkward position when hostile Blackfoot and other tribes began to cross the crest of the Rockies, raid their villages for horses, and drive the people back into the mountains. Historians theorize that this may be one reason the Idaho Indians were so ready to welcome white explorers and traders: they needed all the help they could get in holding off the Blackfoot.

LEWIS AND CLARK EXPEDITION

Perhaps 8,000 Native Americans lived in Idaho in 1805, when **Meriwether Lewis** (1774-1809) and **William Clark** (1770-1838) became the first white men to pass through the region that became this state. There is little doubt that it was the last of the contiguous 48 states to be seen by European-American eyes.

Even before the United States purchased the vast Louisiana Territory (extending to the Continental Divide) from France in 1803, President Thomas Jefferson had begun preparing Lewis, an Army officer and his private secretary, to head an expedition through this wilderness to the Pacific Ocean. He and Clark, a soldier and frontiersman, departed from St. Louis in May 1804 with a party of about three dozen men, all aged 29 to 33 and skilled in sciences or practical trades. They headed up the Missouri River and wintered with the friendly Mandan Sioux in what is now North Dakota. Upon heading out again in the spring of 1805, they employed a French-Canadian interpreter, Toussaint Charbonneau, who brought along his 19-year-old wife, **Sacagawea**, a Lemhi Shoshone native of what is now Idaho, and their infant son.

Kidnapped at about the age of 12, Sacagawea (ca. 1786-1812) was a Mandan slave until Charbonneau bought her. Her part in the journey's success has almost certainly been overly romanticized, but she did play a key role in identifying landmarks and easing tensions with potentially hostile tribes. The most famous example was in August 1805, when the expedition climbed to the Missouri headwaters and sought horses and guides for crossing the Continental Divide. Native bands were

William Clark by Charles Willson Peale, from life. (Independence National Historic Park, Philadelphia)

suspicious until Sacagawea recognized her long-lost brother, Cameahwait, leader of a Shoshone band. Their emotional reunion clinched the deal and allowed the trek to continue.

Lewis and Clark crossed the Divide at 7,373-foot Lemhi Pass in the Bitterroot Range a few days after the horses were obtained, and gazed westward across range after range of wild Idaho mountains. They followed the Lemhi River north into the upper Salmon River, but this notorious "River of No Return" was too fierce even in late summer to allow their party to continue downstream beyond the confluence of its short North Fork.

So the expedition crossed again into what is now Montana, followed the Bitterroot River downstream nearly to modern Missoula, then reentered what is now Idaho at 5,233-foot **Lolo Pass,** en route surviving a mid-September blizzard. By the end of the month, they had descended the Clearwater River and found hospitality among the Nez Percé near modern Orofino. They left their horses with this tribe, built five dugout canoes, and made it down the Clearwater to the Snake River, the Columbia River and (by the second week of November) the Pacific Ocean.

The party spent a stormy winter at hastily built Fort Clatsop, and the following March began their return journey via a similar route. Heavy snow in the Bitterroots forced them to spend a month encamped on the Clearwater near modern Kamiah, among the Nez Percé. By late June, however, they had recrossed Lolo Pass. They were back in St. Louis on Sept. 23, 1806, the journey over.

Lewis and Clark's journals and maps went a long way toward educating the young nation about the topography, native peoples, and animal and plant life of the American West. Of most immediate impact, they sparked a rush of fur trappers attracted by the prospect of valuable pelts from beavers, otters, and other mountain creatures. Fur hats were the rage of the high-fashion world on the East Coast and in Europe, and merchants sought 100,000 beaver pelts a year to meet the commercial demand.

TRAPPERS AND TRADING POSTS

John Colter (ca. 1775-1813) was the first of these wilderness adventurers in the Idaho region. A member of the Lewis and Clark party, he set off on his own during their return journey. Between 1806 and 1810, he made three lengthy journeys through the Missouri and Yellowstone River headwaters areas, stumbling across the geothermal wonders of Yellowstone National Park (which became known in the East as "Colter's Hell"), as well as Idaho's Teton Valley region.

The first trading post in what is now Idaho was **Kullyspell House,** established by British-Canadian trapper-surveyor David Thompson (1770-1857) on the shore of Lake Pend Oreille in 1809. Thompson explored the upper reaches of the Columbia River system in what is now the U.S.-Canada border region, and in 1811 became the first man to follow the Columbia from its source to its mouth. Kullyspell House operated for only about two years.

Another short-lived settlement was **Fort Henry,** near modern St. Anthony in eastern Idaho. When a battle with hostile Blackfoot drove trader Andrew Henry and a group of trappers across the Continental Divide in late 1810, they built their winter outpost on a branch of the Snake River that has ever since borne the name Henry's Fork.

The following spring in Wyoming, Henry's brigade encountered another party of westbound traders, this one sponsored by New York fur magnate John Jacob Astor. Astor had sent one contingent by sea around Cape Horn, and this second one (headed by Wilson Price Hunt) by land, to meet at the mouth of the Columbia River and there establish a post to buy Northwest furs and ship them across the Pacific to China. Hunt's party of about 50 was unprepared for the rigors of the overland journey, and was beset by one scourge after another, from hunger and thirst to disease and Indian attacks. Novelist Washington Irving's 1836 account of their trek, *Astoria,* gave the American public a better understanding of their arduous journey and discovery of the Snake River Plain.

In early 1812 the travelers finally straggled into Fort Astoria, which had been raised several months earlier by the seafarers. As a post for the China trade, however, Astoria failed. The British took over the fort in late 1813 during the War of 1812, but it was returned to the United States in 1818.

All of Idaho was a part of the Oregon Territory, which extended west from the Continental Divide to the Pacific. Unlike Louisiana, which comprised the Mississippi River drainage east of the Divide, Oregon was disputed territory until 1846, jointly claimed by the U.S. and England. Thus Britain's powerful Hudson's Bay Company was able to establish itself at Fort Nez Perces (Walla Walla), at the confluence of the Snake and Columbia rivers (in what is now Washington), and use the post as a staging point for annual trapping expeditions.

Between 1820 and 1832, such self-reliant men as Donald Mackenzie and Peter Skene Ogden led annual Hudson's Bay parties into the Snake River country from the west, leading to extensive exploration and rampant exploitation. Under orders to ruthlessly trap as many beavers as possible to discourage American interests, they nonetheless encountered dozens of competing U.S. trappers in the Henry's Fork area by 1825.

The Americans had moved into Idaho from the Missouri River corridor to the northeast. Whereas the Hudson's Bay Company salaried its employees, St. Louis-based trader William Ashley employed freelance mountain men, colorful characters like Jim Bridger (1804-81) and Jedediah Smith (1799-1831), whose legends became part of the lore of the American West.

Ashley launched his Rocky Mountain Fur Company in 1822, and in 1825 hit upon the idea of replacing permanent trading posts with an annual summer "rendezvous." Trappers invited friendly Indian tribes to join them at an appointed location, where they were met by a wagon train from St. Louis laden with pack animals and a year's supply of goods. They traded cached pelts and spent most of a month gambling, drinking, undertaking contests of strength and skill, and generally raising hell.

Most rendezvous—which continued until 1840—were held on the Green River in what is now southwestern Wyoming, but the 1828 rendezvous was held at Bear Lake on the southeastern edge of modern Idaho. The rendezvous of 1829 and 1832 were staged at Pierre's Hole, now known as the Teton Valley, near Driggs in easternmost Idaho. The second Pierre's Hole rendezvous ended atypically when hostilities flared between a band of Blackfoot, who crashed the party, and several hundred Shoshone, Bannock, Nez Percé, and Flathead participants. Six trappers (of about 200 present) and 17 natives died, and the incident sparked many years

Alfred Jacob Miller's famous painting of the Green River Rendezvous in 1839 hangs in Laramie, Wyoming's American Heritage Center. (American Heritage Center, Univ. of Wyoming)

of unpleasantries with the Blackfoot. Today the Pierre's Hole Mountain Men Rendezvous Days held in Driggs each August reenact the peaceful 1829 event, not the contentious 1832 one.

The contract to supply trade goods to the 1834 rendezvous was won by a Boston merchant named Nathaniel Wyeth. But when Wyeth's caravan reached the Green River, he discovered he had been beaten to the punch: his customers had been stolen by St. Louis traders. Rather than return east with unsold merchandise, Wyeth continued west to the Snake River, and near modern Pocatello built a trading post he named Fort Hall.

For the next 20 years, Fort Hall was an important oasis for transcontinental travelers, though Wyeth sold out in 1836 to the British Hudson's Bay Company which had matched the Fort Hall enterprise by constructing Fort Boise at the confluence of the Boise and Snake rivers in 1834. By the 1840s the need for lengthy trapping expeditions was obviated, especially as aristocratic fashion trends were turning from furs to silks.

Few early visitors to the land that would become Idaho were concerned with environmental conservation, but spiritual salvation . . . well, that was another story. In 1831 William Clark was toiling in St. Louis as federal superintendent of Indian affairs—a quarter-century after the Lewis and Clark expedition—when he received a visit from old friends. Speaking in sign language, three Nez Percé men and a Flathead requested that he send them "the book" and "black robes."

MISSIONARIES

The call for missionaries went out quickly. In 1834 Methodist minister Jason Lee, en route to Oregon's Willamette Valley, accompanied Wyeth as far as Fort Hall and conducted services there. In 1836 another Protestant mission group sent two couples west to the Oregon Country. Marcus and Narcissa Whitman settled near modern Walla Walla, Washington; Henry and Eliza Spalding founded their mission at Lapwai, Idaho, about 13 miles east of modern Lewiston. They were joined in 1839 by Sarah and Asa Bowen Smith, who moved in among the Nez Percé on the Clearwater River, near modern Kamiah.

Spalding devoted his energies to altering the Nez Percé culture from semi-nomadic to agrarian; within a few years his community included a church, a school, a blacksmith shop, a water-powered sawmill and flour mill, and a small printing press on which he printed the Gospel of John in the Nez Percé language. Asa Smith, more a linguist than a missionary, compiled the first Nez Percé dictionary, but openly ridiculed Spalding's efforts to convert the natives to farming. The

A restored room in Old Fort Hall.

Spaldings abandoned Lapwai after Cayuse natives murdered the Whitmans in late 1847; they left behind 44 cultivated acres, 164 stock animals, but only 21 baptized Nez Percé.

Jesuit missionaries were meanwhile active in northernmost Idaho. A Belgian, Father Pierre Jean De Smet, first founded a mission among the Flathead people in the Bitterroot Valley of what is now Montana in 1841, then moved northwest to Coeur d'Alene country. The **Mission of the Sacred Heart** was established on the St. Joe River in 1842; it was rebuilt on higher ground beginning in 1850. The Greek Revival-style church, near modern Cataldo east of the city of Coeur d'Alene, still stands: a state historic park, it is the oldest building in the state of Idaho.

The Jesuits were much more successful than the Protestants had been in converting the native peoples: about two-thirds of all Coeur d'Alene tribe members were baptized as Catholics, either at Cataldo or at a second mission at De Smet (now in the heart of the Coeur d'Alene reservation).

Meanwhile, a third strain of Christianity was making its mark in Idaho. In 1848 Brigham Young led his Mormons out of Illinois and established a new spiritual colony at what has become known as Salt Lake City, Utah. By the mid 1850s they were a major presence in what became southeastern Idaho.

The single greatest influence of the trappers and missionaries, however, was not in seizing furs or saving souls. It was in clearing the way for the great American westward movement of the 1840s and 1850s.

EARLY SETTLEMENT

Between 1842 and the 1860s, more than 50,000 Americans crossed the continent in covered wagons on the **Oregon Trail.** The first "highway" for vehicular traffic through Idaho, the famous trail followed the course of the Snake for much of its journey through southern Idaho. Few if any travelers considered settling in what was to become Idaho. They sought either the golden earth of Oregon's Willamette Valley or the golden ore discovered in California in 1848. By the time the first town had been platted in 1860 (though at the time the founders of the Mormon community of Franklin refused to accept that they had crossed the border from Utah), Oregon was already a state and Idaho was a part of the sprawling Washington Territory.

Then gold fever struck Idaho, and suddenly there was a reason to take up land in this remote wilderness. The first strike was made in August 1860 on Orofino

Father Pierre Jean De Smet.
(Library of Congress)

Creek in the Nez Percé Reservation by prospector Elias Pierce. By the following summer the entire Clearwater River system was crawling with tent and log-cabin cities. Lewiston emerged as the head of river transportation and service center for the mining camps of the region.

In August 1862 a second, larger find was made on Grimes Creek, a Boise River tributary some 200 miles south of the Clearwater. A year later, **Idaho City** (with a population of 6,275) was the largest city in the Pacific Northwest and the hub of the Boise Basin mining district. The area produced more than $250 million worth of gold by sluicing and placer mining in the next 20 years. (Today the settlement has about 300 residents; but unlike most of its mining-town neighbors, it has avoided becoming a ghost town and preserved its architectural heritage.)

When Idaho was accorded territorial status by Congress in 1863, establishing its western border where it is today but incorporating much of modern Montana and Wyoming, Idaho City was declared its capital. It remained there only briefly, however, moving first to Lewiston, then to Boise by late 1864, when Congress set the present boundaries of Idaho (except for a strip of western Wyoming that was chiseled away in 1868). Boise (named by early 19th-century French Canadian trappers, who were delighted to see woods—*bois*—along its river after a long desert crossing) had been founded shortly after the Grimes Creek gold strike as a service center for the many mining camps in the rugged foothills.

THE OREGON TRAIL

The Oregon Trail was the measuring stick by which all other pioneer paths were gauged. During the two decades beginning in 1842, when 18 covered wagons and about 100 brave migrants left Independence, Missouri, this rutted route was the principal thoroughfare for some 53,000 Americans headed to the "promised lands" of the West.

The wayfarers quickly discovered that the 1,900-mile, seven-month ordeal was not a picnic---and the stretch through Idaho was one of the hardest. After surviving such hardships as the Great Plains, the Rockies, Indian attacks, buf-

falo stampedes, violent storms, and a full complement of accidents and illnesses, they entered Idaho-to-be via the muddy Bear River Valley, in what is now the state's southeastern corner. Skirting the hissing geysers of the Soda Springs area, they crossed the Portneuf River and descended to Fort Hall on the Snake River. Abandoned in 1856, the old Fort Hall has since disappeared, and is today marked by a monument on the Fort Hall Indian Reservation. A full-scale replica of the fort stands in Pocatello's Ross Park.

Beyond Fort Hall, Oregon Trail travelers faced a daunting march of more than

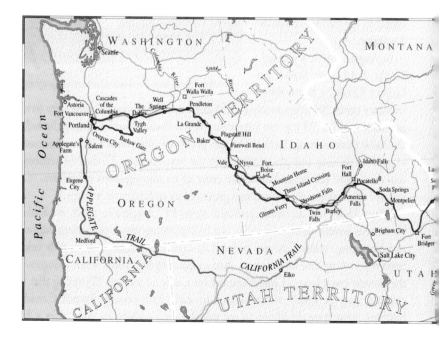

300 miles across the forbidding Snake River Plain before reaching Fort Boise, the next outpost of civilization. Following the course of the Snake for most of its long arc through southern Idaho, wagon ruts can still be seen in the sagebrush along the south rim of the basalt cliffs that line much of the canyon. There were few places where thirsty pack animals could descend to the river. Passages that led to the river, such as Massacre Rocks (now a state park west of American Falls), often bear grateful graffiti painted in axle grease. On the other hand, these places were also most prone to attacks from hostile Shoshones. Massacre Rocks got its name from an attack that took the lives of 10 travelers in 1862. Eighteen were slain in an 1854 ambush (the Ward Massacre) on the Boise River near Middleton.

Travelers indulged their thirst at the Thousand Springs west of Twin Falls, but could not find a good place to ford the Snake River to its north bank until they reached the site of modern Glenns Ferry, about 180 miles west of Fort Hall. Three Island Crossing State Park preserves the site where a series of islets made the transit more manageable. History buffs recreate the crossing each August.

OREGON TRAIL

Modern Freeways Shown in Gray

The trail joined the Boise River near the location of modern Boise, and followed it downstream 40 miles to Fort Boise. The fort, which marked the end of the Snake River Plain and the beginning of the migrants' ascent of Oregon's Blue Mountains, was closed in 1854 after the Ward Massacre. It washed away in the floods of 1862, and the site today is part of a waterfowl refuge. A replica of Fort Boise stands in the nearby town of Parma.

Whereas most migrants followed the Snake River west, engineers were searching farther north for a better route to the Pacific. In the mid-1850s the U.S. Army Corps of Topographical Engineers began building a 624-mile wagon route linking Walla Walla, not far from navigable Columbia River waters, and Fort Benton (now Montana), the uppermost steamboat port on the Missouri River. The Mullan Road---named for the engineer in charge of the project, Captain John Mullan---took nearly a decade to complete, due in large part to the difficult passage across the steep and heavily forested Bitterroot Range. Although it never achieved major importance in the 1800s, it became a principal traffic corridor in the 20th century, and is today paralleled by Interstate 90.

The name "Idaho," incidentally, means . . . absolutely nothing. Originally proposed in Congress a few years earlier as a name for Colorado, it was chosen for the new territory over "Shoshone" and "Montana" by senators who claimed that "Idaho" came from the Shoshone words *e dah hoe*, "gem of the mountains." In fact, the name had been invented by a steamboat operator.

The earliest difficulties the new Idaho territory faced were dealing with lawlessness and Native American tensions. Idaho had no criminal or civil code, and vigilante justice ruled early on. Particularly troublesome were the mining camps, where prospectors' Civil War loyalties were split between Union and Confederacy.

INDIAN WARS

The various tribes, meanwhile, had begun to rebel against government efforts to move them onto reservations and force them to give up their traditional semi-nomadic lifestyles. In 1858 the Coeur d'Alenes banded with other Salish-speaking tribes to battle the U.S. Army; their punishment for failure was utter destruction of their food caches and horses. In 1863 more than 350 Shoshone men, women, and children were slaughtered by a cavalry unit in the Bear River Massacre, the worst such atrocity in American history. (A 10-foot monument on U.S. 91, three miles north of Preston, today marks the site.) During the 1878 Bannock War, Chief Buffalo Horn led the Bannocks and northern Paiutes against settlers in the Snake River Valley. There were dozens of deaths on both sides, but the end result was the same: the Indians were subjugated.

Best known nationally was the Nez Percé War of 1877. In the wake of missionaries' activities and the Clearwater Basin gold boom, the acquiescent Christian majority of Nez Percés, seeking to avoid conflict at all costs, accepted an 1863 treaty that restricted them to a reservation barely 10 percent the size of their traditional lands. But about a third of Nez Percé rejected the treaty, which would have forced them to abandon their ancestral home. Their leaders were **Chief White Bird,** whose people lived on the lower Salmon River (south of modern Grangeville), and **Chief Joseph** (ca. 1840-1904), whose home was Oregon's Wallowa Valley on the west side of Hells Canyon.

Frustrated with the rebel Nez Percés' 14-year refusal to comply with orders to relocate, the U.S. Army gave Joseph and White Bird a 30-day ultimatum in mid-May 1877. Still seeking a peaceable resolution, the tribes had begun their move when three impetuous young warriors from White Bird's band murdered four antagonistic white settlers. Cavalry forces struck back, but White Bird was ready for them: in the Battle of White Bird Canyon on June 17, 34 U.S. soldiers died, while only two braves were wounded.

This skirmish seemed to leave no choice for the dissident Nez Percé. With a more formidable cavalry sure to be assembled against them, they decided to flee to sanctuary among the Crows of northern Montana or, failing that, retreat into Canada. For the ensuing four months, 800 men, women, and children, and about 2,000 horses, followed Joseph and White Bird on a desperate run for freedom.

The collective bands first headed north to the Kamiah area, where they held off a cavalry attack on July 11 and 12 until they could start over the Lolo Trail toward the crest of the Bitterroots. With soldiers on their tails, their odyssey took them to Montana's Big Hole Valley, where a surprise militia attack killed 83 Nez Percé, only 30 of them adult men. The tragedy disheartened Joseph and White Bird, who until then hadn't realized the size and organization of their foe.

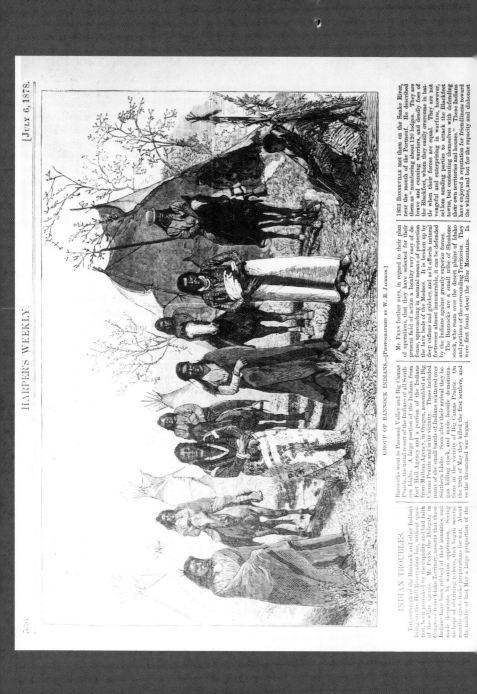

GROUP OF BANNOCK INDIANS.—[Photographed by W. H. Jackson.]

INDIAN TROUBLES.

The outbreak of the Bannock and other Indians living on the Hall Reservation has, without question, been provoked by the cupidity and bad faith of the white agents. Mr. Fenn, the Delegate in Congress from Idaho Territory, asserts that these Indians have been robbed of their annuities, and made desperate by wanton oppression. Seeing no hope of obtaining redress, they began several months ago to make preparations for war. About the middle of last May a large proportion of the

Bannocks went to Passmi Valley and Big Camas Prairie, the usual resort of the Indians of all Southern Idaho. A large portion of the Indians from Fort Hall Agency and a portion of the Indians from Malheur Agency, in Oregon, assembled at Big Camas Prairie and in its vicinity. These included many of the small bands of Indians scattered over Southern Idaho. Soon after their arrival they began killing stock, and made hostile demonstrations in the vicinity of Big Camas Prairie. On the 29th of May they killed the first settlers, and so the threatened war began.

Mr. Fenn further says, in regard to their plan of operations, that they have selected for their present field of action a locality very easy of defense, approaching in natural means of protection the lava beds of the Modocs. It is broken up by deep cañons and gulches, and as it affords natural fortresses almost innumerable, it can be defended by the Indians against greatly superior forces.

These Indians are a small but warlike stock, who roam over the desert plains of Snake and portions of the surrounding Territories. They were first found about the Blue Mountains. In

1833 Bonneville met them on the Snake River, near the mouth of the Portneuf. He described them as "numbering about 120 lodges. They are brave and cunning warriors, and deadly foes of the Blackfeet, whom they easily overcome in battle when their forces are equal. They are not revengeful and enterprising in warfare, however, seldom sending parties to attack the Blackfeet forts, but contenting themselves with defending their own territories." These Indians have enjoyed a reputation for friendliness toward the whites, and but for the rapacity and dishonest

The Nez Percé retreated southeastward, back through Idaho's Lemhi Valley and Island Park areas and across Targhee Pass into Yellowstone National Park, scattering frightened tourists. Here Joseph successfully fooled the U.S. troops into thinking he had turned southward into Wyoming; instead, he struck out almost due north across Montana. When the Crows refused to offer support, their own self-preservation in mind, the exhausted Nez Percé continued toward Canada. Having already come 1,500 miles, they were just 42 miles short of the border, at Bear's Paw, when a cavalry contingent from eastern Montana stopped them.

White Bird and 233 Nez Percé escaped during the night and continued north into Canada, where they settled. Joseph remained with 418 other survivors of the trek, surrendering his rifle with a poignant speech:

> I am tired of fighting. Our chiefs are killed. . . . The old men are all dead. . . . It is cold, and we have no blankets. The little children are freezing to death. My people, some of them, have run away to the hills. . . . I want to have time to look for my children, and to see how many of them I can find; maybe I shall find them among the dead. Hear me, my chiefs: My heart is sick and sad. From where the sun now stands, I will fight no more forever.

Joseph and his people were exiled to Oklahoma until 1885, when most of them were "repatriated" to the Nez Percé reservation east of Lewiston. The chief himself, and 150 of his staunchest followers, were relocated to the Colville Indian Reservation in Washington, where Joseph died and was buried in 1904.

Most of the locations associated with the Nez Percé War have been incorporated into Nez Percé National Historical Park, created in 1965. The park has 38 sites in four states, 29 of them in Idaho.

MORMON SETTLERS

The Native Americans were not the only harassed group in late-19th-century Idaho. Soon after Brigham Young's Mormons had established themselves in Utah in 1848, they extended their influence into southeastern Idaho. **Franklin,** founded in 1860 on what is now the Utah border, was Idaho's first permanent settlement. (Today it is a state historic district.)

An unusually sympathetic report on the Indian troubles of 1878 appears in this edition of *Harper's Weekly*. (Idaho State Historical Society)

Historic Franklin Co-op Mercantile Institution in Idaho's oldest settlement. Note the beehive in the building sign, a symbol derived from the word "Deseret" in the Book of Mormon, meaning "honeybee."

The tenets of Mormon faith, including polygamy and the concept of eternal marriage, led Protestant fundamentalists to mount campaigns of intolerance unheard of in Utah. Congress passed an anti-polygamy act in 1882; territorial (and later state) laws denied Mormons the right to vote or hold public office for many years. Idaho's last anti-Mormon laws were not repealed until 1982. Mormons are the largest religious group in the state today (about half of all declared church members); in southeastern Idaho they comprise a heavy majority of the population.

Anti-Mormonism was just one of several factors contributing to a strong sectionalism that developed in Idaho in the 19th century and remains to this day. With social and economic activity focused on Salt Lake City in the southeast and Spokane in the north, and with only a single road (and that unpaved until 1938) connecting Boise with Lewiston and the Panhandle, statewide unity was difficult to achieve. Congress actually approved the annexation of northern Idaho by Washington in 1887, but the bill was vetoed by President Grover Cleveland. To placate angry northerners, the University of Idaho was located in the Panhandle town of Moscow in 1889.

RAILROADS AND SILVER MINING

Pocatello was linked by rail to Salt Lake City and Butte, Montana, in the late 1870s, but most freight and passengers were delivered throughout Idaho by stagecoach until a pair of silver strikes promised the territory new riches. They inspired the development of transcontinental rail lines through both southern and northern Idaho, beginning in 1884.

The first silver strike occurred in 1880 in the Wood River Valley, not far from the modern Sun Valley resort. The boomtown of Hailey quickly became the richest in Idaho. It implemented the territory's first electric lighting system and its first telephone exchange.

The Wood River Valley boom fizzled by 1893. In the meantime, a much larger strike had taken hold of the Coeur d'Alene valley, on the western slope of the Bitterroots in the northern Panhandle. Gold was found in 1883, but that event

Members of the Pacific Railroad Survey and Nez Percé leaders meet in the 1850s, as drawn for Isaac I. Stevens's report of his part of the survey. (Idaho State Historical Society)

The Idaho Northern boasts of having just shipped the first carload of silver-lead ore out of the Black Horse Mine. (Idaho State Historical Society)

was soon eclipsed by the 1885 discovery of a major lode of silver. In fact, a century after the initial silver strike, the Coeur d'Alene district surpassed one billion ounces mined—a world record.

Unlike gold, which could be panned or sluiced, silver required hard-rock mining technology, smelters, and railway lines. Investors from major U.S. urban centers plunged their money into the necessary equipment, and were quickly repaid many times over. Kellogg, Osburn, and Wallace became pollution-spewing industrial towns, and Spokane grew as the main shipping center for the district.

The new mining wealth helped boost Idaho to statehood as the 43rd member of the Union in 1890.

POTATO FARMING AND RANCHING

In the 1860s the Treasure Valley area was already producing enough grain to feed the miners. The Mormon lands of the southeast and the rolling Palouse Hills north of Lewiston proved to be fine wheat and barley country as well. But it wasn't until large-scale irrigation projects were undertaken that the sage-riddled Snake River valley became the proverbial "fruited plain."

Although irrigation had been practiced on a small scale earlier, it really took off after 1894, when Congress passed the Carey Act, offering up to one million acres of federal land to any state that could irrigate and farm it within 10 years. Orchardist Ira Perrine, who had left Indiana to settle in Idaho, took the legislation as a personal challenge. Amassing investors, he built a 65-mile canal system that turned 244,000 acres of desert on the south side of the Middle Snake into fertile farmland, founding the market town of Twin Falls as he did so. A second canal system added 141,000 acres on the north side of the Snake. And Perrine was not alone as an irrigationist.

By 1902, when the Newlands Act created the U.S. Reclamation Service (now the Bureau of Reclamation), Idaho was a national showcase for the Carey Act, with 60 percent of all lands irrigated under that bill. In subsequent years the Bureau of Reclamation created much more Snake River farmland with a series of dams and new canals.

The Caswell brothers struck gold at Thunder Mountain.
(Idaho State Historical Society)

A harvest of potatoes pours onto a truck .

Among the great beneficiaries were potato farmers. The tuber for which Idaho now has a worldwide reputation was not a big success in the state until the blight-resistant Russet Burbank variety proved perfect for the state's high-desert conditions and volcanic soil. Idaho farms raised their yield from 700,000 bushels in 1900 to 25 million in 1929, and finally passed Maine as the nation's number-one potato producer in 1950.

No person played a greater role in that boom than the late J. R. Simplot. Born in Iowa in 1909, Simplot moved to Idaho as a boy. Legend says he parlayed a highway mishap—he discovered a load of seed potatoes inadvertently dumped by a farm truck—into his first crop, on 160 acres he rented near Burley. During World War II, Simplot supplied American troops with dehydrated potatoes; after the war he created frozen potatoes for the domestic market (including McDonald's french fries). Later he expanded his enterprise into phosphate fertilizers, ranching, mining, and wood products. At the time of his death in 2008, his fortune was estimated at over $3 billion.

Since long before the potato boom, Idaho's vast rangeland has been ideal for raising cattle and sheep. In the 1870s some herds had as many as 30,000 head of cattle, and cowboys roamed the plain. Sheep were prized for their wool, which was

Extensive irrigation has made agriculture possible on the otherwise arid Snake River Plain.

The late Jack R. Simplot, America's potato king.
(Idaho State Historical Society)

shipped to textile mills in Oregon. Ketchum, in the Wood River Valley, evolved from a silver camp into the largest sheep-shipping center in the western United States in the early 20th century.

FORESTS AND DAMS

In northern Idaho, aside from mining, timber has always been a big income producer. Demand for the Panhandle's extensive stands of ponderosa and white pine began around 1890 with the start of rail service, and boomed in the early 20th century after Minnesota timber lord Frederick Weyerhaeuser built mills in Lewiston, Coeur d'Alene, and Potlatch, midway between the two. Today Boise Cascade and Potlatch are Idaho's biggest wood-products firms.

Forest lands are conserved in national forests, which occupy 35 percent of Idaho's land—the largest percentage of any of the lower 48 states. Where there are forests, however, there are fires. The scars of a great fire that swept across the Panhandle in 1910 are still visible. Today Boise is home to the National Interagency Fire Center, which coordinates firefighting efforts throughout much of the western United States.

Fortunately, Idaho is blessed with a surfeit of water to fight fires. What's more, its rivers supply hydroelectricity that makes the economy run and provides modern conveniences to private users.

The dams built by the U.S. Reclamation Service in the early years of the 20th century were only the first of about two dozen that tap the water resources of the Snake River Plain. At 348 feet high, Arrowrock Dam on the Boise River east of the capital was the tallest in the world from 1915 until 1934, when Hoover Dam was completed. American Falls Dam, on the Snake west of Pocatello, created Idaho's largest reservoir, 25 miles long, when it opened in 1927.

The most controversial dams were the trio (Brownlee, Oxbow, and Hells Canyon) built by the Idaho Power Company on the Snake, at the upper end of Hells Canyon, between 1955 and 1968. Designed without fish passage facilities, they prevented salmon from continuing upriver to spawn. Thousands of fish piled up against the face of the dam and died. Hatcheries downstream couldn't come close to duplicating the traditional runs. The creation in 1973 of Hells Canyon National Recreation Area, flanking the Snake in Idaho and Oregon, prevented further dam building from taking place. Environmental groups in the 21st cen-

Peruvian sheepherder Rodolfo Serva Arca at an autumn sheep camp in central Idaho. Peruvian immigrants have become a major part of Idaho's shepherding community.

tury are calling for the redesign—or, in radical cases, removal—of existing dams to give the salmon a chance to reestablish their run.

Another energy producer covers 890 square miles of desert west of the city of Idaho Falls. The Idaho National Engineering and Enviromental Laboratory (INEEL), established in 1949, has 52 separate nuclear reactors (the largest concentration on earth), including the world's first to produce electric power with atomic energy. None are currently operational.

Sun Valley, established in the Wood River Valley in 1936, was at the vanguard of a growing public interest in recreational development, and especially of wilderness preservation. Urged on by Senator Frank Church, a Democrat who served in Washington from 1956 to 1980, Congress designated some four million acres of Idaho land (more than any state but Alaska and California) as wilderness, accessible only by boat or small aircraft.

Another major figure in environmental preservation in Idaho has been **Cecil Andrus.** As governor (1971-77 and 1987-95) and Secretary of the Interior in the Carter Administration (1977-81), he set aside the Birds of Prey National Conservation Area on the Snake River and took a hard line against permanent nuclear-waste storage at INEEL.

IDAHO TODAY

Outside of Idaho, however, the state has an unfounded image of radical conservatism, an image not helped by the Aryan Nations, a militant white-supremacist group founded in the mid-1970s. Its leader, Richard Butler, left California for the isolation and predominantly white Anglo-Saxon population of the northern Panhandle, where he built a fortified 20-acre compound near Hayden Lake, 10 miles from the burgeoning lake resort town of Coeur d'Alene. Butler surrendered the land in 2000 after declaring bankruptcy; on his death in 2004 the grounds were turned into a peace park.

In this state of nearly 1.5 million, only about 11,000 are black, though they comprise the fastest-growing segment of Idaho's population, having increased by more than 50 percent in the past decade. There are about 14,000 Idahoans of Asian ancestry and just over 20,000 Native Americans, predominantly of the Nez Percé, Coeur d'Alene, and Shoshone-Bannock tribes. Together, these groups comprise three percent of the population.

A large number of Basque immigrants first came to Idaho from the Atlantic coastal boundary area of Spain and France between 1900 and 1920; many first took work herding sheep. Today Boise has the largest Basque community out-

Basques have traditionally eaten communally at large tables.

side Europe, and although many of its members are third- or fourth-generation Americans, they maintain great pride in their heritage.

Beginning in the 1990s with a boom in high-technology industry and adventure tourism, Idaho began to attract relocating out-of-state urbanites. Science- and technology-related industries now provide more than 25 percent of the state's revenue, more than agriculture, forestry, and mining combined. Crime, safety, and other social concerns are not big problems here; they take a back seat to economics and environmentalism in the eyes of most Idahoans.

In the early 21st-century Idaho, as population booms, concerns grow over availability of water, both for drinking and for agriculture. Governor Butch Otter is leading a call to resolve a three-decade-old controversy over water rights in the eastern Snake River Plain, and to head off potential similar arguments in southwest Idaho's Treasure Valley.

Environmentalists, meanwhile, continue to dispute the importance of a series of dams on the Snake River, especially in the Hells Canyon area along the Oregon border, citing their existence as a primary reason for reduced runs of wild salmon in Idaho rivers. In this state, however, agriculture and hydroelectricity are the first priority.

FRANK LESLIE'S ILLUSTRATED NEWSPAPER

NEW YORK—FOR THE WEEK ENDING APRIL 19, 1884. [PRICE, 10 CENTS.

OUR ARTIST'S WANDERINGS IN THE FAR WEST—THE FIRST WOMAN IN CAMP IN THE COEUR D'ALENE MINING DISTRICT, IDAHO.

Idaho has been attracting out-of-state urbanites for quite some time, as this illustrated weekly from 1884 attests. The caption reads "Our artist's wanderings in the far west—the first woman in camp in the Coeur d'Alene mining district, Idaho." (Idaho State Historical Society)

BOISE & THE SOUTHWEST

A verdant oasis in a dry landscape, "The City of Trees" got its name from the cottonwoods, birches, and willows that line its namesake river. Early-19th-century French-Canadian fur trappers are said to have seen this swath of greenery after a long desert passage and exclaimed "Les bois! Les bois!"—essentially, "Hey, check out those woods!"

Boise was founded on the Oregon Trail in 1863 as a farming and supply center for nearby mining towns Idaho City and other gold camps in the hills to the north, Silver City in the Owyhee Mountains to the south. Construction of Fort Boise began on July 6 that year; the new town was platted on July 7. By the following year it was the territorial capital and a town that, unlike the mining boomtowns, supported family life. Some of the 400 buildings erected during the city's first five years can still be seen today.

Many more structures date from the last three decades of the 19th century, the period in which Idaho became a state. A handsome collection of these late-19th-century structures stands in the wedge of downtown known as Old Boise, while others grace the Warm Springs district, Boise's first upscale neighborhood. Town engineers also developed irrigation canals and an extensive geothermal heating system (the world's first) emanating from hot springs at the east end of Boise.

By 1910 Boise had 20,000 residents. Thereafter, the population increased by about 1,000 people a year until the 1970s. The Second World War brought substantial growth and prosperity to Boise, as the engineering company Morrison-Knudson won defense contracts and two Air Force training bases were built in the area.

The big companies that have formed the core of Boise's economy—the Washington Group International (engineering and construction; formerly Morrison-Knudsen), J.R. Simplot (agriculture), and Boise Cascade (wood products)—were later joined by high-tech industries like Hewlett-Packard and Micron Technology, which drew increasing numbers of urban refugees from America's Midwest and West Coast, especially California. By 2006 Boise's population had surpassed 200,000, making it by far the largest city in the three states (Idaho, Wyoming, and Montana) of the northern Rocky Mountains.

Today Boise has evolved from a town to a city. High-rise buildings are commonplace. Sidewalk cafés line Eighth Avenue near Main and Idaho streets. A cultural district is emerging at the edge of downtown, just west of Capitol

Looking down Boise's Capitol Boulevard to the State Capitol dome.

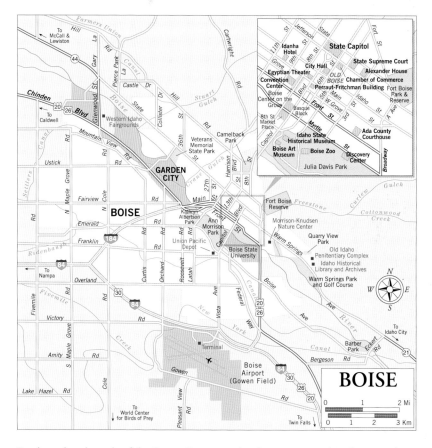

Boulevard and south of the Boise Center on the Grove, a central pedestrian plaza. Nearby, the Basque Block is devoted to the living heritage of the city's most visible minority. Towering above is the State Capitol building, the only one in the U.S. to be heated by geothermal energy. Capitol Boulevard divides the Old Boise historical blocks, to its east, from the main downtown shopping and financial district, to its west.

A few blocks away, at the heart of the Boise River Greenbelt, is Julia Davis Park, home to the city's zoo and its most important museums. Boise's artistic fringe is settling into the newly developing Linen District, along Grove Street west of downtown. The bohemian Hyde Park neighborhood is flourishing in the north end of the city.

And recreation is just outside the door. The Boise River cuts through the heart of the city, and both kayakers and fly fishermen are common sights. In the mountains that flank Boise to the north, Bogus Basin offers a ski season that may extend from Thanksgiving into April.

GREENBELT

The Boise River Greenbelt truly sets Boise apart from other cities of similar size. Starting in 1968, civic leaders directed a cleanup and renovation of the neglected river corridor and created a series of parks linked by 19 miles of walking and bicycle paths. In doing so, they not only instilled a sense of community pride and created Boise's leading recreational attraction; they reestablished a prime habitat for a great variety of urban wildlife, from beavers and muskrats to bald eagles and great blue herons.

The Boise River rises on the western flank of the craggy Sawtooth Range and flows 130 miles to the Snake River. A few miles above Boise it is twice dammed; the Greenbelt begins opposite the spillway from Lucky Peak Reservoir at the Discovery Unit of **Lucky Peak State Park** (Rte. 21, 9 miles east of Boise; 208/334–3360). A bike path follows the river through a narrow canyon to **Barber Park** (Eckert Rd., 0.5 mile south of Warm Springs Ave.; 208/343–1328), known as the put-in point for rafters and inner-tubers.

By some estimates, a quarter-million "river rats" (more than the population of Boise itself) float the 5.5-mile section of the river from Barber Park to **Ann Morrison Memorial Park** (Ann Morrison Park Dr.; 208/384–4240) every summer. (The Greenbelt continues past Kathryn Albertson Park and Veteran's Memorial State Park, several miles farther downriver.) When the August air temperature is 95 degrees, the 60-degree water is shockingly refreshing. Floaters traverse gentle rapids that flow within sight of the State Capitol, avoiding the arc and sweep of fly-fishermen's lines and the Tarzan-like screams of Boise State University students who swing from ropes before plunging into the 100-foot-wide stream. Rental outfits in both Barber and Ann Morrison parks shuttle floaters between put-in and take-out.

Below Barber Park the Greenbelt passes numerous residences, their property lines backed to the river's high-water mark, then skirts Municipal Park—a patch of green popular for group picnics—and the **Morrison-Knudsen Nature Center.** Adjacent to the Idaho Department of Fish and Game headquarters, the center comprises a simulated mountain stream, emptying into a wetland pond, and a

Floating along Boise's river is a popular summer activity.

museum of riparian ecology. Underwater windows enable visitors to follow the development of trout and other fish, from eggs to full-size adults. *600 S. Walnut St.; 208/334–2225.*

Downstream from Broadway Avenue, the river divides ★ **Julia Davis Park** (Julia Davis Park Dr.; 208/384–4240) from the campus of **Boise State University** (1910 University Dr.; 208/385–1011), a 19,500-student institution and Idaho's largest center for higher learning. BSU's main claims to fame are the Morrison Center for the Performing Arts, a state-of-the-art facility designed by the same firm responsible for New York's Lincoln Center, and one of the nation's finest mid-sized college football teams. (BSU's 2007 Fiesta Bowl upset of heavily favored Oklahoma, marked by a series of trick plays, is already regarded as one of the greatest college football games in history.) A footbridge links the university with the park.

Named for the wife of a pioneer whose 7,000-tree orchard once graced this expanse, Julia Davis Park is truly the heart of Boise from a tourist standpoint: it has two museums, a zoo, a boating lagoon, and an impressive rose garden.

At the **Idaho State Historical Museum,** you can trace Idaho history from the fossil past, through the fur-trading and mining-boom eras, to the growth of urban Boise. There's special emphasis on ethnic cultures, including the Shoshone natives, Chinese miners, and Basque immigrants. Several early-Boise buildings of adobe, log, and wood-frame construction have been relocated to a Pioneer Village next to the museum. *Julia Davis Park, 610 N. Julia Davis Dr.; 208/334–2120.*

The **Boise Art Museum** is the home of one of the nation's most highly regarded displays of American-realist paintings, the Glenn C. Janss Collection. The museum also features a rotating annual calendar of at least 15 touring exhibitions and a sculpture garden. *Julia Davis Park, 670 S. Julia Davis Dr.; 208/345–2247.*

The **Discovery Center of Idaho** has 100 permanent exhibits encouraging experimentation in electricity, magnetism, motion, and other physical sciences. Children and their parents are encouraged to do more than just look: here you can participate in the exhibits also through hands-on manipulation. *Julia Davis Park, 131 Myrtle St.; 208/343–9895.*

Zoo Boise has more than 200 animals of some 90 species—most of them native to the region, like elk, moose, bighorn sheep, and diverse birds of prey. The exotic collection is much more limited: zebras, Amur tigers, monkeys, and ring-tailed lemurs. It's a great place for a family afternoon. *Julia Davis Park, 355 N. Julia Davis Dr.; 208/384–4260.*

TOOTIN' TATER AND BIG MIKE

You can get a good introduction to the city by hitching a ride aboard the **Boise Tour Train**. Two motorized 1890s-replica locomotives (The Tootin' Tater and Big Mike), based in Julia Davis Park beside the Pioneer Village, pull a pair of trolley cars on one-hour journeys through the city's historic streets. *Julia Davis Park, 600 N. Julia Davis Dr.; 208/342–4796.*

After circling the park, the Tour Train rambles east down Myrtle Street and crosses Broadway Avenue to the world headquarters of Washington Group International, one of the world's largest engineering-construction firms, which acquired the Morrison-Knudsen Co. in 1996. Founded in Boise in 1912, Morrison-Knudsen declared bankruptcy in 1995 after a well-publicized scandal involving its CEO. The company's projects rise in all 50 states and 75 foreign countries, and have included the likes of Hoover Dam, the Trans-Alaska Pipeline, and the Cape Canaveral launch towers.

Warm Springs District, which stretches east from Broadway, claims to be the world's first residential neighborhood since the last days of Pompeii to be geothermally heated. In 1890 the Boise Hot and Cold Artesian Water Co. began

CLARENCE DARROW ON IDAHO'S ATHENS

Attorney Clarence Darrow came to Boise in 1907 to defend William "Big Bill" Haywood against charges that he had assassinated the former governor, Frank Steunenberg.

Until entering this case I had never been in Boise. I had read of it, and knew that it was far away out West. I had pictured it to myself, but I never found an unfamiliar person or place that proved to be anything like my mental picture. Boise was approached from the east through hundreds of miles of dreary, dusty desert with no living thing in sight but gophers and sage-brush . . . Through the whole region of desert waste, a long strip of green wound and twisted its tortuous way in loops and zigzags across the desolate plain . . . As we neared Boise the scene changed. The fields were fresh and green, the orchards were luxuriant, the town was resplendent with lawns and flowers, shrubs and trees; the houses were neat and up-to-date. The Snake River had been intersected with dikes, which irrigated the barren wilderness and made it a beautiful garden-spot. The landscape was most pleasing, and out beyond, a circle of mountains enclosed the little city; so that after the long, wearisome journey Boise seemed like a bright green gem in a setting of blue.

Darrow won Haywood's acquittal, and afterwards his client described him thus: "When Darrow rose to address the jury he stood big and broad shouldered . . . While he spoke he was sometimes intense, his great voice rumbling, his left hand shoved deep in his coat pocket, his right arm uplifted. Again he would take a pleading attitude, his voice would become gentle and very quiet. At times he would approach the jury almost on tiptoe."

pumping 172-degree water from a well drilled into a rhyolite aquifer at the east end of the young town. Today three-quarters of a million gallons each day are still drawn from the restored pump house at **Quarry View Park** (Bacon Dr. and Old Penitentiary Rd.; 208/384–4240), heating more than 400 homes and eight government buildings, including the State Capitol.

Among the notable homes along Warm Springs Avenue are the 1925 English country-style **C.C. Anderson House** (No. 929), now designated as the home

The electrifying entrance to the Boise Art Museum.

of the officiating Boise State University president; the 1868 Greek Revival-style **G. W. Russell House** (No. 1035), the district's oldest residence; and the 1891 French chateau-style **Moore-Cunningham House** (No. 1109), the nation's first geothermally heated home, still sheltering descendents of its original family.

Upon leaving the Warm Springs district, the Tour Train swings up Fort Street and through the **Fort Boise Reserve** (Fifth and Fort Sts.; 208/384-4486), site of the original U.S. Army post that motivated the settlement of Boise. Preserved in its original location is Boise's oldest building—the 1863 log cabin of soldier John O'Farrell and his 17-year-old bride—as well as the fort's original sandstone guard houses. Fort Boise operated until 1912; since 1938 it has been the site of the Idaho State Veterans Home and Veterans Administration Hospital. From Fort Boise, the Tour Train circles past the State Capitol through downtown Boise and back to Julia Davis Park.

A CAPITAL DOWNTOWN

To truly get a feel for downtown Boise, you'll have to disembark from the tour train and walk. There's no better place to start than at the ★**State Capitol,** a neoclassical structure whose design mimics that of the U.S. Capitol. Construction of the 200,000-square-foot building began in 1905. The center portion, featuring a rotunda dome capped by a man-sized, bronze-dipped copper eagle, was completed in 1912. The east and west wings, which house the state legislative bodies, were added in 1919 and 1920. Boise sandstone laid over a steel framework comprises the Capitol's exterior, but the marble in its interior was imported from Alaska, Georgia, Vermont, and Italy. Historical photographs, a gem display, and a gilded statue of George Washington on horseback are among the four floors of exhibits within the Capitol. *700 W. Jefferson St.; 208/334–2470.*

Facing the Capitol from a small park triangle is a statue of Frank Steunenberg, the Idaho governor whose 1905 assassination, after his term of office had ended, led to the celebrated trial of labor leader "Big Bill" Haywood that pitted the renowned lawyer Clarence Darrow against the equally formidable Borah. Note the state flag: the image it bears is Idaho's state seal, the only one of America's 50 designed by a woman, Emma Edwards Green.

Extending east and north from the State Capitol is a governmental complex of some eight square blocks. The **Ada County Courthouse** (200 W. Front St.; 208/287–7500) is an art deco creation of the 1930s Works Progress Administration. Two blocks east of the Capitol is the **State Supreme Court** (451

The Idaho State Capitol houses four floors of exhibits.

W. State St.; 208/334–2210), built of travertine from eastern Idaho. The Queen Anne-style **Alexander House** (304 W. State St.; 208/334–2119), built in 1897 as the home of America's first Jewish governor, Moses Alexander, is opposite the library; it is now the home of the Idaho Commission on the Arts. The **Idaho Historical Library and Archives** (2205 Old Penitentiary Rd.; 208/334–3356) is on the east side of town.

Back on the front steps of the Capitol, you can look in a southerly direction straight down Capitol Boulevard to the old **Union Pacific Depot** (2603 Eastover Terrace; 208/384–9591), about a mile away across the Boise River. This former Union Pacific station was built in mission style in 1925, and exhibits various memorabilia from Idaho railroad history.

Walk three blocks south of the State Capitol to where the boulevard meets Main Street at the modern Boise City Hall. The flags of all 50 states fly above its sidewalk plaza. Then turn east into **Old Boise.** The two-block-long core of the city's original downtown is now mainly occupied by restaurants, bars, galleries, and small shops. Many of the buildings are of stone or brick construction; the

The Chinese have played a role in the development of Idaho since the middle of the 19th century. Here a New Year's parade passes the corner of Main and Capitol in Boise. (Idaho State Historical Society)

OVERLAND HOTEL. PROPERTY OF EASTMAN BROS. BOISE CITY. IDAHO.

The Overland Hotel in Boise, 1876, somehwat resembles the Idanha Hotel
(see photo following page), which was bult in 1901. (Bancroft Library, U.C. Berkeley)

oldest, the **Perrault-Fritchman Building** (104 S. Capitol Blvd., at W. Main St.; 208/342–6320), was erected in 1879 of local sandstone.

Rising from Fifth and Main is an eye-catching stone structure resembling a castle: the Belgravia, Boise's first apartment house, is now an office building with a gourmet basement restaurant. To the immediate south is **C.W. Moore Park** (Fifth and Grove Sts.), a quiet corner that displays a variety of 19th-century cornerstones from buildings long since razed, and a water wheel—the remains of one of the city's earliest canal systems. Two blocks east, at Third and Main, is the **U.S. Assay Office** (210 W. Main St.; 208/334–3861), a national historic landmark built in 1872. Impregnable in appearance, with two-foot-thick sandstone walls, the cube-shape building processed $75 million in gold and silver ore before it closed in 1933. Today it houses offices of the Idaho Historical Society, which displays a collection of native gemstones.

Walking west on Main Street from City Hall, immediately on your right is the unmistakable ★**Egyptian Theater** (700 W. Main St.; 208/342–1441), built in

1926 at the height of the Egyptian Revival fad brought on by the discovery of King Tutankhamen's tomb. The high-camp interior, which includes a working pipe organ that once provided music and sound effects for silent films, makes this Boise's best place to take in a movie. Idaho's tallest building—the 20-story US Bank Plaza, a bank office building completed in 1978—is directly across Main from the theater. Construction of a 30-story building at Eighth and Main streets is expected to begin soon.

When it opened in 1901, the six-story **Idanha Hotel** (pronounced EYE-dahn-hah) was Idaho's tallest structure, operating the state's first elevator. Theodore Roosevelt and Will Rogers are among the many dignitaries who have slept in this French chateau-style building with corner turrets and crenellated rooftop. The hotel has more than once been saved from the wrecker's ball, most recently in 1981. *928 W. Main St.; 208/341–3611.*

Opposite the Idanha is the international headquarters of the J. R. Simplot Co., the world's largest privately owned agribusiness. More than anyone, Jack Simplot was responsible for making the name of Idaho synonymous with spuds. As legend

The Idanha Hotel (left) and the historic Egyptian Theater (above), both in downtown Boise, have been saved from the wrecker's ball on several occasions.

has it, he started out with a few gold coins. At the time of his death in 2008, he was one of the richest people in America.

South of Main Street, downtown Boise is mostly new. One of the benefits of a massive urban renewal project in the 1970s was creation of the ★**Boise Center on the Grove,** a public plaza extending south from Main along Eighth Street. A fountain at the heart of this pedestrian mall is the focal point for year-round activity, highlighted by the live bands and food vendors of Alive After Five, every Wednesday evening in summer. Across Front Street is the **Eighth Street Market Place,** where several stories of shops, restaurants, night clubs, movie theaters and offices have taken over a renovated early-20th-century warehouse district. A farmer's market of fresh produce is staged outside on summer Saturday mornings.

BOISE'S BASQUE BLOCK

A block west of the Grove, between Capitol Boulevard and Sixth Street on Grove Street, is ★**Boise's Basque Block.** The Euzkaldunak, as they call themselves, first came to North America's Great Basin country in the late 19th century and found work mainly as sheepherders. Now fully assimilated into the general population, southwestern Idaho's 20,000 Basques—the largest Basque community outside of

A Basque sheepshearers' band. (Idaho State Historical Society)

Europe—maintain strong ties with their motherland along the mountainous border between Spain and France.

The **Basque Museum and Cultural Center** is the cornerstone of the Basque Block. Incorporating an adjacent former boardinghouse—Boise's oldest brick building, the 1864 Cyrus Jacobs—Uberuaga House, now converted to a living-history exhibit—this museum is the only one in the United States devoted entirely to Basque culture. Displays that describe Basque history, language (the unique tongue has no known linguistic relatives), and culture can be found in the main museum building, along with a library and gift shop. *607 Grove St.; 208/343–2671.*

Across the street is **The Basque Market** (600 W. Grove St.; 208/433–1208), an importer of food and wine from the Basque Country. Down the block are the Basque Center, home of the acclaimed Oinkari Dancers, who perform internationally; a pair of Basque bar-restaurants; and a fronton where Idaho Basques play *pelota*, a traditional form of handball similar to jai alai.

BEHIND PRISON WALLS

One of Boise's most intriguing attractions, albeit a bittersweet one, is the ★**Old Idaho Penitentiary** (2445 Old Penitentiary Rd.; 208/368–6080), 2 miles from downtown at the east end of the Warm Springs District. Convicts themselves built the prison of hand-cut stone in 1870, quarrying sandstone from Table Rock—a geological formation that still towers over the site, though it now has a lighted cross and telecommunications transmitters on top.

During more than a century of operation, more than 13,000 inmates saw the inside of the prison's high turreted walls. Among them were gubernatorial assassin Harry Orchard, who was sentenced to life imprisonment in 1908 and who died here in 1954 at the age of 88; Diamondfield Jack Davis, acquitted of a murder charge in 1902, on the eve of his scheduled hanging, after five years behind bars; and Lyda "Lady Bluebeard" Southard, who served 19 years (including 15 months on the lam, after a daring escape) for poisoning her fourth husband. (The first three husbands had also died mysteriously.)

A series of riots in protest over living conditions persuaded state officials to open a new penitentiary in south Boise in 1973. Barely a year later, this venerable complex, known locally as The Old Pen, was admitted to the National Register of Historic Places. Today owned by the Idaho State Historical Society, it is operated as a museum, or rather a series of museums.

JAIL FOR THE RIGHT SORT

*Idaho weathered the Great Depression of the 1930s better than most states, thanks in large part to President Franklin Roosevelt's New Deal. The Works Progress Administration had the wisdom to make noted Idaho novelist Vardis Fisher (*Toilers of the Hills, In Tragic Life*) the primary author of its guidebook to Idaho.* Idaho: A Guide in Word and Picture *(1937) was the first of 48 guides to individual states.*

The following excerpt on the Idaho City jail is classic Fisher:

Its [Idaho City's] jail was the first in the large territory once called Idaho, and this jail, used until 1870, was the scene of some stirring episodes . . . There was Ferd Patterson, for instance: gambler, gunman, and murderer, he killed the captain of a boat in Portland, scalped his ex-mistress, and climaxed his playfulness by slaying the sheriff of Idaho City. Ferd was, records declare, a pulp villain of the first water: he affected high-heeled boots, plaid trousers reinforced with buckskin, a fancy silk vest spanned by a heavy gold chain of California nuggets, and a frock coat of beaver cloth trimmed with otter. But the sheriff whom he killed is described by an early historian as one of 'nature's noblemen,' and not fewer than a thousand men awaited Mr. Patterson's return with a deputy who sailed out to capture him. The mob was bent on lynching, but the deputy outwitted them and got his prisoner safely into the jail; whereupon the vigilantes met in the graveyard, went to Boise and got a cannon, and resolved to attack. But the deputy, a man who apparently was remarkably nimble of wit, got a cannon also, cut portholes in the jail wall, manned his fortress with a bunch of desperadoes, and waited. And he won. It is not recorded that he almost died of chagrin when Patterson went to trial and was freed.

Guided or self-guided tours of the prison grounds begin with an 18-minute slide show on the facility's history. Open for inspection are several cell blocks, including the cramped women's ward, the maximum security wing, the solitary confinement chambers (known among inmates as "Siberia" or "The Corner Pocket"), the cells of Death Row, and the gallows that performed Idaho's last hanging in 1957. Among special exhibits are photos and replicas of inmates' tattoos (from demonic to erotic), a frightening array of confiscated weapons, and a

The Union Pacific train depot is now filled with railway memorabilia.

rose garden that the Jackson & Perkins Rose Co. used as a test garden (and where the first Tropicana roses were bred in the early 1960s).

Several small museums are housed within the **Old Penitentiary complex** (2445 Old Penitentiary Rd.; 208/368–6080). The Old Pen's former shirt factory has been converted into the **Idaho Transportation Museum,** a collection of vehicles ranging from a traditional Shoshone travois—a two-pole sled dragged by a dog—to horse-drawn buggies, early farm machinery, and classic automobiles. In the former commissary, the **History of Electricity in Idaho Museum** follows a timeline from Benjamin Franklin and Thomas Edison to the modern hydropower industry. The **Idaho Museum of Mining & Geology** is in the new trusty quarters, built outside the prison walls in 1928 as a dormitory for trusted inmates with supervisory responsibilities; this museum's exhibits tell the story of the state's early gold and silver mining communities with artifacts and photographs.

The **Idaho Botanical Garden,** outside the prison's northeast wall, is worth a visit while you're at the Old Pen. The nine separate theme and display gardens here bloom from late April through mid-October. Some feature roses, irises, or herbs; some follow cultural themes, such as Chinese and Basque; some are designed specifically to attract hummingbirds and butterflies, or to encourage meditation. *2373 Old Penitentiary Rd.; 208/343–8649.*

NEARBY NATURE PRESERVES

Speaking of hummingbirds, this corner of Idaho is also home to the world's largest nesting populations of raptors—birds of prey. To protect these birds, two principal (but administratively unrelated) natural preserves have been established near Boise.

★**The World Center for Birds of Prey** was established in 1984 to breed threatened and endangered eagles, hawks, falcons, and owls. Since that time, more than 4,000 birds of 22 species have been released in places as far from Idaho as Madagascar and the Philippines. Trained docents guide visitors on tours of the interpretive center, where they can see raptor incubators and demonstrations with live birds. Owned by the Peregrine Fund, the reserve is 6 miles south of Boise via South Cole Road. *5666 W. Flying Hawk La.; 208/362–2376.*

The **Snake River Birds of Prey National Conservation Area,** administered by the Bureau of Land Management, is 30 miles south of Boise, but it is well worth the trip. Three resident species of hawks and seven types of owls, as well as golden eagles, prairie falcons, kestrels, harriers, and turkey vultures, nest on ledges and crevices in the walls of the Snake River Canyon. More than 800 pairs of raptors nest on the basalt cliffs, some of them hundreds of feet high. The 81-mile stretch of canyon preserves the largest concentration of nesting raptors on earth. Bald eagles, ospreys, peregrine falcons, and six other migratory species make extended visits to the preserve.

In search of mice, ground squirrels, and jackrabbits, the birds ride updrafts from the prevailing canyon winds over the surrounding desert. May and June are the best months for human visits, when eggs have hatched and bird populations are highest. Good riverside viewing points are posted turnouts 5 miles south of Melba via Can-Ada Road, and at Dedication Point, 15 miles south of Kuna via Swan Falls Road. The best way to see the birds, however, is from the river itself, by raft or boat: contact the BLM (208/384–3300) or local river outfitters.

TREASURE VALLEY

A prescient public-relations man deserves credit for bestowing the name of Treasure Valley upon the immensely rich bottomlands of the Boise, Payette, and Snake rivers. The local riches aren't gold and silver, however; they're sugar beets and potatoes, corn and wheat, barley and alfalfa, apple and cherry orchards, and vineyards. But there's more to be seen than fruits and grains on a one-day loop trip from Boise.

With 52,000 people, **Nampa** is Idaho's fourth-largest city. But it is best known as the home of one of America's biggest rodeos, the **Snake River Stampede** (208/323–8555). A five-day event held the third week of July at the Idaho Center (below), the Stampede draws leading professional rodeo circuit riders to compete for prize money in bull riding, calf roping, bareback bronco riding and other traditional events. There are also parades, dances, and an Indian powwow. Nampa is only 15 miles west of Boise.

Nampa was founded in 1883 as a railroad town. Its early 20th-century Oregon Short Line depot, Idaho's finest example of Baroque Revival architecture, is now the home of the **Canyon County Historical Museum** (1200 Front St., Nampa; 208/467–7611). Still resting beside the tracks, it displays an engrossing assortment of railroad artifacts and other items that shed light on Nampa area history. The small campus of **Northwest Nazarene University** (623 Holly St., Nampa; 208/467–8011), a tiny liberal-arts school, attracts national attention once a year when basketball teams from 16 colleges throughout the nation converge on Nampa to vie for the Division II title of the National Association of Intercollegiate Athletics (NAIA).

Though not as rapidly as Boise, Nampa is also growing and gentrifying. A focal point is southwestern Idaho's largest arena complex, the **Idaho Center** (Can-Ada Rd., at Garrity Blvd., Nampa; 208/463–4700). The Snake River Stampede makes good use of its outdoor coliseum, which accommodates 800 horses along with 20,000 spectators, and the Idaho Stampede (and NBA Development League team) plays in its 15,000-seat indoor arena. The adjacent Sweetwater Junction complex has a water park, hotels, restaurants, and retail outlets.

Several World War II aircraft (including two Curtiss P-40s and a Fokker triplane replica) are exhibited at the **Warhawk Air Museum** (201 Municipal Dr., Nampa; 208/465–6446), along with wartime uniforms, photographs, and a variety of unusual souvenirs.

Hungry travelers can pick up a self-guided brochure, "Farm to Market Agricultural Tours," from the **Nampa Chamber of Commerce** (1305 Third St. S, Nampa; 208/466–4641). In addition to roadside fruit and vegetable stands and "U-pick" orchards, the brochure will lead you to the Swiss Village Cheese Factory, which manufactures blue cheese, and to wineries.

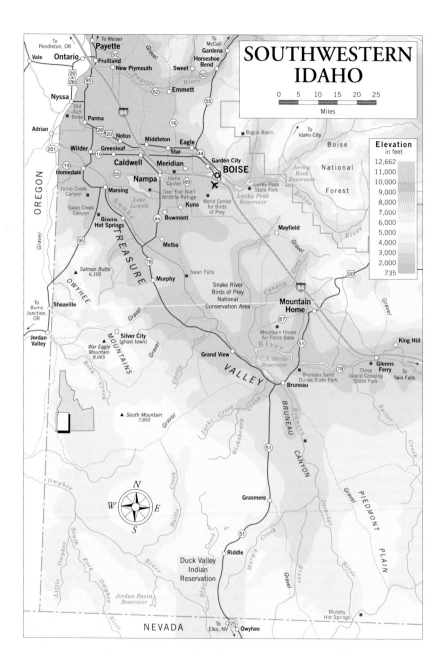

SOUTHWESTERN IDAHO

Elevation in feet

12,662
11,000
10,000
9,000
8,000
7,000
6,000
5,000
4,000
3,000
2,000
735

Branding time on a ranch outside of Nampa.

Wineries? In Idaho? Absolutely! Although Idaho is one of the nation's newer viticultural areas, this corner of the state produces excellent Johannesburg Rieslings, chardonnays, and pinot noirs. The **Ste. Chapelle Winery** (19348 Lowell Rd., Caldwell; 208/453–7843), founded in 1978, is the largest, producing 100,000 cases of varietals a year. Its white wines, including award-winning Rieslings, gewurztraminers, and ice wines, are especially strong. Ste. Chapelle hosts a popular summer Sunday jazz series. Tours and tastings are offered here and at several other nearby wineries. Look for Hells Canyon Winery, Indian Creek Winery, Pintler Cellar, and Weston Winery. For more on Idaho wineries, visit www.idahowines.org.

Idaho's wine country is south and west of sparkling blue Lake Lowell. Created for irrigation purposes by the diversion of the New York Canal from the Boise River in 1909, the reservoir is completely surrounded by the **Deer Flat National Wildlife Refuge.** An executive order of President Theodore Roosevelt established the refuge, one of the first in the United States. Visitor-center exhibits describe many of the 200 species of resident and migratory birds that inhabit the refuge, parts of which are open for hunting and fishing in season. As many as 100,000 ducks and 10,000 geese congregate in late fall on the lake and nearby Snake River. *Orchard Ave., 6 miles west of Nampa; 208/888–5582.*

Wildlife also flocks to **Wilson Ponds,** about 3 miles south of downtown Nampa. The small creek connecting the wetland pools makes for some great trout and bass fishing, not to mention bird-watching. Nature trails link the state Department of Fish and Game offices at the ponds' north end with a hatchery at the south, where you can observe trout by the thousands, from fingerlings to full-sized adults. *3101 S. Powerline Rd., Nampa; 208/465–8465.*

Nampa's sister city, **Caldwell,** with a population over 26,000, is the home of one of Idaho's most progressive schools, **College of Idaho,** formerly Albertson College (2112 Cleveland Blvd., Caldwell; 208/459–5011). Founded by a Presbyterian minister in 1891, the school now has an annual enrollment of about 800. William Judson Boone Hall, the science building on the splendid campus quadrangle, is home to several museum collections. Foremost is the **Orma J. Smith Museum of Natural History** (2101 Fillmore St., Caldwell; 208/459–5507); its research collection comes from throughout the western U.S. and Baja California. Boone Hall also has a gem and mineral display, planetarium, and herbarium.

In Caldwell's Memorial Park, the open-air **Van Slyke Agricultural Museum** (S. Kimball and Irving Sts., Caldwell; 208/459–7493) preserves a pair of 1864 log cabins, a variety of antique machinery, a freight-train boxcar, and a caboose. The site is not often open, but it can be viewed through a chain-link fence.

The original site of Fort Boise, the Hudson's Bay Company trading post built on the Oregon Trail in 1834, was about 20 miles northwest of Caldwell at the confluence of the Boise and Snake rivers. The adobe fort, its usefulness outlived, was destroyed by flood in 1853; and although Snake River ferry service operated from this location between 1864 and 1902, there's nothing to see at the site today. A replica known as **Old Fort Boise,** however, stands near the Boise River on U.S. 95 at the eastern edge of the small town of Parma, five miles upstream. A pioneer cabin and a historical museum are within its concrete walls. *East Main Ave., Payette; 208/722–5138.*

U.S. 95 follows the Snake north 20 miles through the little town of Fruitland, a center of apple orchards since the early 20th century, to **Payette,** at the mouth of the Payette River. Founded in 1867 and named for French-Canadian trader François Payette, who ran old Fort Boise in the 1830s and '40s, Payette has a downtown historic district that dates from 1885. Foremost among the structures is a Methodist Episcopal church, designed in Gothic Revival style in

Walter "Big Train" Johnson is considered by some the greatest pitcher of all time. He once pitched 85 straight scoreless innings. (Idaho State Historical Society)

1904, that now is home to the **Payette County Historical Museum** (90 S. Ninth St., Payette; 208/642–2362). Exhibits there include antique furniture and clothing, and a corner devoted to Payette native Harmon Killebrew, one of the greatest sluggers in Major League Baseball from 1954 to 1975. A member of the Baseball Hall of Fame, Killebrew hit 573 home runs in his career, a total bettered only by Hank Aaron, Babe Ruth, Willie Mays, and Frank Robinson.

Another Baseball Hall of Famer—a charter member, at that—is inextricably linked with nearby **Weiser,** although he spent only a few months there. Walter "Big Train" Johnson, rated by some as the greatest pitcher ever, was a 19-year-old Kansan who came to Idaho via California in 1907. He took up pitching for the Weiser Kids of the semi-pro Idaho State League. (Other teams had nicknames like the Nampa Beet Diggers, Payette Melon Eaters, and Emmett Prune Pickers.) By the time his contract was bought by the Washington Senators of the American League, he had pitched 85 straight innings without surrendering a run, averaging 16 strikeouts a game. In his 21 years with the Senators he won 416 games, the second-best record of all time.

Weiser's main claim to fame today is its **National Old-Time Fiddlers' Contest and Festival** (208/414–0255), a spirited event held the third week of June every year since 1963. Memorabilia from this favorite of bluegrass fans can be seen year-round in the **Weiser Chamber of Commerce** (8 E. Idaho St., Weiser;

208/549–0452). The town of over 5,000 people is one of the most architecturally intriguing in Idaho. Its numerous turn-of-the-20th-century buildings include the Pythian Castle, a crenellated, cut-stone manor with a Tudor facade, pressed-tin ceiling, and stained-glass windows; and the Intermountain Cultural Center, a former college preparatory school that now incorporates the **Washington County Museum** (2295 Paddock Ave., Weiser; 208/549–0205).

Where the Payette River pours into the Treasure Valley, the town of **Emmett** grew up in the midst of apple, plum, peach, cherry, and apricot orchards. It is the site of Boise Cascade's largest mill and plywood plant in southern Idaho. Emmett's **Gem County Historical Museum** (501 E. First St., at Hawthorne St., Emmett; 208/365–4340) encompasses five pioneer buildings with displays on local history, including early Shoshone culture.

ELMORE AND OWYHEE COUNTIES

The Elmore County town of **Mountain Home** gives the feeling of being out in the middle of nowhere. It is not in the mountains at all, in fact, but in the midst of a flat sagebrush desert 13 miles north of the Snake River, and 48 miles southeast of Boise. Idaho's warmest community was given its name by a stagecoach driver who thought wistfully of the cooler climes of his own mountain home.

Mountain Home was founded on Rattlesnake Creek by Oregon Short Line railroad construction crews in 1882, and within a couple of decades became an important shipping point for more than one million pounds of wool a year. Artifacts in the **Elmore County Historical Society Museum** tell the story of its development. Today the economic mainstay of this town of more than 11,000 is the Mountain Home Air Force Base, 11 miles southwest. Established in 1942 as a training school for Second World War bomber crews, it has become the home of the U.S. Air Intervention Composite Wing, a division of the Tactical Air Command. Crews from Mountain Home are on immediate call to be deployed anywhere in the world, as they have been in the Persian Gulf, Somalia, Bosnia, Afghanistan, Iraq, and elsewhere in recent years. Civilians can call ahead for tours. *Rte. 67, Mountain Home; 208/828–6800.*

Owyhee County stretches to the horizon beyond the Snake River. This largely barren region has a population density of fewer than one resident per square mile. Idaho's southwesternmost county is different from any other part of the state. The aberration begins with its name: Owyhee was the original spelling of Hawaii. Three Hawaiians in the employ of the Hudson's Bay Company failed to return from a fur-trapping expedition in the winter of 1818-19; this sector was named in their memory.

Among Idaho's most unusual geological sights are the Bruneau Sand Dunes preserved within **Bruneau Sand Dunes State Park,** a short drive from Mountain Home. Formed 15,000 years ago, in the wake of the Bonneville Flood, the 470-foot piles of sand are the tallest free-standing dunes on the continent. A small museum at the visitor center describes the formation of the dunes and their natural history. *Rte. 78, 20 miles south of Mountain Home; 208/366–7919.*

Even more spectacular is **Bruneau Canyon,** a 60-mile-long chasm with vertical walls rising 800 to 1,200 feet above the river. Geologists are fascinated by the rhyolite strata revealed by the cut, which proves that this volcanic region predates the Snake River Plain and the Yellowstone Caldera. Outfitters run rafting trips down the Bruneau and a tributary stream, the Jarbidge. Landlubbers can gaze down into the northern end of the canyon by driving 18 miles southeast from the tiny town of Bruneau, on unsurfaced roads.

Much of the high sagebrush desert rangeland south of Bruneau is accessible only by small plane or hardy four-wheel-drive vehicle. The mountains to the west of here, some exceeding 8,000 feet in elevation, were once rich in gold and silver; now, only ghost towns remain. At the Nevada border, an hour's drive from Bruneau, the highway passes through the Duck Valley Indian Reservation, an arid tract established in 1877. About 850 members of the Western Shoshone-Northern Paiute tribe (the Sho-Pais) live there today.

Along the southern bank of the Snake River, Route 78 traverses the 80 miles of Owyhee County between Bruneau and Marsing, just west of Nampa. The worst Indian massacre in Oregon Trail history took place on Castle Creek, about 28 miles from Bruneau, in September 1860. Thirty-two of the 44 members of the Elijah Otter wagon train were killed during a two-day siege by Shoshones.

Only 75 people live in **Murphy,** the county seat. At one time in the early 20th century, when it had a rail link to Nampa, Murphy shipped more livestock than any other terminal in the Pacific Northwest. The town's **Owyhee County Historical Museum** (190 Basey St., Murphy; 208/495–2319) has a reconstructed mining-stamp mill, a schoolhouse, and a homesteader's cabin, its kitchen untouched.

A dirt road (best avoided in the rain) leads 28 miles southwest from Murphy to the foot of War Eagle Mountain and **Silver City,** Idaho's best-preserved ghost town. The discovery of placer gold here in 1863 and silver lodes in 1864 led to a classic mining boom, with towns like Ruby City and DeLamar springing up

The Owyhee Mountains
near Murphy, in spring.

around the Owyhee Mountains. Silver City had Idaho Territory's first telegraph service and its first newspaper; by 1912 $30 million had been taken from its mines. Only $10 million more was taken in the next three decades, however, and then World War II mining restrictions rang the death knell for Silver City.

The mines, alas, are not safe for public tours, but 40 wood-frame buildings still stand today, though most are privately owned and not in particularly good condition. You can stay at the 1866 Idaho Hotel, which has 20 spartan rooms (with shared bath), a café, and a licensed lounge. Learn more about the area's mining history at the two-story **Old Schoolhouse Museum** (Morning Star Mill Rd., Silver City; no phone), built in 1892. And you can pray for new riches outside Our Lady of Tears Catholic Church, which dates from 1898.

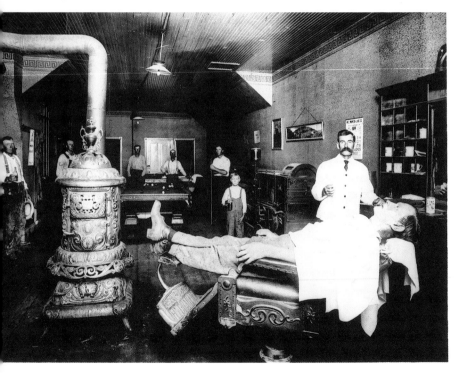

A Silver City saloon doubles as a pool hall and barbershop.
(Idaho State Historical Society)

Owyhee County's two largest towns stand at the edge of the Treasure Valley. Homedale (with about 2,500 people) and Marsing (with over 900) are both farming communities. Twelve miles southeast of Marsing, the commercial Givens Hot Springs still flows where the ancestors of Shoshones and Paiutes camped as long as 4,500 years ago. The small **Givens Hot Springs Resort** (Rte. 78, Marsing; 208/495–2000), first established in 1881, has a thermal swimming pool as well as camping and picnicking facilities. At **Jump Creek Falls,** 10 miles south of Homedale, a 60-foot ribbon of water drops dramatically over a sheer lava wall into a pristine pool.

Silver City is now a ghost town and its 1892 schoolhouse is now a museum.

LOCAL FAVORITE PLACES TO STAY

Doubletree Club Boise. 475 W. Park Center Blvd., Boise; 208/345-2002. $$-$$$

Geared heavily toward weekday business travelers, this classy, contemporary hotel cuts its rates in half for weekend visitors. It's in a quiet part of town and some rooms have lovely mountain views. The pool is for lap swimming only. Rates include a full breakfast.

Doubletree Hotel-Boise Riverside. 2900 Chinden Blvd., Boise; 208/343-1871. $$$

This rambling riverfront property about 2 miles from downtown has a stately charm and 300-plus large rooms, though with outdated decor. The grounds are attractive, with a pool, a pretty garden and gazebo, the river, and access to a 25-mile hiking and biking trail.

The Grove Hotel. 245 S. Capitol Blvd., Boise; 208/333-8000. $$$

One of Boise's finest hotels, this four-star property in the heart of the city has contemporary rooms with neo-classical accents; some have impressive city views.

★Hotel 43. 981 Grove St., Boise; 208/342-4622. $$$

Idaho, the 43rd state, is crossed by the 43rd parallel, hence the name of this six-story boutique-style inn. The 112 rooms have mahogany furnishings, playful pops of color, and amenities like flat-screen TVs. The steakhouse/lounge/martini bar is swanky-modern, in blue neon and black leather.

Idaho Heritage Inn. 109 W. Idaho St., Boise; 208/342-8066. $$

Listed on the National Register of Historic Places, this geothermally heated B&B was once a governor's mansion. The six rooms are furnished with antiques. Two overflow rooms are available in the nearby Flamingo Station cottage.

★Modern Hotel. 1314 Grove St., Boise; 208/424-8244. $$

A marvelous art-deco renovation of a former TraveLodge in the heart of the new Linen District, the Modern has 41 rooms with cutting-edge interior design, plus a chic bar and interior courtyard where a continental breakfast is served each morning.

Owyhee Plaza Hotel. 1109 W. Main St., Boise; 208/343-4611. $$

Built in 1910, this three-story city-hub boutique inn is contemporary with antique accents. Rooms are individually decorated, though some are outdated. Rates include a full breakfast and it has a pool and restaurant.

LOCAL FAVORITE PLACES TO EAT

Chapala. Sixth and Main Sts., Boise; 208/331-7866. $

A family from Guadalajara runs this longtime Mexican favorite in Old Boise. The huge menu includes many varieties of burritos, enchiladas, and fajitas, plus specialties such as *sopitos,* homemade corn shells filled with beans, beef, cheese, and tomatoes.

★Cottonwood Grille. Corner of Ninth and River Sts., Boise; 208/333-9800. $$$

One of Boise's best restaurants, this lovely spot has wonderful food and an extraordinary atmosphere, on the banks of the Boise River. A menu of contemporary Northwest cuisine ranges from stuffed prawn Florentine to roast Muscovy duck to braised lamb shank.

Donnie Mac's. 1616 W. Grove St., Boise; 208/338-7813. $-$$.

Self-dubbed "trailer-park cuisine"— meatloaf, mac-and-cheese, some of Idaho's finest burgers—is served in this commercial garage turned diner. One of the tables is actually inside an old sedan.

Emilio's. 245 S. Capitol St., Boise; 208/333-8002. $$$

Cherry-paneled walls and neoclassical chandeliers usher you into the elegant restaurant of the Grove Hotel, with a display kitchen and adjoining piano bar.

The focus is on regional cuisine, including well-aged steaks.

Epi's, A Basque Restaurant. 1115 First St., Meridian; 208/884-0142. $$

There's a real family feel to this outpost in suburban Meridian, 8 miles west of downtown Boise. Come for dishes like beef tongue in a peppery tomato sauce; squid, cooked with green peppers in its own ink; and savory rice pudding.

BarDeNay. 610 Grove St., Boise; 208/938-5093. $$

A handsome, brick-front restaurant in a historic building on the Basque Block, BarDeNay has its own distillery. Its menu of comfort food includes barbecued ribs and fresh pan-seared trout.

Bar Gernika. 202 S. Capitol Blvd., Boise; 208/344-2175. $-$$

Tender *solomo* (pork) sandwiches, deep-fried chicken croquets, and a delicious lamb stew are just some of the Basque-style foods offered at this casual and historic restaurant, a gathering place for the local Basque community.

Brick Oven Beanery. The Grove on N. Eighth St., Boise; 208/342-3456. $

Generous portions of soups, salads, sandwiches, and blue-ribbon specials— shepherd's pie, salmon meatloaf—are dished up cafeteria-style. Seating is in a homey dining room or outside on the pedestrian plaza.

Cazba. 211 N. 8th St., Boise; 208/381-0222. $$

Lebanese brothers serve wonderful Greek and Middle Eastern dishes, such as kebabs and gyros, as well as moussaka, spanikopita, and dolmades. A belly dancer performs on weekends in a casually elegant room decorated with Middle Eastern art.

The Gamekeeper. Owyhee Plaza Hotel, 1109 W. Main St., Boise; 208/343-4611. $$$

Dress to impress for dinner at the Gamekeeper, where steaks are carved tableside and desserts are flambéed before your eyes. Fresh seafood dishes and dishes made with elk and buffalo make up the menu.

The Grape Escape. 800 W. Idaho St., Boise; 208/368-0200

On one of downtown's busiest corners, this small but popular sidewalk wine bar serves a wide range of vintages, some from Idaho wineries, along with light bites such as bruschettas and cheese-and-charcuterie plates.

Moon's Kitchen Cafe. 815 W. Bannock St., Boise; 208/385-0472. $

A downtown tradition since 1955, Moon's expanded in April 2008 under new ownership, but kept its nostalgic ambience. Famous milk shakes attract a steady clientele, who also enjoy the classic diner offerings in home-style breakfasts, lunches, and light dinners.

The MilkyWay. 205 N. 10th St., Boise; 208/343-4334. $$$

Jazz combos and chamber musicians regularly play at this classy downtown restaurant with eclectic comfort food. Three-course prix-fixe meals include entrées like duck breast and cioppino, or you can order à la carte.

★Mortimer's Idaho Cuisine. 110 S. Fifth St., Boise; 208/338-6550. $$$

The quarried sandstone walls of the 1904 Belgravia Building surround diners at this basement restaurant in Old Boise. Idaho products like trout, catfish, lamb, and local produce are presented in flavorful, light dishes.

TableRock BrewPub & Grill. 705 Fulton St., Boise; 208/342-0944. $

Serving custom beers and comfort food, this spot a block from the Eighth Street Market Place, on the edge of the Cultural District, is a good place to meet Boiseans.

SOUTHEAST
THE FERTILE CRESCENT

The Snake River describes a broad, south-bending arc as it sweeps through southern Idaho. Thanks to a series of dams that have slowed the Snake's flow and diverted its life-giving waters, the desert that once pushed clear to the banks of the Snake has been pushed back beyond a crescent of rich farmland. Where sagebrush once thrived farmers now cultivate a diversity of crops that brings life and prosperity to the farming towns that hug the river: Idaho Falls, Blackfoot, Pocatello, American Falls, Burley, and Twin Falls.

The Russet Burbank potato is king here, especially in the region surrounding Pocatello. They thrive in the region's light, moist, volcanic soil, its hot days and cool nights, and its 4,500-foot elevation. Idaho's "famous potatoes" are even celebrated on state license plates.

Idaho overtook Maine as the center of American potato production in the years following World War II. Some 500 square miles of Idaho are planted in potatoes. Especially in May and June, you'll see the tuber's vinelike leaves and yellow flowers as you drive the backroads of the Snake River valley. If you pass through in the fall, you may catch harvesters digging them out.

If you're traveling east from Boise through southern and southeastern Idaho, you'll be following the interstate highway corridor up the Snake River toward its source in Yellowstone National Park. Indeed, the Snake is the thread that binds this region. Though the river is extensively diverted for irrigation, travelers' eyes may also be extensively diverted by a series of aquatic attractions.

The Thousand Springs, for instance, cascade from apparently sheer rock, and Shoshone Falls is a spectacular, 1,000-foot-wide horseshoe-shaped waterfall. There are parks and reservoirs and wildlife refuges throughout the region. And in the corner of the state bordering Montana and Wyoming, hard by Yellowstone, is Henry's Fork of the Snake River, widely regarded as the country's finest trout stream.

MIDDLE SNAKE

Unfortunately, most folks are in a hurry and see no more than is possible from a car window zooming along the interstate. Those who detour from time to time, who meander off onto old U.S. 30 or other side routes, find a region that fascinates and delights.

Glenns Ferry, about an hour's drive southeast of Boise on I–84, is the first important freeway exit that encounters the Snake River. From here to Lake Walcott reservoir, about 100 miles east, the river is known to Idahoans as "the Middle Snake." The flow of this southernmost reach of the river is diverted by a half-dozen dams to farms and public water supplies.

Glenns Ferry is the gateway to a park that commemorates the single most important Snake River ford for Oregon Trail pioneers. Every August, **Three Island Crossing State Park** hosts a reenactment of this crossing, when covered wagons risked all to traverse a trio of gravel bars that turned one broad stream into four narrow ones. Before it was dammed upstream, the flow of the Snake was considerably more formidable than it is today. (The ferry for which the town is named didn't begin service until 1869.) Some pioneers regretted their decision to continue west along the southern bank's hot, dry Owyhee Plateau. Wagon ruts are still visible today behind the park's interpretive center. Bison and longhorn

A covered wagon makes its way along the banks of the Snake River in this vintage 19th-century photograph. (Library of Congress)

cattle are pastured by the riverbank, and overnight campers angle for trout and catfish. *Madison Ave., Glenns Ferry; 208/366–2394.*

Another interesting exit from I–84 is at **Bliss,** 18 miles east of Glenns Ferry. Follow the Old Bliss Road down a steep canyon wall to the River Road, where there are two worthwhile stops virtually side-by-side about 2 miles southeast. One is **Snake River Pottery** (555 River Rd., Bliss; 208/837–6527), the oldest ceramics studio in Idaho. Drich Bowler founded the shop in the days following World War II; today his son, Peter Bowler, manages the quirky shop, where you'll find everything from terra-cotta wares to porcelain and raku. The other is **Teater's Knoll,** the only building in the state designed by Frank Lloyd Wright. It was built on a riverfront bluff in 1953–57 for artist Archie Teater. Today it remains a private residence and is not open to the public, but its simple and distinctive prowlike design of stone, wood, and glass, characteristically blending into the basalt landscape, can be easily seen overlooking the Snake from the Bowlers' pottery shop.

A few miles farther on, just after the River Road joins U.S. 30, the highway crosses a bridge over the Malad River Gorge. Look for a left turn another 2 miles south where you can backtrack to **Malad Gorge State Park.** A steel footbridge spanning the 250-foot-deep abyss affords the most impressive view of its glaciated, million-year-old rock walls.

The Big Wood and Little Wood rivers meet just above the gorge, then pour 60 feet into the yawning Devil's Washbowl. From here the Malad River churns threadlike through a narrow chasm for two miles before entering the Snake. *1074 E. 2350 Rd. S, 6 miles east of Bliss; 208/837–4505.*

Malad Gorge is but a preamble to the geological phenomena of the next 30 miles of river, as you proceed upstream on U.S. 30.

First up is the lush green Hagerman Valley, where fields of melonlike boulders alternate with grassy pastures. Cattle and horses now graze here, but this was once the stomping ground of *Equus simplicidens.* A zebralike ancestor of the modern horse, this creature became extinct three million years ago. Since a team of Smithsonian Institution paleontologists uncovered its first

SOUTHEASTER
IDAHO

partial skeleton in the 1930s, more than 150 separate similar sets of *Equus* bones have been exhumed from bluffs on the west bank of the Snake. So rich are the Hagerman Fossil Beds—they also have yielded fossil mastodons, saber-toothed tigers, and other denizens of subtropical marshes—they are considered the finest repository of Upper Pliocene Epoch mammals on the planet.

A visitor center in the small town of Hagerman will tell you more about **Hagerman Fossil Beds National Monument,** established in 1988. Study the full-cast replica of the original "Hagerman horse" and view an artist's impression of how this area must have looked three million years ago. There's an interpretive overlook above Upper

Salmon Falls Reservoir, 5 miles south of Hagerman (on W. 2700 South Rd.), but as yet there are no facilities at the unmarked bone quarry. The visitor center will give you directions, but it's best to join a National Park Service tour on summer weekends. Collecting and removing fossils from the site is prohibited. *221 N. State St., Hagerman; 208/837–4793.*

Highway 30 from Bliss to Twin Falls is nicknamed the ★**Thousand Springs Scenic Route,** and with good reason: keen-eyed observers will see dozens of waterfalls—some gushing, some trickling—pouring from sheer black cliffs along the northeast canyon wall. Irrigation diversion has significantly reduced their numbers; 19th-century pioneers saw several hundred springs. These Thousand Springs emanate from the Snake River Plain Aquifer, a vast, spongelike, subterranean reservoir that underlies south-central Idaho's lava desert. The aquifer is filled annually by runoff from several mountain streams, including the Big Lost River and Little Lost River, which disappear into the porous Snake River Plain more than 120 miles to the northeast.

You can get closest to the outflow at **Niagara Springs State Park,** a national natural landmark south of the community of Wendell. Each second, hundreds of gallons of icy water cascade from the cliffs at Niagara Springs and adjacent Crystal Springs. Drivers beware: the road to the small park is steep and narrow, not advisable for trailers or large RVs. *Niagara Springs Rd., 8 miles south of Wendell; 208/837–4505.*

A century and a half ago, Oregon Trail pioneers traded with native Shoshones in the Hagerman Valley for fresh trout. Today a series of fish farms produce two-thirds of all commercially raised trout in the United States. More than two million rainbow and steelhead trout, plus smaller numbers of catfish and tilapia, come from a 30-mile stretch of the Snake between Twin Falls and Hagerman. The largest of many hatcheries—in fact, the largest commercial trout farm on earth—is **Clear Springs Foods,** north of Buhl. From underwater windows, behold numerous giant trout and some remarkable white sturgeon, including one that is more than 70 years old and 10 feet long. *Clear Lakes Rd., Buhl; 208/543-4316.*

Southwest of Buhl, amid other basalt formations in the canyon of Salmon Falls Creek, is **Balanced Rock.** Geologists say the mushroom-shaped boulder, 40 feet in diameter, has been poised precariously atop another, larger rock for thousands of years. Apparently not everyone was certain it would stay that way: concrete now reinforces its base. *Orchard Dr., 13 miles from Buhl via Castleford Rd.*

MAGIC VALLEY

It's not far from Buhl to Twin Falls, hub of the so-called Magic Valley. The moniker is ascribed not so much to the Thousand Springs' reappearing act as to the water wizardry applied to this semi-arid plain by turn-of-the-century pioneer Ira B. Perrine. Amassing financial backers after Congress passed the Carey Act in 1894, Perrine directed the construction of a series of canals that turned 385,000 acres of desert into farmland. **Twin Falls,** which straddled the Union Pacific rail line, became the regional center. Its population is now over 35,000.

Where the Snake River marks the northern edge of the city of Twin Falls, it does so in dramatic fashion. Observation decks at the **Buzz Langdon Visitors Center** (U.S. 93 North; 208/733–3974) provide an awesome panorama of the Snake River Canyon, carved 15,000 years ago by the great Bonneville Flood. Stark palisades as high as 600 feet tower above a pair of golf courses and a city park that occupy the canyon floor. The Perrine Bridge, 933 feet long and 486 feet above the canyon, was the world's highest bridge when it was built in 1927. Now reconstructed, it links Twin Falls with I–84, just to the north.

Evel Knievel mounts his "motorcycle" in a futile attempt to jump the Snake River Canyon near Twin Falls. *(Twin Falls Times-News)*

Balanced Rock,
a landmark near
Castleford, just
west and south of
Twin Falls

In 1974 Montana motorcycle stuntman Evel Knievel tried to jump the Snake River Canyon here on a rocket-powered two-wheeler. Like Wile E. Coyote, he failed. Unlike the Roadrunner's foe, he parachuted to the canyon floor. The launch ramp from Knievel's fiasco, a couple of miles upriver from the Perrine Bridge, has been removed, but locals can show you the site.

Knievel should have known he couldn't compete with ★**Shoshone Falls,** a little farther upriver, as the canyon's leading attraction. "The Niagara of the West" pours its waters 212 feet—that's 52 feet higher than Niagara—over a horseshoe-shaped, 1,000-foot-wide basalt face. Its most spectacular season is spring, when the Snake is swollen with snowmelt; at other times it can be little more than a trickle. There's a dedicated lookout point opposite a powerhouse in **Shoshone Falls–Dierkes Lake Park** (3300 East Rd., Twin Falls; 208/736–2265). The actual Twin Falls from which the city takes its name are another two miles upriver at **Twin Falls Park** (3500 East Rd., Kimberly; 208/423-4223).

A quiet midtown pedestrian area marks downtown Twin Falls, which huddles near Rock Creek 3 miles south of the canyon. Other than the surrounding natural curiosities, it's of interest as the location of the College of Southern Idaho, a junior college with one of the finest Native American museums in the West. The

A few of the dozens of waterfalls along the Thousand Springs Scenic Route.

Herrett Center for Arts and Science (315 Falls Ave., Twin Falls; 208/733–9554 Ext. 2655) displays 18,500 artifacts that range from pre-Columbian Mayan treasures to modern American tribal art, including examples of stone tools used by Clovis Man. It also has the Pacific Northwest's largest planetarium, a gem and mineral collection, and a student art gallery.

Idaho gamblers make Twin Falls their launch pad for trips to Jackpot, Nevada. Its four roadside casinos, less than an hour's drive south on U.S. 93, legally encourage the rapid disposal of hard-earned wages. Cactus Pete's is the best casino of the bunch, with more roulette and blackjack tables and a regular big-name entertainment schedule.

East from Twin Falls, U.S. 30 follows the old Oregon Trail route along the Snake to Burley. Among intriguing detours is the **Stricker Store,** south of Hansen about 12 miles from Twin Falls. It was built in 1864 as the first trading post and stagecoach station between Fort Hall and Boise. By 1901 it had a ranch house, a 40-horse stable, a saloon, a dance hall, and numerous other outbuildings, as well as a cemetery. Today the surviving buildings—the log store and the two-

Flag Day is celebrated at Shoshone Falls with a speech by Ezra Meeker. (Idaho State Historical Society)

BASEBALL'S BLOOMER GIRLS

The evenings, in that season of the year in Southeastern Idaho were long and lingering, so that after work and supper, the members of the baseball team had time for snappy practice. The local fans who did not play would gather in the grandstand or along the baselines. . . .

At an early hour that Sabbath morning, the special train bearing the Boston Bloomer Girls and their small male retinue appeared at the southern rim of the flat and steamed into Ashton. Because the visiting athletes were still sleeping in the first flush of dawn, the train, with drawn curtains, was shunted onto our Reclamation side track, beyond Roby's warehouse, and it was not until breakfast time, 6 A.M. in those parts, that the official committee of welcome, consisting of Doc Puckett, the town marshal, Doc Show, Tod the typist, our captain, Howard Wise, Norman Torrance, and me, strolled down the track to greet the Bloomer Girls.

There were ten girls in all, seven of whom were first-string players, and the remaining three were utility women. They had a male manager, who looked like a Broadway promoter, a male pitcher who could throw overhand, underhand or in side-arm style and could have played in a minor league if the minors had women so handy, and a male

shortstop who had been expelled from some of the leading Eastern institutions of learning and also was a sprinter. I remember most clearly Big Liz, a rangy girl who hit like a female Hans Wagner and covered first base like a veteran; "Little Eva," a blonde who took care of the keystone sack; Cleo, the Catcher, who had an astonishing arm; Lulu, the center fielder who became the idol of the inmates of The Lake; and Coney Island Mary, the third baseman. . . .

Reinforced by the boys from the reform school . . . we gave, thanks to the Bloomer Girls, a good show to the Mormons, Jack Mormons and Gentiles that day. Doc Shaw, always alert for more information about his fellow creatures, enumerated carefully the reactions of the bums. Those who shuffled across the railroad track, to see the game free of charge and offered to spit in the hat when it was passed, for the benefit of delinquents and orphans, our new doctor decided were reclaimable. He pointed out to the horrified Frank Crowe that since the Government was spending so much to water the dry land, a little more to save its resentful wandering citizens might well be appropriated.

"What are you? A God-damn anarchist?" Crowe asked.

—Elliot Paul, *Desperate Scenery*, 1954

Newly hatched and full-grown Canada geese.

story frame ranch house—are owned by the Idaho State Hisorical Society, and are undergoing preservation work. *Rock Creek Rd., Hansen; 208/423–4000.*

AROUND BURLEY

The farming town of **Burley** is unique in two regards. In early settler days, five pioneer paths (including the Oregon, California, and Mormon trails) extended in all directions from the community like spokes on a wheel; and each June it hosts Idaho's only nationally known speedboat races, the **Idaho Regatta**. The races take place at serpentine Milner Reservoir; stretching 15 miles west from Burley to the Milner Dam and another 10 miles east, it is yet only a few hundred yards wide. During the Regatta, a hundred or so hydroplanes, flatbottoms, and other stream-lined boats share the water.

The riverine reservoir also divides Minidoka County, to its north, from Cassia County, to its south. Rupert, 8 miles northeast of Burley, is the seat of Minidoka County. Platted in 1904 during a federal irrigation project, it is built around Idaho's most traditional town square, complete with a bandstand and turn-of-

American white pelicans in breeding plumage at the Minidoka National Wildlife Refuge.

Morning light illuminates the
City of Rocks National Reserve
in Cassia County.

the-20th-century storefronts on all four sides. A few miles farther northeast, the Minidoka Dam holds back the waters of Lake Walcott. **Minidoka National Wildlife Refuge** (961 E. Minidoka Dam, 10 miles east of Rte. 24; 208/436–3589) surrounds the 11-mile-long reservoir and an additional 11 miles of Snake River. In the fall, hunters throng here to bag some of the quarter-million ducks and geese that gather in the wetlands; at other times, 208 avian species, from great blue herons to tundra swans and white pelicans, find safe haven.

South of Burley, Cassia County has several interesting towns and locations worth a day's loop trip. Start your tour by driving south 20 miles on Route 27 to historic **Oakley,** a hamlet of 700 founded by Mormon colonists in 1880 as a farming and silver-mining town. It foundered early in the 20th century but survived when Idaho quartzite, quarried at several locations in the surrounding Goose Creek Mountains, found an international market. Oakley is an official National Historic District, with more 19th-century buildings than any other town of its size in Idaho. Numerous colorful Victorian and Edwardian mansions and businesses, including banks, an opera house, and the 1883 Oakley Cooperative Mercantile, highlight walking tours. Note the three-story Marcus Funk home, built in 1895. A polygamist, like some Mormons of his time, Funk supposedly planned each floor's decor to satisfy the taste of a different wife. The **Daughters of Utah Pioneers Museum** (300 N. Main St., Oakley; 208/678–7172), in the old Worthington Hotel, displays artifacts from the region's first settlers.

Technical rock climbers from around the world find their way through Oakley to **City of Rocks National Reserve** (Rte. 77, Almo; 208/824–5519). Granite columns that once guided pioneer travelers to the crossroads of the Kelton Stage Road and California Trail are now scaled by adventurers armed with ropes and pitons. Their routes ascend past 150-year-old graffiti scrawled in axle grease near the base of the huge pillars, some of which loom 60 stories above the sagebrush. At two billion years old, the Precambrian crystalline exposed in the City of Rocks is some of the oldest rock known in western North America. The 14,300-acre preserve is administered by the National Park Service and the Idaho Department of Parks and Recreation. The gravel road through the City of Rocks leads east to the hamlet of Almo, where you can pick up another series of county and state roads to return via Albion to Burley, 47 miles from the reserve's visitor center.

Several byways lead west into the Albion Range of the Sawtooth National Forest, home of 9,265-foot Mount Harrison. Lake Cleveland and the Pomerelle Ski Area cling to its timbered slopes.

DIAMONDFIELD JACK

The best time to visit tiny Albion is July, when local citizens stage a reenactment of the trial of "Diamondfield" Jack. A Virginian who came west to pursue reports of a diamond mine, Jackson Davis was hired in 1895 by Oakley cattle baron John Sparks to patrol his land against trespassing sheepherders. One such conflict ended with Davis shooting and wounding a sheepman, and Cassia County erupted in a range war. Later that year, when two herders were found shot and killed in their camp wagon, fingers pointed at Davis. Davis maintained his innocence, but in a one-week trial in the county courthouse in Albion in April 1897, a jury found him guilty of murder and sentenced him to hang.

A year and a half later, with Davis on death row, Sparks's ranch manager and a partner confessed that they had slain the sheepherders in self-defense. Their argument was sustained by a jury that acquitted them of the crime. But still Davis was scheduled to hang. In fact, he had eight stays of execution until his sentence was commuted to life imprisonment, and he was moved to the state penitentiary in Boise in 1901. Eighteen months later—more than five years after he was convicted of a crime he didn't commit—the state Board of Pardons finally released Davis.

A postscript: Davis's defense lawyer, James Hawley, became Boise's mayor and later governor of Idaho. The prosecuting attorney, William Borah, became the state's most famous U.S. senator. Davis's employer and financial supporter, John Sparks, became the governor of Nevada. Davis himself moved to Tonopah, Nevada, where he became rich and famous as president of the Diamondfield Triangle Gold Mining Company. He squandered his wealth, however, and was an aged drifter when he died after being hit by a Las Vegas taxicab in 1949.

"Diamondfield" Jack Davis looking rather glum at the Idaho State Penitentiary. (Idaho State Historical Society)

With a modern population of less than 300, **Albion** is but a shadow of its former self. Founded in the 1870s, the ranching center was once the seat of Cassia County and the site of Southern Idaho College of Education, which closed in 1951. (The college reopened from 1957 to 1967 as Magic Christian College of the national Church of Christ, but that school also failed.) The 40-acre campus, its dozen structures built of locally quarried stone and brick, survives.

AMERICAN FALLS

About 14 miles east of Burley, I–84 turns suddenly southeast away from the Snake River, crossing a vast and arid basin en route to Utah and the Salt Lake City metropolis. As an explorer of Idaho, you'd do well to continue northeast on its spur freeway, I–86, toward Pocatello.

The main point of interest along this stretch of the Snake is **Massacre Rocks State Park** (3592 N. Park La., off I–86; 208/548–2672), 11 miles southwest of American Falls. Natural and human history share the spotlight at this 1,000-acre oasis. High cliffs overlook a narrow gap through which Oregon Trail travelers passed with trepidation, ever fearful of attacks from hostile Shoshones. Their fears were rarely justified, but an ambush in 1862 took the lives of 10 immigrants. You can still find wagon ruts here. Three miles downstream at Register Rock, pioneers used axle grease or stout knives to immortalize their names on a 20-foot stone. One carving in particular is worthy of note: in 1866, seven-year-old J.J. Hansen chiseled and initialed an Indian's head. In 1913 the 54-year-old Hansen, by then a noted sculptor, returned and again dated the rock. Three hundred different desert plants and more than 200 species of birds have been recorded at Massacre Rocks by state park personnel, who offer summer interpretive programs and evening campfires.

Just east of American Falls sprawls **American Falls Reservoir** (Rte. 39, American Falls; 208/226–2688), the largest lake on the Snake River. Twenty-three miles long, the resevoir is enormously popular with fishermen, water-skiers, sailors, and the like. Boat rentals and board sailing lessons are offered at Willow Bay, the largest of numerous recreation areas around the lake shore. When the Bureau of Reclamation built the first dam here in 1927, eradicating its namesake 50-foot waterfall in the process, the old town of American Falls had to be relocated. Sometimes you still can see parts of the former townsite when the reservoir is low. The current dam, more than a half-mile long, was built in 1976 by the

Idaho Power Company at a cost of $46 million. The new town, a potato processing and shipping center, has more than 4,000 people.

One of the most remarkable volcanic landscapes in North America lies less than an hour's drive north and west of American Falls on gravel Bureau of Land Management roads. **Great Rift National Landmark** comprises the longest exposed geological cleft on the continent, running southeast some 45 miles from Craters of the Moon National Monument near Arco. Highlights include the Crystal Ice Cave, whose constant 31-degree cold freezes water that seeps into it through a fissure, and the King's Bowl, a dramatic crater created just 2,100 years ago by a violent eruption. *11 miles west of Rte. 39 (5 miles north of American Falls) on N. Pleasant Valley Rd., 4 miles north on Winters Rd., 13 miles northwest through BLM land on gravel Crystal Ice Cave Rd.*

East of the Great Rift and north of American Falls Reservoir lie some of eastern Idaho's premier potato fields. Communities like Aberdeen, Springfield, Pingree, and Rockford draw life from an 86-mile network of canals issuing from the reservoir.

Pocatello was the largest rail station in the region at one time. Here locomotives line up at a coaling station. (Union Pacific Railroad, Idaho State Historical Society)

POCATELLO AND VICINITY

With over 53,000 residents, Pocatello is the biggest city in eastern Idaho, and the second largest in the state. Once the largest railroad center in the United States west of the Mississippi River, Pocatello was established in 1887 at the crossing of the tracks of the Utah Northern (Salt Lake City to Butte, Montana) and the Oregon Short Line, a Union Pacific subsidiary.

A timetable for the Oregon Short Line railroad from 1900.

As rail transportation declined in importance, so did Pocatello. But the city remains a favorite of train buffs. Its downtown historic district, for instance—12 square blocks beside the Portneuf River—clearly shows its former splendor. No less a dignitary than President William Howard Taft attended the 1915 opening of the three-story **Oregon Short Line Depot** (Union Pacific Ave. and Bonneville St.; no phone). Within a year, the four-story, terra-cotta-trimmed **Yellowstone Hotel** (230 W. Bonneville St.; no phone) was erected across the street. A few blocks away, the 1902 **Stanrod Mansion** (648 N. Garfield St.; 208/234–6184) is considered by architectural historians to be Idaho's finest Victorian home.

Ross Park, at the south end of Pocatello, is the city's pride and joy. The **Bannock County Historical Museum** will tell you everything you ever wanted to know about southeastern Idaho's development. When you check out the display of antique Union Pacific railroad cars, you may be reminded of Chief Pocataro, the Shoshone leader who signed the treaty granting the railroad a right-of-way through his land (and who inadvertently gave his name to the new city). *Avenue of the Chiefs, Pocatello; 208/233-0434.*

The zoo at **Ross Park** has a fine little display of denizens of the northern Rocky Mountain states. In addition to a rose garden and the requisite sports fields and aquatic center, the park is developing a facsimile townsite of 1890s Pocatello. Close to both the townsite and the historical museum is a full-scale replica of Fort Hall, the Oregon Trail trading post that operated a few miles north of here from the 1840s to the mid-1860s. The original plans were used to reconstruct the fort's living quarters, guardhouse, and working areas. *Avenue of the Chiefs, between Second and Fourth Aves.; 208/234–6232.*

Before you leave Pocatello, swing by the campus of Idaho State University (ISU)—one of the state's three major institutions of higher learning—to visit the **Idaho Museum of Natural History.** The museum is noted for its exhibits on endangered species and on Idaho's fossil record. Of special interest are artifacts, such as intricate basketry, unearthed at the 2,000-year-old Wah'-Muza archaeological dig. *Hutchinson Quadrangle, Fifth Ave. and Dillon St.; 208/236–3168.*

Both **Wah'-Muza** and the ruins of **Fort Hall** are on the Fort Hall Indian Reservation, some 20 miles north of downtown Pocatello. To visit either, you'll

Inside the replica of Fort Hall in Pocatello.

have to get permission from tribal officials via the Shoshone-Bannock Tribal Museum (below); a guide must accompany you to Wah'-Muza. ISU students and faculty have discovered four separate periods of occupation of the site in house foundations, fire pits, and a large midden. Fort Hall's original location is designated by a small obelisk on Sheepskin Road; Oregon Trail ruts run nearby. If you're a keen amateur archaeologist, it may be worth the effort to visit; the Shoshone-Bannock are pleased to share their heritage with those who respect it.

The casual visitor may be satisfied to peruse the small **Shoshone-Bannock Tribal Museum** just off I–15 north of Pocatello. Of special interest are early black-and-white photographs of Fort Hall. About 3,000 "Sho-Bans" live on the 820-square-mile reservation, Idaho's largest. Culturally melded by intermarriage over the last century and a quarter since they were ushered onto the same reserve, the tribes now jointly operate a phosphate mine and Snake River fishery. *Simplot Rd., Fort Hall; 208/237–9791.*

BEAR RIVER COUNTRY

Idaho's hilly southeastern quadrant has two unifying threads that give it an identity distinct from the rest of the state. One is the Bear River, Idaho's only significant stream that is not a part of the Columbia and Snake River watershed. The other is the Mormon religion.

The meandering Bear River rises in the Wasatch Mountains of northern Utah, swings briefly into Wyoming before cutting westerly into Idaho. It then scribes a horseshoe turn and runs abruptly south into Utah's Great Salt Lake. More than half of its 300-mile course is in Idaho, and the largest towns of this part of the state—Montpelier, Soda Springs, and Preston—are along its course.

Mormons, the largest religious group in the state (about 400,000 strong), have dominated life in the southeast ever since they founded **Franklin** as Idaho's first permanent white settlement in 1860. From the beginning, Brigham Young's Salt Lake City–based Church of Jesus Christ of Latter-day Saints had a difficult time winning acceptance in Idaho, but the Mormons persisted and won respect for their hard work and strong communities.

Malad City's chief distinction is the notoriety it gained in the 1870s as the home (however briefly) of outlaw Jesse James. James quietly moved to town, married a local girl, and then just as quietly left her and never returned. Once a major stage stop on the Salt Lake-to-Butte road, Malad (named "Sick" by French-Canadians who grew ill here) boasts numerous 19th-century buildings including a working flour mill built in 1867. **Curlew National Grassland** (Rte.

Franklin's historic Hatch House is a good example of pioneer architecture.

38; 208/766–4743), a federally administered sustained-yield management area, begins 20 miles west of Malad. Covering 47,000 acres in three parcels along Rock Creek and Deep Creek, the reserve has permitted an area seriously overgrazed by homesteaders in the 1920s and 1930s to recover. Fall brings hunters in search of sharp-tailed grouse, pheasants, and other game birds.

To explore this region at its Mormon roots, make a beeline for Franklin, 76 miles from Pocatello. Turn off I–15 at Exit 36 and continue southeast on U.S. 91. En route, a pair of historical markers invite you to pause and contemplate. **Red Rock Pass** (U.S. 91, 8 miles southeast of Downey) was the point at which ancient Lake Bonneville escaped its banks 15,000 years ago and started the great Bonneville Flood. Near the **Bear River Massacre Site** (U.S. 91, 12 miles northwest of Preston), noted by a historical marker, more than 350 Shoshone men, women, and children were slain by a U.S. cavalry unit in 1863, one of the saddest moments in Native American history.

For a dozen years after Mormon colonists platted **Franklin,** they were convinced they were Utahns. Their surprise came when an 1872 survey indicated they were one mile north of the border. The entire town center is now an Idaho State Historic District, which preserves the likes of the 1870 Greek Revival–style Lorenzo Hatch Home and the 1895 Pioneer Relic Hall, a two-story stone

The turquoise color of Bear Lake is caused by limestone particles and other carbonates.

store that now contains a settlers museum. Five hundred people today call Franklin home.

Travelers east of Franklin must surmount the Bear River Range, a northern spur of the Wasatch Mountains, to reach Bear Lake. There are several ways to make—or to avoid—the crossing. Four-wheel-drivers can take the direct approach around the flank of 9,575-foot Paris Peak, via backcountry roads through Caribou National Forest. Paved Route 36 follows a more northerly course between Preston and Montpelier. U.S. 89 goes south through Logan, Utah, to Bear Lake.

If only to soak up its remarkable turquoise color, **Bear Lake** is worth the trip to Idaho's southeasternmost corner. Half in Idaho, half in Utah, this large lake—20 miles long and 7 miles across—was well known to fur trappers, who gathered on its shores with Shoshone, Ute, and other native tribes for rendezvous in the summers of 1827 and 1828. Soluble carbonates, principally limestone particles, are responsible for its unusual hue.

Not including the mythical Bear Lake Monster, Idaho's answer to Scotland's Nessie, Bear Lake is home to several species of fish unknown elsewhere. Foremost, perhaps, is the Bonneville cisco, a silvery whitefish that runs in schools beneath the winter ice. (At an elevation of 5,923 feet, the surface typically freezes.) Hardy fishermen chop holes and dip buckets and fine-mesh nets to snare the swift, sar-

Limestone formations in Minnetonka Cave near Bear Lake.

The Electric Hotel of Paris, Idaho. (Idaho State Historical Society)

dinelike fish, which rarely exceed 7 inches in length. Their daily limit: 50 fish. Commercial angling is not allowed.

Idaho water sports enthusiasts approach the lake via **Bear Lake State Park** (U.S. 89, Montpelier; 208/945–2790), with white-sand beaches in the two separate units. The eastern unit is the larger of the two, and has a campground. A larger resort and marina center is at the south end of the lake around Garden City, Utah. The marshes of **Bear Lake National Wildlife Refuge** (Merkley Lake Rd., Montpelier; 208/847–1757), divided from Bear Lake's north shore by a sandbar, protect thousands of Canada geese, sandhill cranes, white pelicans, and a dozen species of ducks.

A premier natural attraction in the Wasatch Range west of Bear Lake is **Minnetonka Cave,** 10 miles up a creek canyon from the village of St. Charles. The mouth of this cavern in Caribou National Forest is at an elevation of 7,700 feet. Guided tours in summer lead visitors through nine rooms and up and down 448 steps, past walls of ice crystals (wear a jacket!) and chambers of stalactites and stalagmites. You may see prehistoric plant and marine-animal fossils in the lime-

A classic southeastern-Idaho sight: a barn surrounded by recently harvested fields.

stone cave. *St. Charles Creek Rd., St. Charles; 208/945–2407 summer, 208/847–0375 winter.*

Several small communities are on U.S. 89 between Bear Lake and Montpelier. St. Charles, at the lake's northwest corner, is notable as the birthplace of the sculptor of Mount Rushmore's presidential mugs. Gutzon Borglum (1867–1941) is remembered by a monument on church grounds in the heart of town.

Eight miles north of St. Charles is **Paris,** the second Mormon settlement in Idaho. It was founded in 1863. The town's chief claim to fame today is its **Paris Idaho State Tabernacle** (Main St., Paris; 208/945–2112), designed by Brigham Young's son Joseph and built between 1885 and 1889. Swiss masons cut and carved the temple's red sandstone, which was quarried on the east side of Bear Lake and, in winter, sledded 18 miles across the ice to town. The Romanesque building has an 80-foot tower and room in its sanctuary for 3,000 people, five times the town's modern-day population.

The full population of **Montpelier** could also fit into the tabernacle, but that hasn't kept the old Oregon Trail settlement from becoming the urban hub of Bear Lake County. At the junction of U.S. 89 and U.S. 30 northeast of Paris, the town recalls almost fondly the visit paid by Butch Cassidy in 1896. The quirky

Interior of the historic Mormon Tabernacle, built in Paris in 1869.

The only "captive geyser in the world" at Soda Springs.

outlaw and his Wild Bunch robbed the town bank of $7,165, a princely sum in those days.

U.S. 30 north from Montpelier (it was named after Brigham Young's birthplace in Vermont) follows the Bear River 32 miles, through aspen forests whose leaves turn a brilliant gold in autumn, to **Soda Springs.** The economy of this town is tagged to the phosphate industry. You'll see phosphorus slag piled outside the Monsanto Company plant on the north side of town; the mound began growing when the factory opened in 1953. There are other plants nearby, and the J. R. Simplot Company's phosphate-ore mine is a few miles northeast. Phosphorus is used in fertilizer, detergents, and water treatment.

Soda Springs got its name from geothermal springs located near the modern town. Many Oregon Trail migrants also remarked on Steamboat Springs, whose three-foot geyser roared before it spurted; it's now beneath the surface of the reservoir west of town. Hooper Springs, whose bubbling water was commercially marketed 100 years ago, is now preserved in a city park north of downtown, and is still good for drinking.

Perhaps it's a comment on the modern proclivity for the artificial, but Soda Springs' biggest attraction today is a "captive" geyser in **Geyser Park.** It was created in 1937 when a drill crew hit a pocket of carbon dioxide 315 feet below the earth's surface. Now capped, the geyser erupts to 150 feet at timed intervals: on the half-hour in summer, hourly the rest of the year. *First St. S. and First St. W., Soda Springs; 208/547–2600.*

Geothermal phenomena are the raison d'être for **Lava Hot Springs,** a handsome little resort community a few minutes' drive west of Soda Springs along U.S. 30. The 104- to 110-degree mineral pools, which lie at the foot of lava cliffs that overlook the Portneuf River, may be 50 million years old. They were a neutral zone for warring Bannock and Shoshone Indians, who considered them sacred. Their modern descendants, in bathing suits, still frequent the hot baths, today beautifully renovated into handsome pools of varying temperatures. In the evening locals and visitors alike come to take the waters, which are rich in carbonates but free of sulfur. The Sunken Gardens on the cliff walls add color. For more vigorous exercise, try the two large swimming pools in town. *430 E. Main St., Lava Hot Springs; 208/776-5221.*

From Lava Hot Springs, it's an easy return trip to Pocatello—but first, a couple of side trips beckon from U.S. 30. Northeast of Soda Springs, Route 34 meanders past 9,600-foot Caribou Mountain to Wyoming's Star Valley. The mountain, as well as surrounding Caribou National Forest, were named for Jesse "Cariboo Jack" Fairchild, a Canadian prospector who ignited a gold rush when he struck it rich here in 1870. By 1890, $50 million worth of gold had been taken from these slopes. The remains of a ghost town still reward the curious, off-road adventurer.

In the western shadow of Caribou Mountain is **Grays Lake National Wildlife Refuge,** encompassing a large shallow marsh. There's not much lake, but 200 species of birds, mainly waterfowl, consider the cattails and bulrushes to be avian paradise. More than 200 pairs of greater sandhill cranes nest here, a greater number than anywhere else on the planet. Thousands more join them in the early fall

Storm clouds gather over a barn on Railroad Ranch in Harriman State Park.

The landscape of Grays Lake National Wildlife Refuge resembles that of Alaska's North Slope.

before they migrate to New Mexico for the winter. *74 Grays Lake Rd., Wayan; 208/574-2755.*

Listed on the National Register of Historic Places, **Chesterfield** is an early Mormon farming village stuck in the 19th century, 15 miles north from the road connecting Soda Springs and Lava Hot Springs. Platted in 1879, it is now a virtual ghost town with 23 surviving buildings, all but two of them constructed before 1910. For a tour, contact the nonprofit **Chesterfield Foundation** (1300 East Rd.; 208/548–7625), which maintains this community.

IDAHO FALLS AND VICINITY

For travelers heading northeast along I–15 from Pocatello to Idaho Falls, a mandatory midway stop is at **Blackfoot,** a city of more than 10,000 people that is firmly rooted in potatoes. In the community's 1913 railroad depot you'll find **Idaho's World Potato Exposition,** whose name may be overly grandiose but which really does put this state's potato industry in an international context. The museum's exhibits and videos beautifully illuminate the biology, history, economy, and production methods of the lovable spud. And don't miss the gift shop/cafe, which advertises "Free Taters for Out-of-Staters." *130 N.W. Main St.; 208/785–2517.*

With 51,000 people, **Idaho Falls** is the state's fourth-largest city. A launch

pad for fly fishermen and snowmobilers, it remains a gateway both to the Yellowstone wilderness and the Idaho National Engineering Laboratory. Named Eagle Rock when it was founded at a Snake River bridge crossing in 1865, it had no falls until a weir was built in 1911, 20 years after boosters changed its name to attract prospective settlers. The plan worked.

Miss Idaho, "Queen of the Fair," presents her apples and potatoes. (Idaho State Historical Society)

TOWN OF BLACKFOOT, 1937

Blackfoot, 27 m. (4,505 alt., 3,681 pop.), was named for the Blackfeet Indian tribe. The Indians were called Siksika (meaning 'black of feet') because their feet are said to have been blackened by constant wading in the ashes of the regions devastated by fire. If a town can be summarized by a single quality, then perhaps the most notable characteristic of Blackfoot is the fact that its indefatigable librarian made of this city not only probably the most book-conscious one in the State but also lifted its taste in reading far above the usual levels. This circumstance is all the more remarkable when the books in this small library are compared with those in other public libraries in Idaho, and when it is remembered that all the books in all the public libraries in the State do not add to more than half a million. So awakened has this town become to the cultural possibilities to be found in a good library that it recently made an extensive drive to enlarge its resources in reading.

—Idaho, A Guide in Word and Picture (by Vardis Fisher for the WPA), 1937

Today the 20-foot falls just north of the Broadway Bridge between I–15 and downtown, are at the southern end of the city's Snake River Greenbelt. The two-mile-long riverfront park strip has bike paths, picnic tables, and authentic Japanese lanterns in its **Rotary International Peace Park.** A northerly Greenbelt extension leads to the impressive **Idaho State Vietnam Veterans Memorial** (Science Center Dr.; 208/529–1478) in Russell Freeman Park. Dedicated in 1990, the inverted steel "V" is inscribed with the names of all Idahoans killed or missing in action during the war in Southeast Asia. Another oasis in this city of parks, **Tautphaus Park** (Rollander Ave., at 25th St.; 208/529–1470) has a fine zoo with more than 50 species. City heritage is represented at the **Bonneville County Historical Museum** (200 N. Eastern Ave.; 208/522–1400) in the 1916 Carnegie Library building.

From Idaho Falls, I–15 turns sharply north toward the Montana border, 77 miles away at Monida Pass. Not quite halfway, the freeway passes the **Camas National Wildlife Refuge** (I–15, Exit 150, Hamer; 208/662–5423), a 10,500-acre waterfowl sanctuary on the northeastern fringe of the arid Snake River Plain.

Closer to the state line is an exit for North America's only commercial opal mine. The **Spencer Opal Mine** (Idmon Rd., Spencer; 208/374–5476), opened in 1948, welcomes rock hounds in search of colorful star opals.

HENRY'S FORK

Way back in 1810, a U.S. exploratory expedition led by Major Andrew Henry crested the Continental Divide on what is now the Montana border and descended to an alpine lake surrounded on three sides by high mountains. The lake was dubbed Henry's Lake, and the river that flows from it, a major Snake River tributary, Henry's Fork. Today that river is perhaps the most acclaimed trout stream in the United States for fly fishermen.

U.S. 20 more or less follows Henry's Fork from near Idaho Falls to West Yellowstone, Montana, a distance of 112 miles. Immediately north of Idaho Falls, the farming town of **Rigby** makes a fair claim to being the birthplace of television. Back in 1920, a 14-year-old prodigy with the unlikely name of Philo Taylor Farnsworth III was daydreaming as he plowed his family's fields after school. Encouraged by an intrigued and supportive science teacher, young Farnsworth visualized dissecting images to their component electrons, transmitting them to a receiver, and reconstructing them into a picture. Dropping out of school when his family moved to Utah two years later, he continued to exercise his electronic genius. In 1928 Farnsworth invented the first cathode-ray tube and thus the first television. He died in 1977 with 300 patents and an honorary doctorate to his name.

The center of **Rexburg**, a thriving city of 18,000 people 12 miles from Rigby, is dominated by **Brigham Young University–Idaho** (S. Center St. and W. 4th St.; 208/496–1150), formerly Ricks College, operated by the Mormon church and with an enrollment of about 13,500. Dance troupes from all over the world travel to Rexburg each August for the **Idaho International Folk Dance Festival** (208/356–5700). Three blocks north of campus, the **Upper Snake River Valley Historical Museum** (51 N. Center St.; 208/359–3063), built in twin-towered Italianate style as a tabernacle in 1911, has a fascinating exhibit on the Teton Dam disaster.

Just 23 miles upriver from Rexburg on the Teton River, the dam collapsed on June 5, 1976, causing Idaho's worst flood since the Bonneville cataclysm 15,000 years earlier. When the Bureau of Reclamation dam gave way just before noon, 80 billion gallons of water poured out. Rexburg was inundated by about 1:30 that afternoon, Idaho Falls by dinnertime, Blackfoot the next morning. By the time flood waters were contained in American Falls Reservoir on June 8, 25,000 people had been driven from their homes, 18,000 head of stock had died, and $800 million in damage had been done. Amazingly, only 11 people drowned.

St. Anthony, northeast of Rexburg on U.S. 20, is famous for its sand dunes, which lie eight miles to the northwest. Running 35 miles in a northeasterly direction, the St. Anthony Sand Dunes range up to five miles wide and reach an average height of 250 feet. Prevailing winds have blown the alluvial white-quartz sands, deposited over millions of years, to this far corner of the Snake River Plain. Off-road vehicle riders test their mettle at a **BLM recreation site** (Red Rd., Parker; 208/354–2500) at the edge of the shifting sands.

Many scenic side routes strike out from Ashton. The ★**Teton National Scenic Byway** (Routes 31, 32, and 33) drops south from here (*see* Teton and Swan Valleys, below). The **Cave Falls Road** probes tentatively into the remote Cascade corner of Yellowstone National Park, a distance of 26 miles from Ashton to the park's Bechler Ranger Station near 35-foot Cave Falls. It's a four-day backpack from here, along the Belcher River Trail through grizzly country, to Old Faithful.

More readily traveled is the **Mesa Falls Scenic Byway** (Rte. 47), which loops to the northeast through Targhee National Forest. The latter route offers glimpses of two beautiful, unspoiled falls tumbling from the rim of the ancient Island Park Caldera: Upper and Lower **Mesa Falls,** which drop 114 feet and 65 feet, respectively, within less than a mile of one another on Henry's Fork. You can see the lower falls from the campground, and hike a boardwalk to an observation point at the upper falls. Modern geologists now consider the caldera, a collapsed volcano identified only in 1939, to be among the world's largest. Dense pine forests and expansive meadows now hide much of its 18-by-23-mile expanse, but aerial observations reveal a quarter-mile scarp on its south and west sides. Many lakes stand in the caldera.

At the south end of the caldera, along a nine-mile stretch of Henry's Fork, **Harriman State Park** (Green Canyon Rd., Island Park; 208/558–7368) preserves the former "Railroad Ranch" of W. Averell Harriman, founding father of Sun Valley, chief executive of Union Pacific Railroad and later the governor of New York. After 75 years as a private retreat, the ranch was donated to the state of Idaho in 1977. More than two dozen original log structures, known as the Railroad Ranch, remain and are open for tours in summer. Visitors to the park are encouraged to fish and ride horses in summer, cross-country ski in winter. Grazing moose and elk share the pastures with birdlife such as sandhill cranes and

FISHING HENRY'S FORK

From its source in the spring-fed streams that feed Henry's Lake, for about 50 miles downstream to Ashton Reservoir, Henry's Fork of the Snake River is legendary among trout fishermen. President Theodore Roosevelt and statesman William Jennings Bryan, rail magnate Roland Harriman, and the family of novelist Ernest Hemingway have all cast their dry flies here for rainbow and other trout, and with remarkable success. And even those who don't snag a big fish have stories to tell about the natural beauty of this area just west of Yellowstone National Park.

Henry's Lake has a thriving fishery of brook trout, larger cutthroat trout, and huge (up to 12 pounds) cutthroat-rainbow hybrids. The 10-mile stretch of Henry's Fork from the lake to Big Springs is a major trout spawning area and thus closed to fishing. The 15-mile "blue ribbon" stretch of Henry's Fork below Island Park Reservoir has the best angling, although it is designated strictly catch-and-release. This section includes Box Canyon, whose tumbling rapids recommend drift fishing to wading for fish. Below Last Chance and through Harriman State Park, Henry's Fork is wider and slower, with pockets and pools that enable trout to hide effectively and demand anglers to place a fly perfectly to have any chance at success. Still, this section of river can be easily waded, especially in late summer and fall, and it's not unusual to bring in a rainbow trout of 20 inches or more.

After the river drops over Upper and Lower Mesa Falls, its nature changes. Anglers casting a line above or below Warm River may as easily catch a brown trout as a rainbow, or perhaps even bring in a rare Yellowstone cutthroat.

Fishing season opens on Memorial Day and runs through November. The Island Park area has many fishing-guide services, including **Henry's Fork Anglers** (800/788–4479); **Three Rivers Ranch Fly Fishing Outfitters** (208/558–7501); and **Trouthunter** (208/558–9900). All are reliable and have accommodation at area lodges. **André Puyans Fly Fishing Seminars** (208/558–7017) has full-week angling tours with room and board for about $3,000.

Casting a line on Henry's Fork, one of the country's best places for trout fishing.

An evening view of the Tetons from Teton Basin. Most Americans are only familiar with the profile of the mountains' crest as seen from Grand Teton National Park in Wyoming.

rare trumpeter swans, which nest in the surrounding wildlife refuge, once a private hunting preserve for the Harrimans and their guests.

Just below the Continental Divide and the Montana border, the highway forks, with the right branch (Rte. 20) heading over Targhee Pass to West Yellowstone and Yellowstone National Park. The left branch (Rte. 87) climbs past **Henry's Lake State Park** (Goose Bay Rd., Island Park; 208/558–7532), discovered by Major Henry nearly two centuries ago, and then over Raynolds Pass to Montana's Madison River Valley.

TETON AND SWAN VALLEYS

State highways eastbound from Rexburg and Ashton follow spectacular routes past rolling hills of grain and potatoes. Above them, to the east, rises the silhouette of the spectacular Teton Range, whose summits and eastern flanks are encompassed by Wyoming's Grand Teton National Park, the highest peak of which is the Grand Teton at 13,776 feet. The highways lead to the village of **Tetonia,** northern gateway to Idaho's 30-mile-long Teton Valley.

In the early 19th century, the Teton Valley was known as Pierre's Hole, after a French Canadian–Iroquois fur trapper named Pierre Tevanitagon. Pierre was two years in the grave, a victim of a Blackfoot attack in Montana, before this valley hosted its first summer traders' rendezvous. Three years later, hostile Blackfeet crashed the rendezvous, leading to 23 deaths and putting an end to rendezvous in Pierre's Hole. Now, however, the rendezvous spirit is re-created each August with mountain men's encampments, black-powder shoots, and such whimsical activities as the Mr. Pierre Tall Tale Contest and the John Colter Indian Escape Dash.

The valley's economy, while traditionally sustained by cattle ranching and hay farming, has begun to turn more toward tourism in recent years. Its hub is Driggs, a community of 1,200 people that offers the sole road access to **Grand Targhee Ski & Summer Resort** (Ski Hill Rd., Alta, WY; 307/353–2300). More than 40 feet of light, dry champagne snow falls at Targhee in winter, making it a national favorite of "powder-hound" skiers. Summer recreation includes hiking, horseback riding, mountain biking, golf, and tennis. The resort also hosts summer music festivals and ecology classes. Though geographically in Wyoming, Grand Targhee is just 12 miles east of Driggs but an hour's drive from the nearest Wyoming town, Jackson.

Route 33 to Jackson is worth a trip in itself to enjoy the fine views from 8,429-foot **Teton Pass.** The main route between Idaho Falls and Jackson is U.S. 26, which follows the South Fork of the Snake River upriver nearly to its source. A favorite day's destination for regional residents is **Heise Hot Springs** (Heise Rd.,

LOCAL FAVORITE PLACES TO EAT

Butch Cassidy's. 260 N. Fourth St., Montpelier; 208/847-3501. $$

This steak-and-seafood spot is named for the famous outlaw who held up the bank in this southeasternmost Idaho town in 1896. Open for three meals daily, the dining room is casual and family friendly; an adjoining saloon has pool tables and live bands on weekends.

Continental Bistro. 140 S. Main St., Pocatello; 208/233–4433. $$–$$$

In the heart of Pocatello's historic district, this restaurant serves European cuisine, primarily French and northern Italian, in a jazz bar–like space. There's outdoor dining when weather permits.

Hawg Smoke Café. 4330 N. Yellowstone Hwy., Idaho Falls; 208/523–4804. $$

Owner Dave Musgrave is a huge Harley-Davidson fan, so you'll find plenty of biker memorabilia on the walls here. The eclectic daily menu typically includes fresh fish and beef tenderloin dishes.

La Casita. 111 S. Park Ave W, Twin Falls; 208/734–7974. $

In a small yellow house by the railroad tracks, this family-owned Mexican restaurant specializes in authentic, homemade south-of-the-border cuisine in an alcohol-free environment. Regulars rave about the tamales.

North Highway Cafe. 460 Northgate Mile, Idaho Falls; 208/522–6212. $

One of Idaho's great "greasy spoons," this classic diner serves huge portions of chicken, seafood, and hickory-smoked beef 21 hours a day, from 5 AM to 2 AM daily. Local cowboys love it.

Senang Wine Bar and Tapas Bistro. 815 S. First Ave., Pocatello; 208/478-6732. $$–$$$

Diners share small plates, including crab cakes with cucumber salad and beef saté with a mango-cilantro emulsion, at this intriguing and colorful Indonesian-themed restaurant. Some 150 international wines are available by the glass.

Snake River Grill. State St. and Hagerman Ave., Hagerman; 208/837–6227. $$–$$$

Fresh rainbow trout from nearby farms and Snake River sturgeon make appearances at this classy, colorful restaurant, along with rack of lamb and Idaho alligator. Owner-chef Kirt Martin, a wild-game specialist, will even prepare your own catch of the day. Try your meal with Hagerman's own Rose Creek wine.

LOCAL FAVORITE PLACES TO STAY

Back O'Beyond B&B. 404 S. Garfield St., Pocatello; 208/232–3825. $$

This Victorian home, built in 1893 by a prominent publishing family, has four antiques-furnished rooms with private baths, a short walk from the downtown historic district.

Bar H Bar Ranch. 1501 Eight Mile Creek Rd., Soda Springs; 208/547–3082. $$

You can help with the branding and calving of 2,000 head of beef cattle when you stay at this 9,000-acre working ranch, 8 miles southeast of Soda Springs. Guests are served three hearty meals a day and stay in private rooms in a refurbished bunkhouse.

Best Western Burley Inn. 800 N. Overland Ave., Burley; 208/678-3501. $$

A central park area with swimming and volleyball make this family-oriented motel-and-convention complex the best choice for lodging between Boise and Salt Lake City, despite somewhat outdated decor. It's a short walk from the north bank of the Snake River.

Best Western Cottontree Inn. 1415 Bench Rd., Pocatello; 208/237–7650. $$

This 147-room hotel with traditional furnishings and big rooms has tennis and racquetball courts as well as an indoor pool and whirlpool. Kids stay for free and have a big playground where they can cut loose.

Grand Targhee Resort. Ski Hill Rd., Alta, WY, via Driggs; 307/353–2300. $$–$$$

Three alpine lodges at 8,000 feet elevation offer Southwestern-style accommodation for skiiers, mountain bikers, hikers, and other sports lovers. Choose between the hotel-style Teewinot Lodge, the motel-style Targhee Lodge, and the condo-style Sioux Lodge, with its bunk beds and kiva fireplaces.

Lava Hot Springs Inn. 94 E. Portneuf Ave., Lava Hot Springs; 208/776–5830. $$

This art-deco inn on the banks of the Portneuf River, built as a hospital in the 1920s, has its own mineral pools and includes full breakfasts in its rates. It retains an institutional feel from that

Ririe; 208/538–7312), on the north bank of the Snake 23 miles from Idaho Falls. The facilities include two outdoor mineral pools and a log lodge that dates from 1898. A small ski resort is 4 miles away in Kelly Canyon.

Wildlife abounds through Antelope Flat and the Swan Valley, the 35 miles of river between Heise and Palisades Dam. In particular, the cottonwood botera, somewhat supplanted by an eclectic garage-sale-find décor.

Le Ritz Hotel and Suites. 720 Lindsay Blvd., Idaho Falls; 208/528- -0880. $$

Beside the Snake River in the heart of town, this updated inn is friendly and well maintained, with a big complimentary breakfast, indoor pool and hot tub, fitness center, and business facilities. Some rooms have fireplaces, all have refrigerators and microwaves.

Lodge at Palisades Creek. 3720 Swan Valley Hwy., Irwin; 208/483–2222. $$$

This small, Orvis-endorsed lodge is a refuge for urban fly fishermen willing to pay top dollar to stay in rustic luxury and hook brown and rainbow trout. Accommodations are in cozy cabins. It's closed late-September to mid-June.

Red Lion Canyon Springs Hotel. 1357 Blue Lakes Blvd. N, Twin Falls; 208/734–5000. $$–$$$

Built around a central courtyard with a swimming pool and playground, this 112-room motel, just a block from the Snake River Canyon, has a restaurant, lounge and espresso shop. Rooms have matching hardwood furnishings but are otherwise utilitarian. Kids stay for free.

Rock Lodge Resort. 17940 Rte. 30, Hagerman; 208/837–4822. $$

Billingsley Creek, one of the Thousand Springs of the Hagerman Valley, tumbles past this eight-room resort. Each knotty pine-paneled unit has its own wooden patio on the creek.

Teton Ridge Ranch. 200 Valley View Rd., Tetonia; 208/456–2650. $$$

A luxurious guest lodge spread over 1,600 acres, the Teton Ridge is open for summer and winter seasons, with one-week minimum stays in midsummer. Accommodations are in a two-bedroom cottage and five suites.

tomlands attract bald eagles, ospreys, and other raptors to feed on the river's huge cutthroat and brown trout. There are tourist facilities at several locations in and around the village of Swan Valley. **Palisades Reservoir,** a popular fishing lake, backs up 17 miles behind an earthen dam built in 1959 by the Bureau of Reclamation. Its eastern end pokes into Wyoming's beautiful Star Valley.

CENTRAL IDAHO
ROCKIES TO SNAKE RIVER

Central Idaho is the roof of the state, where dozens of Rocky Mountain sub-ranges climax in the Sawtooths and the White Clouds, the Lemhi Mountains, and the Lost River Range. Most of Idaho's major rivers, including the Salmon, the Payette, the Boise, and the Wood, spring from the mountains' alpine lakes and snows. The state's highest mountain—12,662-foot Borah Peak—spawns creeks that feed the Big and Little Lost rivers, which flow nearly 100 miles southeast before disappearing into the porous lava of the Snake River Plain, a 10,000-square-mile ancient volcanic depression extending westerly from the Yellowstone region to the Thousand Springs near Hagerman. Also here are two monuments to past and future meltdown: Craters of the Moon National Monument and the Idaho National Engineering and Environmental Laboratory.

A winter's afternoon in the Boulder Mountains just north of Sun Valley.

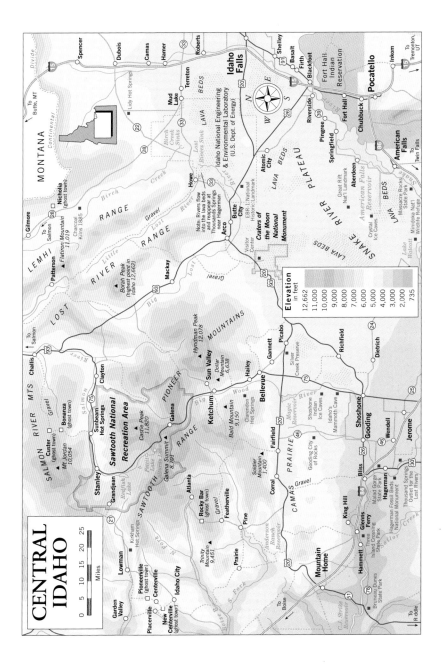

CENTRAL IDAHO

0	5	10	15	20	25
Miles

MONTANA

Continental   *Divide*

To Butte, MT

15

LEMHI   **RANGE**

Gilmore
Nicholia (ghost town)
Patterson   To Salmon   Flatiron Mountain 11,019
Charcoal Kilns 1885

Borah Peak (highest point in Idaho 12,662)

Birch   *Creek*

Little   *Lost*   **RIVER**   **RANGE**   *Gravel*

Mackay

Spencer   Dubois   Camas   Hamer   Roberts

Lady Hot Springs

22   **26**

33

Mud Lake   Terreton

LAVA   BEDS

Bowes Sink   *Lost*

Birch Creek Sinks

Note: Rivers flow into the lava beds and reappear at Thousand Springs near Hagerman

Howe   Atomic City   Arco   Butte City   EBR-1 National Historic Landmark

Idaho National Engineering & Environmental Laboratory (U.S. Dept. of Energy)

Idaho Falls   Shelley   Basalt   Firth   Blackfoot   Fort Hall Indian Reservation

91   **15**   **26**

Riverside   Pingree   Springfield   Aberdeen

Fort Hall   Chubbuck   Pocatello   Inkom

15   To Tremonton, UT

American Falls   To Twin Falls   **86**

American Falls Reservoir

Great Rift Nat'l Landmark   Massacre Rocks State Park   Minidoka Nat'l Wildlife Refuge

SNAKE   **RIVER**   **PLATEAU**   LAVA BEDS   LAVA BEDS

Crystal Ice Caves

Lake Walcott

To Salmon   **93**   Challis   **75**   Clayton   Bonanza (ghost town)   Custer (ghost town)   Mt Jordan 10,054

SALMON RIVER MTS   *Gravel*   *Salmon*   *River*

Stanley   Grandjean   Sunbeam Hot Springs   Castle Peak 11,820

Sawtooth National Recreation Area

Redfish Lake   Galena   Galena Summit 8,701   *Sawtooth Wilderness*   *SAWTOOTH*

Kirkham Hot Springs   Lowman   Garden Valley

Placerville   New Centerville (ghost town)   Centerville   Pioneerville (ghost town)

Idaho City   Atlanta   Rocky Bar (ghost town)   Featherville   Pine   Prairie

Gravel   Trinity Mountain 9,451

To Boise

21

Payette   *River*   *N. Fork*   *Boise*   *S. Fork*   *River*

Hyndman Peak 12,078   **PIONEER**   **MOUNTAINS**   **RANGE**

Sun Valley   Dollar Mountain 6,638   Ketchum   Hailey   Bellevue   Bald Mountain 9,150   Clarendon Hot Springs

Picabo   Gannett   Silver Creek Preserve   Richfield   Dietrich

Fairfield   Corral   Soldier Mountain 7,400

CAMAS   **PRAIRIE**   *Gravel*   Gooding City of Rocks

Magic Reservoir   *River*   **20**   **46**   **75**   **24**   **25**

Shoshone Indian Ice Caves   Idaho's Mammoth Cave

Shoshone   Gooding   Wendell   Jerome

Big   *Wood*   **River**

Bliss   Hagerman   Thousand Springs Outlet for the Lost Rivers   *Malad Gorge State Park*   Hagerman Fossil Beds National Monument

King Hill   Hammett   Glenns Ferry   Three Island Crossing State Park

Mountain Home   Bruneau Dunes State Park   To Riddle

Anderson Ranch Reservoir   *C.J. Strike Reservoir*

20   **30**   **26**   **46**   **51**   **78**

Elevation in feet

| 12,662 |
| 11,000 |
| 10,000 |
| 9,000 |
| 8,000 |
| 7,000 |
| 6,000 |
| 5,000 |
| 4,000 |
| 3,000 |
| 2,000 |
| 735 |

Craters of the Moon National Monument

Visitor Center   **20**   **93**

Within this rugged landscape, 19th-century prospectors found a wealth of natural resources: gold, silver, copper, and lead. (Recently, molybdenum has been a valuable ore.) The Boise River Basin engendered most of these early bonanzas, sparking instant boomtowns that grew and faded with the miners' fortunes. The population of Idaho City, once the largest community in the Pacific Northwest, has dwindled to about 450; but that's still more than Atlanta, which now has 40 residents, or Placerville, Pioneerville, and Rocky Bar, all of which have gone to the ghosts.

Most of the communities of Central Idaho seem far from the bustle of contemporary urban life, but the Wood River Valley, including the Sun Valley resort region and the adjacent towns of Ketchum and Hailey, is an exception. Here, perhaps more than anywhere else in the state, big-city sophistication comfortably coexists with no-nonsense rusticity.

Four highways provide the primary avenues of travel through this region: U.S. 20, U.S. 93, Route 21, and Route 75. The latter is perhaps the most frequently driven, as it links the resort center of Sun Valley and the spectacular Sawtooth National Recreation Area with the Snake River Plain.

SUN VALLEY

Long before there was any glitz in Aspen, Vail, Park City, or Jackson, people were coming to see (and be seen in) Idaho's ★Sun Valley, the first winter-sports resort in western North America. This glamorous playground of well-heeled skiers was commanded into existence by no less a potentate than W. Averell Harriman, chief executive of the Union Pacific Railroad. A future governor of New York, Harriman had become hooked on skiing during the 1932 Winter Olympics at Lake Placid in his home state. Like many people with money, he wanted a mountain of his own.

Harriman's vision called for a village surrounded by terrain "of the same character as the Swiss and Austrian Alps." That's what he told Felix Schaffgotsch, the Austrian count he hired to conduct an alpine shakedown of the Western ranges. He certainly made it well worth the young count's effort. Schaffgotsch scoured the American West, wandering the Cascades, the Sierra Nevada, Utah, Colorado, and Wyoming before eventually coming to Ketchum in January 1936. He immediately notified Harriman that he had found just the place they were looking for. Ketchum, Idaho, had been a mining hub in the 1880s and a sheep-ranching center in the early 1900s, but was now mainly ranchland. Two weeks after Schaffgotsch called, Harriman arrived. He wrote a $39,000 Union Pacific check for a 3,888-acre ranch on the site—and Sun Valley was his.

Construction of the four-story Sun Valley Lodge began soon thereafter at a cost of $1.5 million. Ski runs were created on two small adjacent hills, Dollar and Proctor mountains. To help skiers climb to the summits, Harriman decided to go one better than East Coast rope tows. He instructed Union Pacific engineers to design a "chairlift." What a novel concept! As luck would have it, one of the engineers, James Curran, had spent time in the tropics, where he had invented a way to hoist bananas onto ships. Curran put chairs where the banana hooks had been, and voila! the chairlift was born.

Harriman hired public-relations *Wunderkind* Steve Hannagan to handle the resort's marketing. Hannagan, who was largely responsible for making Miami Beach a popular destination with East Coast vacationers, coined the name Sun Valley. He also made the resort's December 1936 opening a Hollywood event, bringing in such movie stars as Claudette Colbert, Errol Flynn, and Clark Gable for the extravaganza. Many of their autographed black-and-white publicity stills hang on the walls of the venerable lodge even today.

So successful was Sun Valley's first season that by the resort's second winter another lodge, the chalet-style Sun Valley Inn, had been completed. It didn't hurt, of course, that a major railroad owned the resort and was able to offer packages that delivered cross-country guests almost directly to its doorstep.

Union Pacific sold the resort in 1964. It is operated today by Earl Holding's Little America Corporation.

Sun Valley sits amid the peaks of Idaho's Rockies, in the middle of the **Wood River Valley,** a long, ravishingly beautiful stretch of paradise. Though founded as a resort for skiers, Sun Valley could not help but be just as attractive by summer. Today it boasts four 18-hole golf courses, 85 tennis courts, riding stables, swimming, biking, hiking, fishing, and a world-class ice-skating rink where Olympic medalists like Sasha Cohen, Kristi Yamaguchi, Scott Hamilton, Brian Boitano, and Nancy Kerrigan perform to sell-out crowds on weekend evenings through the summer. Hot springs are another big draw for tourists in the valley. Some, like rustic Worsewick Hot Springs, lie well off the beaten track. Others, like Easely Hot Springs (north of Ketchum) and Bald Mountain Hot Spring (in downtown Ketchum), have been developed into fancier resorts.

Most importantly, Sun Valley has its winter skiing. **Bald Mountain** ("Baldy"), at 9,150 feet, wasn't even in the resort's original plans. It was too big and too challenging for most skiers' abilities (not to mention ski technology) in the 1930s.

Today it is regarded as one of North America's truly Schwarzeneggarian mountains. (And yes, you may run into Arnold on the slopes: the California governor and former film star has a home in Sun Valley, as do other Hollywood celebs, among them Bruce Willis, Demi Moore, Jamie Lee Curtis, and her husband, Christopher Guest.) **Dollar Mountain** still serves beginners. Instead of one banana-hoist chairlift, Sun Valley has 17 doubles, triples, and quads.

The resort itself has a European-village appeal. In addition to the two lodges built in the 1930s, it is now surrounded by hundreds of modern condominiums, as well as a dozen restaurants and perhaps twice as many chic shops. Moreover, it has **Trail Creek Cabin,** a rustic cottage just a short journey from the lodge by horse-drawn sleigh. Four-course dinners around a roaring fire make this a favorite destination of winter visitors. *Trail Creek Rd., 1.5 miles east of Sun Valley Resort; 208/622-2135.*

In spring and summer, the Sun Valley area hosts music festivals and arts-and-crafts shows. The valley also accommodates a range of outdoor activities, including road races and triathlons, paragliding, horseback riding, and multiday mountain-biking or rock-climbing trips with licensed instructors. Three nearby lakes provide windsurfing, waterskiing, jet skiing, swimming, and diving. You can also fish, kayak, or raft on one of the area's many rivers: Silver Creek, Big Wood, and Salmon. The valley has four 18-hole golf courses, over 60 tennis courts, and trap and skeet shooting.

In August 2007 the Castle Rock fire devastated 40,000 acres near the resort and threatened 2,000 homes and several lifts on Bald Mountain. Happily, Sun Valley emerged from the blaze none the worse for wear.

SKIING SUN VALLEY

Expect a winter's day at Sun Valley to emerge clear, cold and glorious. Even when the summit temperature lingers around 5 degrees, the morning rays glint off freshly fallen powder on Bald Mountain's eastern face—from Christmas Ridge to Easter Bowl, Upper College to Exhibition. Skiers and snowboarders shiver but smile as they disembark from the Lookout Express, the second of two quad chairlifts that make the 3,300-foot ascent from River Run Plaza to just beneath the peak of 9,150-foot Baldy.

The easiest way down from the mountain's peak is via Upper and Lower College, into Lower River Run; all of these runs are marked green, or "easier," although they might be rated blue, or "intermediate," at other resorts. Expert skiers seeking a more significant challenge prefer to head into the powder of Lookout

Bald Mountain ("Baldy")

Terrain: 64 runs on 2,067 acres
  38% beg., 45% inter., 17% adv.
Lifts: 13; 7 hi-speed quads, 4 trip., 2 doub.
Vertical drop: 3,400 ft.
Summit elevation: 9,150 ft.
Snowboarding permitted.

Dollar Mountain

Terrain: 13 runs
  Primarily a beginner mountain
Lifts: 4 total
Vertical drop: 628 ft.
Summit elevation: 6,638 ft.
Snowboarding permitted.

Snow Report:
  (800) 635-4150/(208)622-2093

Over 100 miles of groomed **nordic tracks** in the area; **heli-skiing** is also available.

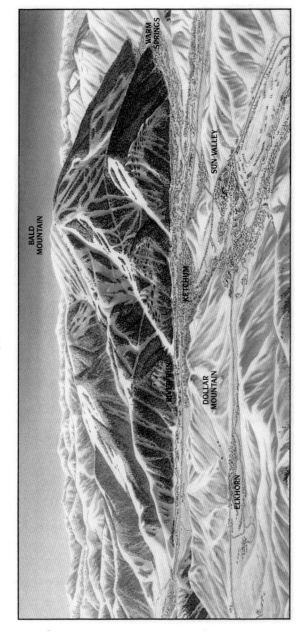

BALD MOUNTAIN
WARM SPRINGS
RIVER RUN
KETCHUM
DOLLAR MOUNTAIN
SUN VALLEY
ELKHORN

Bowl, Easter Bowl, and Little Easter Bowl. Skiers who seek a secret stash head for Frenchman's, which rides a ridgeline on the northeast face of the mountain. Several intermediate runs, including Graduate, Can-Can, and Janss Pass, branch off Lower College to the base of this shorter chairlift.

Baldy has two main access areas with ski shops, restaurants, and the like: in addition to River Run, there is also Warm Springs on its north side. River Run Plaza stands on its own, less than a mile southwest of downtown Ketchum on the Big Wood River. The Warm Springs Day Lodge is about three miles northwest but is surrounded by condominiums and private homes. It sits just off Picabo Street, an avenue named for the female Olympic ski champion.

The longest of Sun Valley's 13 chairlifts, a quad called the Challenger, begins at Warm Springs and climbs 3,142 feet in 10 minutes to the Lookout Restaurant. This is also the terminus of the River Run chairs, making the Lookout the mountain's on-slope hub. And there are two other places to escape the cold on Baldy: the Seattle Ridge Day Lodge, atop an easier section of mountaintop runs, and the mid-mountain Roundhouse Restaurant, a fine-dining spot now connected to River Run by a year-round gondola (constructed in spring 2008).

Alpine skiing isn't the only winter diversion in Sun Valley. More than 100 miles of groomed cross-country track are spread throughout the Wood River area, including 40 km (25 mi) of loop trails from the Sun Valley Nordic and Snowshoe Center. Extended ski and snowshoe trips into the wilderness of the nearby Sawtooth National Recreation Area can be arranged. You can even book heli-skiing and dog-sledding expeditions. The Sun Valley Lodge has an outdoor ice-skating rink, open daily for public skating.

KETCHUM

A scant 2 miles from Sun Valley, Ketchum hasn't been eclipsed by its newer but more famous neighbor. On the contrary, it has grown right alongside it. When Bald Mountain was developed, its lift stations were placed along Big Wood River and Warm Springs Creek, virtually in downtown Ketchum, at an elevation of 5,821 feet. Ketchum today has a gentrified Western charm most apparent along Main Street, where restaurants and bars, bookstores and boutiques, art galleries and espresso shops vie for attention in the community's original brick buildings. Motels, motor lodges, and bed-and-breakfasts cluster near the River Run and Warm Springs areas at the foot of the mountain.

Former modes of transport may be viewed at the Ore Wagon Museum in Ketchum. (Idaho State Historical Society)

The **Ore Wagon Museum** still preserves some reminders of the old days. Long, tall, and narrow, pulled by 20-mule teams, the wagons were used through the 1880s to haul millions of dollars' worth of silver and lead ore from outlying mines to Wood River Valley smelters. As many as nine tons of ore could be lugged 12 to 16 miles a day in a single wagon, up and down grades as steep as 12 percent. On Labor Day weekends the museum unleashes the wagons to again trundle through the streets of Ketchum. Some of their weighty wheels are as large as 7 feet in diameter. *500 East Ave., Ketchum; no phone.*

Ketchum has an active art-gallery scene. Modern American folk artist Jane Wooster Scott heads a roster of local painters who have made their mark nationally; others include Gail Severn and Lynn Toneri. The **Sun Valley Gallery Association** (208/726-4950) sponsors nine gallery walks a year; they are a great way to check out the local art scene. Seven leading galleries line a three-block stretch of First Avenue, two blocks west of Main Street.

In particular, the **Sun Valley Center for the Arts** (191 Fifth St. E, Ketchum; 208/726-9491) always has an intriguing, contemporary exhibit on its walls, often with a political or social edge. **Frederic Boloix Fine Arts** (320 First Ave. N,

HIGH ON HEMINGWAY

In the late 1930s Ernest Hemingway lived in Idaho while writing For Whom the Bell Tolls. *His companion in fishing and hunting was Lloyd Arnold, who wrote a book about their experiences together.*

"Ernie, you write Westerns?" No words to describe Ernest's face, or ours when he jerked his head around, grabbing at his falling hat.

······ ❀ · ❀ · ❀ ······

We took the Salmon River route home, the graveled Highway 93 hugging the river through the scenic heartland of the state for a hundred miles—to cross it as a tiny creek at the foot of Galena Summit, an hour from Ketchum. It would be hard to find a more satisfying hundred miles than following the storied River of No Return to its trickling source. Looking back on it from a high switchback on the snaky old Summit road, Ernest said softly, "You'd have to come from a test tube and think like a machine not to engrave all of this in your head so that you never lose it."

The following dawn the work on the novel continued as scheduled, we learned at a lingering lunch, and it went better in mountain cool than it had in months of heat in a hotel in Havana. He said he was on the rough of Chapter 13, and had worked the name Sun Valley into it. We lifted brows. How could he do it, time-wise?

He grinned. "The freedom of fiction."

—Lloyd R. Arnold, *Hemingway: High on the Wild,* 1968

Ketchum; 208/726-8810) carries Picasso, Matisse, and Chagall. The **Broschofsky Galleries** (360 East Ave., Ketchum; 208/726-4950) are specialists in Western art, both traditional (Catlin prints) and modern (Warhol lithographs). And Robin Reiner's **Gallery DeNovo** (320 First Ave. N, Ketchum; 208/726-8180) introduces European and Asian artists to American audiences.

A series of summer outdoor concerts caters to every musical preference, from classical to rock, jazz to world beat. The Sun Valley Music Festival, Sun Valley Summer Symphony, and Northern Rockies Folk Festival keep July, and especially August, filled with the sounds of music.

The text on the memorial plaque reads:

BEST OF ALL HE LOVED THE FALL
THE LEAVES YELLOW ON THE COTTONWOODS
LEAVES FLOATING ON THE TROUT STREAMS
AND ABOVE THE HILLS
THE HIGH BLUE WINDLESS SKIES
...NOW HE WILL BE A PART OF THEM FOREVER
ERNEST HEMINGWAY · IDAHO · 1939

The Ernest Hemingway Memorial in Sun Valley.

As for writers, Ernest Hemingway (1899-1961) and Ezra Pound (1885-1972) are the best known. Hemingway first visited in 1939 and completed *For Whom the Bell Tolls* there. Twenty years later, having won a Pulitzer Prize for fiction and a Nobel Prize for literature, he fled his home in Cuba upon Fidel Castro's takeover and moved back to Ketchum. Unable to deal with depression and declining health, he ended his life with a self-inflicted gunshot in July of 1961. Hemingway's grave lies in a pine grove in Ketchum Cemetery, and the **Ernest Hemingway Memorial** overlooks Trail Creek—one of his favorite fly-fishing streams—a mile northeast of the Sun Valley Lodge.

Ezra Pound, rated by some as the most important (and most controversial) American poet of the 20th century, was born in the mining town of Hailey (his father was an assayer). At the age of two he moved with his family to Philadelphia. After his college graduation he lived in London, Paris (where he edited some of the young Hemingway's early manuscripts), and finally Italy, where he spent most of the rest of his life, having never returned to Idaho. The state still claims him.

Sixty million dollars' worth of silver, gold, and lead were produced in the Wood River valley during the decade of the 1880s, and **Hailey,** as the Blaine County seat, was the biggest beneficiary. In 1883 the town got a telephone exchange, Idaho's first. In 1889 it installed the state's first electric-light system. The **Blaine County Historical Museum** (218 N. Main St.; 208/788-4185) is housed in an 1882 building, one of a handful surviving from that era. (By the 1890s the mines had been worked out.) Just down the street, Bruce Willis owns a popular nightclub, The Mint, where he occasionally performs. When he does so, his ex-wife and fellow Hailey resident Demi Moore and her husband Ashton Kutcher often attend.

With outdoor recreation primarily responsible for the modern economic success of the Wood River valley, it makes sense that non-motorized means are among the most popular ways to travel from Ketchum through Hailey to Bellevue, a distance of 21 miles. The paved Wood River Trail System, on a former railroad right-of-way that parallels Route 75, seems always to be packed with cyclists, runners, and in-line skaters or, in winter, with cross-country skiers. A pedestrian underpass connects it to 10 more miles of bike trails through Sun Valley.

SAWTOOTH NATIONAL RECREATION AREA

They're called "America's Alps," and those who cast their eyes upon the lofty Sawtooth Mountains would find it hard to argue. These chiseled peaks, 42 of them over 10,000 feet in elevation, tower above the stream valleys that emanate from their heights: the main Salmon River along with its Middle and East forks, the North and South forks of the Boise River, the South Fork of the Payette River, and the Big Wood River. More than 300 alpine lakes speckle the Sawtooth Range and its adjacent Boulder Mountains and White Cloud Peaks, all of them contained within the 1,180-square-mile Sawtooth National Recreation Area (SNRA). Hunters, anglers, horseback riders, and backpackers frequent the mountains during much of the year. The rivers and lakes lure rafters and boaters from several states. Five hundred formal campsites, several guest ranches, and clusters of motels and cabins provide accommodation.

Driving north from Ketchum on State Highway 75, you enter the SNRA just 8 miles from the Sun Valley area. Stop for maps and information at the headquarters station (built to resemble a profile of the Sawtooth Mountains) on your right. You can also borrow an audio cassette (and a tape player, if you don't have one) that will provide narration for your 61-mile drive to Stanley—just be sure to return it to the Stanley or Redfish Lake ranger station.

From SNRA headquarters the road climbs gradually northwest up the Big Wood River, 22 miles to Galena Summit at 8,701 feet. Forests of lodgepole pine and Douglas fir shroud parts of the road, but where the trees open up there are marvelous views to the east across the Boulder Mountains and west to the fire-ravaged Smoky Mountains. This route, built in 1953, was the third to transit the Galena Summit; the first was cut in 1881 to serve the mines of the region.

You won't see a sign for it, but one of the most controversial locations in the northern Rockies is near here. In 1995, 15 wolves from Canada were transplanted into the Frank Church-River of No Return Wilderness by the U.S. Fish and Wildlife Service. A further 20 were introduced the following year. The transplants were deemed successful and no further wolves were introduced. As of late 2007 there were an estimated 15 separate wolf packs thriving, with perhaps as many as 800 wolves throughout the state. Opponents claim the wolves, slaughtered nearly to extinction by bounty hunters in the late 19th and early 20th centuries, will prey upon their livestock. Supporters of the program insist the creatures' reputation as livestock-killers is undeserved, that they prefer wild game and descend to rangeland only when weather conditions are abnormally harsh. The jury remains out. Meanwhile, environmentalists are weighing the possibility of reintroducing grizzly bears to the Idaho mountains.

Just below Galena Summit stands **Galena Lodge,** an old travelers' oasis that's been refurbished as a Nordic skiing center and restaurant. This is but a prelude to

The Sawtooth
Mountains are
often called
"America's Alps."

the magnificent panorama of the 30-mile-long Sawtooth Range from the 8,701-foot summit, which divides the watersheds of the Big Wood and Salmon rivers. *24 miles north of Ketchum on Rte. 75, Ketchum; 208/726-4010.*

Descending to the headwaters of the Salmon, you can see the 11,000-plus-foot heights of the White Cloud Peaks to the east. To the west, nestling at the foot of the Sawtooth Range, are a series of beautiful glacial lakes, the largest of which are Alturas, Pettit, and Redfish. **Alturas Lake** is the site of several church and scouting organization camps. Campgrounds are especially attractive to anglers, who launch their boats to troll for kokanee salmon and rainbow trout. Nearby **Pettit Lake** is also popular with fishermen, as well as backpackers climbing into the Sawtooth Wilderness on the 17-mile Pettit-Toxaway Loop Trail. **Redfish Lake,** with deep indigo waters framed by craggy peaks and surrounded by pine forests, is the single most popular destination for visitors to the National Recreation Area. There are several campgrounds along the lake's northeastern shore, as well as a U.S. Forest Service visitor center with exhibits and detailed maps for backcountry adventurers. The long-established Redfish Lake Lodge has budget-priced cabins, indoor and outdoor dining, and a general store; out front, on the lakeshore, there's a sandy beach and a marina where you can rent motorboats or canoes,

Kokanee salmon spawn in the rivers streaming from the Sawtooth Mountains.

or join a lake excursion that will shuttle you to trails leading into the Sawtooth Wilderness at the head of Redfish Lake.

One of the state's finest guest ranches is located midway between Alturas and Redfish lakes, about 10 miles south of Stanley. The **Idaho Rocky Mountain Ranch** was a private club for East Coast urbanites in the 1930s, and a 1,000-acre cattle ranch for 35 years thereafter. Today its rustic cabins and lodge rooms welcome the public for riding, hiking, hot springs swimming, and other activities. There may be no better place to view the entire vista of the Sawtooth Range than the wide front porch of the ranch's huge, hand-hewn log lodge, especially at sunrise. *Rte. 75, 9 miles south of Stanley; 208/774-3544.*

At an altitude of about 6,600 feet, the **Sawtooth National Fish Hatchery** is the highest-elevation hatchery in the United States, and an important one, raising more than three million chinook salmon each year. Tours, available in summer, take visitors through the various steps of the fish-breeding process, from tiny minnows to fully grown salmon awaiting release. *Rte. 75, 3 mi south of Stanley; 208/774-3684.*

Most Sawtooth activities revolve around the village of **Stanley,** where Route 21 from Boise meets Route 75 from Ketchum. To unsuspecting winter visitors, Stanley must seem more like Alaska than Idaho: the community competes with Gunnison, Colorado, and International Falls, Minnesota, on the "nation's coldest temperature" lists. Sub-zero (Fahrenheit) recordings are the norm in January and February, and snowfall averages nearly eight feet. It's favored only by hardy cross-country skiers and snowmobilers.

But between the spring snowmelt and the next onslaught of winter, Stanley is a glorious place to be. Surrounded by the high wilderness crags of the Sawtooth Range, it is a community of spectacular beauty. The Old West appearance of unpaved **Ace of Diamonds Street** and its other broad avenues recalls that of a 19th-century mining town. Recreation keeps the village afloat (so to speak): white-water rafting operators, horse packers, and other guides and outfitters make their headquarters in Stanley. Town history is recalled at the 60-year-old **Valley Creek Ranger Station,** a half-mile west of the junction on Route 21.

Hudson's Bay Company fur trappers were the first white men to pass through the Stanley Basin. Game was not plentiful—the broad alpine meadows perhaps left most species feeling vulnerable—so the trappers moved on. Prospectors exploring the region in the 1860s also found no good reason to stay. It was not until the second decade of the 20th century that Stanley gained importance as a

A miner's pack train heads for the hills in this 1870s photograph. (Library of Congress)

tiny enclave of civilization at a wilderness crossroads. Fewer than 100 people call Stanley their year-round home even today.

WESTERN SLOPES OF THE SAWTOOTH RANGE

The headwaters of the Boise River and the South Fork of the Payette River rush down the western slope of the Sawtooth Range through ancient moraines and between steep ridges. For thousands of years, the gold washed down by their raging waters remained unclaimed. Then in the mid-1800s argonauts stumbled upon the rich placers. Instantly, riotous camps of treasure seekers sprang up—boomtowns with names like Idaho City, Pioneerville, and Atlanta.

Today Route 21 passes through Idaho City en route from Stanley to Boise. After cresting the Sawtooths near Bull Trout Lake, it follows Canyon Creek to the Payette's South Fork. Adventurous travelers may want to detour here and follow the river upstream 6.5 miles on a gravel road to the community of **Grandjean,** on the opposite side of the Sawtooths from most access points. Grandjean's primitive lodge and campground provide a staging ground for hunters, hikers, and horseback riders.

The canyon of the South Fork of the Payette below the Grandjean junction bears the scars of a devastating forest fire that ravaged this region in 1992. Many summer homes went up in smoke, but some survivors still stand beside the river near the village of Lowman. With the passage of time, as seedling pines begin to rise in the burn, some new, contemporary homes are sprouting up. At nearby **Kirkham Hot Springs,** thermal vents in the South Fork's south bank heat a series of rock pools. Pipes carry the water to four tubs in a Boise National Forest campground.

The heart of Idaho's biggest 19th-century mining boom was **Idaho City,** 34 miles below Lowman, at the confluence of Elk and More's creeks. In the two decades beginning in 1862, more than a quarter-billion dollars' worth of gold was taken from this hill country. In 1864, when the Idaho Territory was created, some 6,200 citizens lived here, making it larger than any other settlement in the Pacific Northwest; in fact, 80 percent of the territory's population called Idaho City home. The citizenry included 5,640 men, 360 women, and 224 children; about one-third of the male population was Chinese. Its 200 businesses included 36 saloons, a couple of churches, and a school.

Gold was first discovered here in August 1862 by three prospectors panning on Grimes Creek, 7 miles northwest of Idaho City. As soon as word got out, the rush was on. Pioneerville, Placerville, Centerville, New Centerville, Quartzburg, and Bannock City (later renamed Idaho City) sprang up almost overnight. Although a few quartz lodes were discovered in the surrounding hills, most Boise Basin gold was taken by hydraulic methods: sluicing and placer mining.

★**Idaho City** stands as a living monument to historic preservation. Although its modern-day population has dwindled to around 450, it has saved blocks of buildings from its boom days, including several that survived a spate of fires between 1865 and 1871. The oldest of the surviving buildings is the **Idaho Territorial Penitentiary** (Montgomery and Wall Sts., Idaho City; no phone), constructed of hand-hewn logs in 1864. The jail was primitive, to say the least. Surrounded by a mere board fence, it had a single guard working a 12-hour shift. Amazingly, of the 106 convicts imprisoned here between 1864 and 1872, only 17 escaped. (None of them was recaptured.)

In 1864 the Independent Order of Odd Fellows (IOOF), a private fraternal society founded in late-18th-century England, chose Idaho City for its Pioneer Lodge No. 1, the first of its lodges west of the Mississippi River. Another fraternal lodge, the **Masonic Temple** (Wall and Montgomery Sts., Idaho City; 208/343-

A winter night sky swirls around the North Star over the Sawtooth Valley of Central Idaho.

4562), Idaho Lodge No. 1, was erected in 1865 and is the oldest Masonic hall in the American West still in active use.

As you wander the planked boardwalks of Idaho City, you may also visit "The Merc," the **Boise Basin Mercantile Co.** (313 Main St., Idaho City; 208/392-4443), a general store that opened in 1865 at its present location—a one-story brick building with a quartet of arched doorways—and has never closed. From 1867 to 1918 the **Idaho World Building** (Main and Commercial Sts., Idaho City; 208/392-4989) was home to the *Idaho World,* the state's longest-published newspaper; it is still printed as a weekly. Up on a hilltop, parishioners rebuilt **St. Joseph's Catholic Church** (200 E. Hill Rd., Idaho City; 208/392-4751) in a single month in 1867 after it was destroyed by fire. Another 1867 building, then Idaho City's post office and news agency, now houses the **Boise Basin Historical Museum** (402 Montgomery St., Idaho City; 208/392-4550). Photographs and memorabilia passed down by the descendants of miners and other townspeople make it a fascinating place to visit.

Today most of the other gold rush towns offer nothing but memories. A few buildings do remain in **Placerville,** 13 miles northwest of Idaho City via Placerville Road. Once home to 3,200 residents, it still has a general store, post office, Episcopal church, and a small museum in its elegant old Magnolia Saloon. A handful of more modern houses are the summer homes of Boise urbanites. A half-dozen abandoned buildings remain in **Pioneerville,** 17 miles north of Idaho City via Grimes Pass Road, while the cemetery is all that remains of nearby Centerville; yet both towns once had populations of about 3,000.

Backroad adventurers can follow Boise National Forest roads 60 miles east from Idaho City to **Atlanta** (it was named by Confederate sympathizers in the wake of General Sherman's raid), another well-preserved relic of the gold-rush era. (Take Rabbit Creek Road east from Route 21 to the North Fork Boise River, continue upstream to Swanholm Creek Road, then cross a ridge to Middle Fork Road and proceed east.) On the south bank of the Middle Fork Boise, Atlanta had 500 residents in the 1870s. A large quartz deposit, rich in gold and silver, was discovered here in 1863, but despite substantial investment, transportation and technology problems kept most of it economically out of reach. There was a mini-boom in 1878-84, but not until the 1930s—with the construction of the Middle Fork Road from Boise and the aid of a new concentrator—did the Atlanta Mining District take off. Between 1932 and 1953 Atlanta produced $16 million in gold and a significant amount of antimony.

Today Atlanta is a gateway to the adjacent Sawtooth Wilderness, immediately northeast of here. The village's four-dozen year-round residents have assembled an economy built around outdoor recreation: hunting and fishing in the warmer months, cross-country skiing and snowmobiling in winter. The old Atlanta jail has been converted into the **Atlanta Historical Society Museum** (Middle Fork Rd., Atlanta; 208/864-2222) where, among other things, you can learn the story of "Peg Leg Annie" McIntyre.

One sunny morning in May 1896, Annie and her friend "Dutch Em" von Losch set out on foot from Atlanta for the neighboring mining town of Rocky Bar, some 14 miles distant. Unfortunately, the weather changed dramatically and they were caught in a spring blizzard near James Creek Summit, at 7,500 feet elevation. The storm raged for two days. When it finally let up, a search party found Em frozen to death and a maniacal Annie crawling through the snow. Annie survived, but her feet were so badly frostbitten that they had to be amputated.

A century ago, prostheses were not what they are today. But "Peg Leg Annie" lived to be an old woman. She remained in Rocky Bar for several years, selling whiskey and doing laundry; she died in Boise in 1934. Her cabin is one of several structures still standing amid the abandoned mining equipment in Rocky Bar.

Fly fishing for steelhead.

The town had a small boom in the late 1860s, and then a bigger one between 1886 and 1892, when $6 million in gold was recovered from its quartz lodes. By the second decade of the 20th century, however, it was almost as empty as it is today.

A gravel road south from Rocky Bar runs 7 miles to **Featherville,** a former stage station on the South Fork Boise River. Another 10 miles south by paved Route 61 is **Pine.** Both communities are outdoor-recreation centers within the Boise National Forest, but Pine has the added advantage of being at the head of **Anderson Ranch Reservoir,** a favorite spot for fishing and waterskiing. A side road from Fall Creek, midway up the reservoir's north shore, leads 13 miles to the **Trinity Mountain Recreation Area,** where a profusion of alpine tarns nestle in the bosom of 9,451-foot Trinity Mountain. If you're in a four-wheel-drive vehicle, or if you're feeling light of foot, you can climb to a mountaintop fire lookout.

Heading south on Castle Rock Road from Anderson Ranch Reservoir toward U.S. 20, the main highway crossing the Snake River Plain, you will pass through the area of the grotesque Castle Rocks. Old-time Idahoans will tell you this is "Charlie Sampson country." Sampson was a piano dealer who, beginning in 1914, made it his personal mission to signpost unmarked country roads leading to his Boise music store. "Pianos/Sampson/Boise" reads the faded orange lettering still visible on a boulder alongside U.S. 20. By 1933 the businessman had created 19 "Sampson Trails" through five Western states, his orange and black paint striping everything from rocks to old barns and bridges. When the state highway department, which itself had made no effort to keep pace, formally objected, Idaho's legislature passed a resolution that applauded Sampson's work and encouraged him to continue. Two years later, Charlie Sampson died, but his legacy persists.

SNAKE RIVER PLAIN

South of the Sawtooths and its neighboring ranges, constrained to the edge of the arid Snake River Plain by the ranks of swelling mountains, U.S. 20 rambles along the 215-mile stretch from Mountain Home to Idaho Falls like a Sunday driver admiring the wide-open scenery. Near its western end, it passes through Camas Prairie (one of three by that name in Idaho), a region well-known to the native Shoshone and Bannock tribes, who for centuries harvested camas bulbs there until they were rooted out by white settlers' livestock. The lily's high-protein bulb was a staple of the Indians' diet. Native Americans inhabited this prairie for at least 10,000 years. Archaeological digs near Fairfield have unearthed some of the

CITY FOLKS TRY FARMING

When Charley actually announced his decision to give up a perfectly good salary from the million-dollar sugar-factory in Garden City, Kansas, to go to a perfectly unknown, sight unseen, undeveloped wilderness farm in Idaho, I almost went on a hunger strike, through horror. I loved the pretty house I was having such fun furnishing, one of my passions being interior decorating, inherited, no doubt, from my ancestors who interior-decorated Windsor Castle, and painted pictures on the side.

･････ ❀ ･ ❀ ･ ❀ ･････

We do not talk, we two women. We must rush, *rush,* RUSH! There is no such pressure on the men out-of-doors as there is on the women in the kitchen. Everything must be ready on the very dot of time when the threshing-machine stops with a great silence. Probably the earth would change its orbit, and a few planets crash, if it should ever occur that the threshing meal was not exactly ready when the first tableful of men was ready for it.

. . . Nerves are stretched taut. I begin adding, in my mind, the different parts of the sum that makes the dinner, peeping into every steaming kettle, prying with a fork, scalding my fingers . . .

･････ ❀ ･ ❀ ･ ❀ ･････

The first tableful are seated, are passing the bread, pickles, preserves, vegetables, meat, everything at the same time, with cross-currents that manage not to collide, while Hen Turner's wife is pouring coffee for all the coffee-drinkers, and milk for all the milk-drinkers, and water for all the water drinkers and coffee, milk, and water for the coffee, milk, and water drinkers, and hot water with a little milk in it for Farmer Stillton. I am already refilling dishes—more hot rolls, more meat, more of everything. The second table is lolling in the shade of the house . . .

･････ ❀ ･ ❀ ･ ❀ ･････

It is just as foolish and dangerous for a city man to take his family out in the sagebrush to farm as it would be for the local barber to attempt an operation for gall-stones with a razor and a shaving-mug. And yet, we city farmers did very well alongside the born farmers, and we might have succeeded entirely were not the world of agriculture ruled by the middlemen who know no law but that of profit to themselves . . .

After we lost our farm, I watched from the living-room windows the sale of the stock. It was all that belonged to us, except our shabby household goods.

—Annie Pike Greenwood, *We Sagebrush Folks,* 1934

Blue camas bloom
on their namesake
Camas Prairie.

finest Clovis points (Stone Age spearheads) found on this continent. Nowadays, it's a forage-crop farming district watered by Camas Creek (a tributary of the Big Wood River) and Mormon and Magic reservoirs, both of which thrill anglers with their giant rainbow and brown trout.

Goodale's Cutoff, an important pioneer route, crossed this plain in the mid-19th century. Blazed by mountain man Tim Goodale, it offered an alternative to the Oregon Trail between Fort Hall and Boise.

Soldier Mountain is a small family-oriented ski area built on a 1,400-foot vertical drop in the Sawtooth National Forest foothills, 12 miles north of Fairfield. The resort, which also offers backcountry skiing, now has two chairlifts. Owners (who include Bruce Willis) have been discussing large-scale development. *Soldier Creek Rd., north of Rte. 20, Fairfield; 208/764-2526.*

An interesting detour leads over Bennett Mountain to the **Gooding City of Rocks,** a 26-square-mile BLM recreation area. The gnarled sandstone formations of this intriguing geological district attract mountain bikers and rock climbers. Naturalists are drawn by a resident elk herd. Ancient petroglyphs are also carved in some of the rocks. To get there, head 14 miles south on Route 46 (the junction is just east of Fairfield) to signs at Flat Top Butte; from there you've got another 9 miles on unsurfaced roads.

Anyone with an interest in speleology should detour to the **Shoshone Indian Ice Caves.** One thousand feet long and 40 feet high, these lava tubes are refrigerated by air currents that range between 28 and 33 degrees year-round. The ice floor varies from 8 to 30 feet thick. Prehistoric fossils have been found within the caves, and Shoshone travelers once escaped desert heat inside. Pioneers quarried ice from the caves for two decades after they were discovered in 1880. Guided tours take 40 minutes. *1561 N. Hwy. 75, Shoshone; 208/886-2058.*

There's no ice in **Idaho's Mammoth Cave,** a mile-long tube of cherry-red lava that was used as a civil-defense shelter in the 1950s. There are no guided tours, but visitors can explore its lofty chambers on their own. An A-frame at its entrance has an exhibit of hundreds of stuffed birds. *Thorn Creek Reservoir Rd., off Rte. 75, 8 miles north of Shoshone; no phone.*

Ernest Hemingway's favorite fishing hole was along a Little Wood River tributary, a meandering wetland stream known as Silver Creek. The Nature Conservancy now owns the **Silver Creek Preserve** (Kilpatrick Creek Rd., Picabo; 208/788-7910), with spring-fed waters whose temperature never climbs much above 50 degrees. Fly fishermen who pursue the creek's oversized rainbow, brook, and brown trout are compelled to "catch and release" with barbless hooks. The

A trapper looks over the lava beds and Craters of the Moon region of Idaho in this lithograph from *Harper's Weekly* in 1878. (Idaho State Historical Society)

nearest community to the Silver Creek Preserve is tiny **Picabo** (pronounced "Peek-a-boo"). This hamlet might have remained forever anonymous were it not for a spunky local woman—named for the village—who established herself as the best downhill skier in the world in the mid-1990s. Picabo Street won the silver medal in the 1994 Olympic downhill and the overall 1995 World Cup women's downhill title.

The eastern half of the Snake River Plain, cauldron of Idaho's most recent violent volcanic activity, embraces some of the most rugged terrain in North America. This is the land of lost rivers, where streams disappear into the aquifer that underlies the porous lava fields. For most travelers, the sightseeing highlight of the Snake River Plain is ★**Craters of the Moon National Monument** (19 miles southwest of Arco, off Rte. 20; 208/527-3257), whose name was not given glibly. American astronauts actually have been trained at this site, whose landscapes are considered the nearest-to-lunar in the country. The reserve's 83 square miles of spatter cones and fissure vents occupy the northern end of a 60-mile-long Great Rift Zone, which cuts across the heart of the plain. Geologists say eruptions and lava flows began here about 15,000 years ago, continued until about 2,000 years ago, and could occur again.

Buckwheat flowers spring up
on the cinder slopes of the Craters
of the Moon National Mounment.

President Calvin Coolidge proclaimed this national monument in 1924, thanks in large part to a daring expedition through these badlands by two men and a dog. Robert Limbert and W.L. Cole were the first to cross the lava beds, traveling 28 miles from Minidoka to the old Arco-Carey Road in 1920. The razor-sharp *'a'a* lava (with chunks of fused stony matter) tore their boots and feet (they had to bandage the dog's paws and carry it) and left them no place to sleep. When they finally encountered smoother *p'ahoehoe* lava flows, they could find no water. Snowmelt sustained them until they reached the Big Lost River. Meanwhile, however, they were awed by the natural features they encountered. Limbert's expedition reports and photographs helped convince Congress and the President of the site's uniqueness.

Numerous short and well-blazed trails still offer modern visitors (including people with disabilities) ample opportunities for exploration. You may want to start at the national-monument visitor center, where you can see a film and exhibits on geology and natural history, then drive a 7-mile loop road past cinder cones and volcanic vents, lava tubes, and petrified trees.

The best time to visit is late spring, when the cinder fields are awash in wildflowers. The worst time is midsummer, when the heat can be suffocating. There's outstanding cross-country skiing here on groomed trails in winter. For overnighters, there are three dozen campsites.

The monument's "gateway" town of **Arco,** 19 miles northeast, bears the distinction of having been the first community in the world lighted by nuclear power. That's because the world's first electricity-producing nuclear plant is just 18 miles east on the grounds of the **Idaho National Engineering and Environmental Laboratory** (INEEL; Rte. 20 West, Idaho Falls; 208/526-0050). Experimental Breeder Reactor No. 1 (EBR-I) operated from 1951 until 1964. Free guided tours during the summer include its four reactors, fuel rods, turbines, control room, and radioactive "hot cell." The redbrick structure is a national historic landmark. EBR-I was only the first of 52 nuclear reactors at INEEL—the greatest concentration of them on the planet. None of the experimental reactors is still in operation, but 8,000 workers, including engineers and scientists, are still employed in the laboratory complexes at this 890-square-mile outpost and at its Idaho Falls headquarters.

Though the lava fields may seem like a wasteland, former Idaho governor Cecil Andrus actively discouraged nuclear waste storage here, with good reason. The Big Lost River, Little Lost River, and Birch Creek (which drain the next two valleys to its east) all disappear into the spongelike Lost River Sinks, and hydrologists say the waters filter through the lava—in some places a mile thick—to an enormous aquifer under the beds. This subterranean reservoir releases its waters 120 miles southwest into the Snake River. Though it take hundreds of years for the underground rivers to make this journey, any nuclear waste they might be carrying will not yet have lost its radioactive potency. Succeeding governor Phil Batt signed an agreement in 1995 allowing more than 1,000 shipments of nuclear waste to be stored in the Snake River Plain, in exchange for a pledge that all waste be removed from Idaho by 2035.

U.S. 93 follows the Big Lost River upstream through **Mackay,** 26 miles northwest of Arco. Established as a copper-mining town in the mid-1880s, Mackay continued to produce and smelt the mineral until about 1930. Today the little town is mainly a ranching and outfitting center, and its mining heritage is not often observed save at its Lost River Museum, in the sanctuary of a turn-of-the-century Methodist church.

Mackay is the staging point for climbers of **Borah Peak,** Idaho's highest summit at 12,662 feet. About 20 miles northwest of Mackay, this jagged apex of the Lost River Range was named for "The Lion of Idaho," Sen. William Borah (1865-1940). The preferred ascent is a 6-mile scramble up the west ridge from a Challis National Forest trailhead on Birch Springs Road. On October 28, 1983, Borah Peak was the site of a 7.3-magnitude earthquake that added 2 feet to the mountain's already lofty height. The quake, which could be felt from Salt Lake to Spokane and beyond, created a fault scarp 21 miles long and as much as 14 feet deep. Look for it off Double Springs Pass Road a mile east of Highway 93, where you also can view displays at an **Earthquake Visitors Information Center** (Double Springs Pass Rd., Mackay; 208/588-2274).

The partially paved road up the Little Lost River valley from Howe is one of the loneliest in the state, with little but scenery to recommend it. But Route 28, which runs up the Birch Creek valley between the Lemhi and Bitterroot ranges, could be of considerable interest to history buffs. For starters, archaeologists have confirmed that ancient Lemhi Indians lived in rock shelters and caves in the Lone Pine area more than 11,000 years ago. Artifacts in Jaguar Cave have yielded evidence of two breeds of domesticated dogs—the earliest such record. Excavations at the Veratic Rockshelter have revealed North America's most extensive record of bison hunting. Neither site, however, is open to the public.

The ghost town of **Nicholia** lies off the highway, about 10 miles north of the archaeological sites, and at the foot of the Beaverhead Mountains that form the Idaho-Montana border. In the 1880s Nicholia's Viola mine produced high-grade

The world-famous trout stream Silver Creek meanders through a Nature Conservancy preserve near Picabo in Blaine County.

lead ore that was smelted here or shipped by rail to smelters in Omaha and Kansas City. Only two ramshackle wooden buildings remain from what was once a town of 400. The principal cause of death? Lead poisoning.

Because lead smelters require large amounts of charcoal, the miners of Nicholia built a row of 16 kilns on the west side of the Birch Creek valley, 13 miles from their town at the foot of Bell Mountain. Fir logs were cut in nearby canyons and hauled to the kilns for regulated burning. Each kiln could produce 500 pounds of charcoal from 35 cords of wood. Only four charcoal kilns still stand, as settlers dismantled the others for their bricks.

About two-dozen abandoned buildings comprise the ghost town of **Gilmore,** a short distance west of Route 28 near Gilmore Summit. The town was an important lead- and silver-mining district until 1929, when the Great Depression kicked the legs out from under it. Explorers can see numerous tunnels and mine-shaft openings, as well as the bed of the Gilmore and Pittsburgh Railroad, which connected the mines with Butte, Montana, from 1910. The rails were removed for scrap iron in 1939.

These historic charcoal kilns in Birch Creek valley were built in 1883.

LOCAL FAVORITE PLACES TO EAT

Globus. 291 Sixth St. E, Ketchum; 208/726-1301. $$-$$$

This cozy wood-frame house at the edge of downtown serves Asian-fusion fare and some of the valley's most creative seafood. Try Indian-style lamb curry or wild salmon in a a lobster-lemongrass broth.

Il Naso. Fifth and Washington Sts., Ketchum; 208/726-7776. $$-$$$

Veal dishes, specialty raviolis (such as duck), and a marvelous beet salad highlight the made-from-scratch contemporary Italian menu at quaint, intimate Il Naso. The wine list is outstanding.

Kneadery. 260 Leadville Ave. N, Ketchum; 208/726-9462. $$

Furnished with life-size animal sculptures, the "Ketchum Zoo," as locals call it, is a Sun Valley favorite for its homestyle menu of great omelets in the morning and soups and salads at midday.

Lodge Dining Room. Sun Valley Lodge, One Sun Valley Rd., Sun Valley; 208/622-2150. $$$

Tuxedoed waiters serve continental cuisine beneath crystal chandeliers as string quartets play on a marble staircase in what may be Idaho's most elegant dining experience. Indulge in a chateaubriand for two, and return for the sumptuous Sunday brunch.

Pioneer Saloon. 308 Main St. N, Ketchum; 208/726-3139. $$

Ketchum's oldest restaurant is still its best for solid steak-and-seafood fare. The rustic tavern in the heart of town has nightly fish specials, tangy ribs, a popular shrimp teriyaki plate, and a classic cheeseburger.

The Sawtooth Club. 209 Main St. N, Ketchum; 208/726-5233. $$-$$$

Snag a seat on the mezzanine overlooking the big stone fireplace to dine on creative international cuisine—from Cajun shellfish pasta to chicken in an apple-brandy curry—and mesquite-grilled seafood, steak, and poultry.

Trail Creek Cabin. Trail Creek Rd., Sun Valley; 208/622-2135. $$$

In winter a horse-drawn sleigh takes diners from the Sun Valley Inn to this rustic log home—accessible by car in other seasons—for a gourmet four-course dinner beside a roaring fire. Entrées include prime rib, Idaho lamb, and the catch of the day. Lunch is sometimes served. Reservations are essential.

Zou 75. 416 N. Main St., Hailey; 208/788-3310. $$-$$$

Fine fresh sushi and creative Japanese-style dishes make this candlelit restaurant a few blocks north of Bruce Willis's Mint nightclub a local favorite.

ELSEWHERE IN CENTRAL IDAHO

Pickle's Place. 440 S. Front St., Arco; 208/527-9944. $

Three meals a day of solid home cooking is available even in the lava desert of the Snake River Plain. At lunch, fresh-made deli-style sandwiches are accompanied by homemade soup.

Galena Lodge. Rte. 75, 37 miles south of Stanley; 208/726-4010. $-$$

Open for lunch, après-ski, and Sunday brunch (popular with locals), the lodge serves hearty burgers, homemade soups and bread, and creative specialties such as a chipotle steak wraps and a cilantro-lime shrimp salad.

Kasino Club. 21 Ace of Diamonds St., Stanley; 208/774-3516. $$

A rustic lodge on a dirt street with a no-frills decor is home to fine cuisine, such as black-and-bleu prime rib and pan-fried trout straight from the Salmon River.

Trudy's Kitchen. 419 Rte. 21, Idaho City; 208/392-4151. $

Famed for its huckleberry cheesecake, Trudy's has more-than-generous portions of standard American fare (including breakfast) and Friday and Saturday prime-rib specials amid antiques-store decor with yellowing photographs on the walls.

LOCAL FAVORITE PLACES TO STAY

SUN VALLEY

Best Western Kentwood Lodge. 180 S. Main St., Ketchum; 208/726-4114. $$-$$$

A notch above the average Best Western, this handsome property just steps from Ketchum restaurants and nightlife has a large pool, ski-lodge-style architecture and furnishings, and some rooms with balconies and hot tubs.

Knob Hill Inn, 960 N. Main St., Ketchum; 208/726-8010. $$$

A small luxury hotel and a member of the prestigious Relais & Chateaux group, Knob Hill is a lovely inn with full gourmet dinners and an indoor-outdoor pool. Each suite has a marble bath, a wet bar, and a balcony opening to the mountains.

Lift Tower Lodge, 703 S. Main St., Ketchum; 208/726-5163. $$

A low-end alternative to Sun Valley's many pricey accommodations, this motel with a hot tub is a short walk from the lifts at River Run Plaza. A 1939 lift tower with four chairs stands outside; Continental breakfast is included.

Sun Valley Lodge & Inn. One Sun Valley Rd., Sun Valley; 208/622-4111. $$$

The majestic lodge and chalet-style inn, built in 1936 and 1937, are the classic accommodations around which the resort grew in the mid-1930s. The four-story lodge and two-story inn are still the center of an integral skiing, golf, and tennis community. On the property are an ice rink, indoor and outdoor heated pools, saunas, hot tubs, fitness rooms, and (in the lodge) a bowling alley.

Wood River Inn. 603 N. Main St., Hailey; 208/578-0600. $$

This pleasant and spacious motel has fridges and microwaves in each of its 57 rooms. An indoor pool and hot tub, ski lockers, and guest laundry make it a popular choice among families who don't want to fight the crowds in nearby Ketchum.

Idaho Rocky Mountain Ranch. Rte. 75, 9 miles south of Stanley; 208/774-3544. $$$

Established in the 1920s, this log-cabin resort in the heart of the Sawtooth National Recreation Area shares its 1,000-acre spread with no more than 50 guests at a time. They enjoy horseback riding, hiking, fishing, and soaking in a natural hot-springs pool. Accommodation is in log cabins or lodge rooms; breakfasts and full gourmet dinners are served family-style.

Mountain Village Resort. Rtes. 21 and 75, Stanley; 208/774-3661. $-$$

Natural hot springs, for guests only, are the main attraction at this tidy log-style motel-and-restaurant complex near the Salmon River headwaters. It has a standard 61-room lodge, a restaurant serving three meals a day, a general store, and a service station.

Redfish Lake Lodge. Redfish Lake Rd., 5 miles south of Stanley; 208/774-3536. $

Surrounded by trees and mountains, this collection of private log cabins and rooms in a log lodge (some with shared bath) sits at the edge of Redfish Lake, with spectacular views. You can rent a canoe to paddle the lake. The restaurant serves everything from a spicy chorizo omelet and a smoked-trout salad to steaks and chops in the evening. The property is closed from mid-September to mid-May.

Wild Horse Creek Ranch. Wildhorse Creek Rd., Mackay; 208/588-2575. $$$.

Hidden in the Pioneer Mountains on a tributary of the Big Lost River, this ranch is just the ticket for a true getaway. Activities include horseback riding, hiking and fishing in summer, Nordic skiing and snowmobiling in winter. Four bunkhouse units share a common area and bath facilities; six other rooms have private baths.

NORTH-CENTRAL
WILDERNESS RIVERS

A rugged wilderness region of rivers, canyons, forested mountinas, wild animals, and a few people divides southern and northern Idaho. A single highway (U.S. 95) traverses the region from Boise to Lewiston, via Riggins and White Bird Hill. To the west is Hells Canyon of the Snake River, the deepest gorge in North America, forming Idaho's western border with Oregon. To the east are national forests, the largest federally designated wilderness area in the lower 48 states, and the fabled Bitterroot Range along Idaho's eastern boundary with Montana. East of the Salmon River, U.S. 93 runs north into Montana through Challis and Salmon.

Out of this vastness flow such rivers as the Payette and the Salmon, eventually adding their waters to those of the Snake. The Salmon is the largest river contained in any one American state, excluding huge and isolated Alaska. Most of the Payette and the smaller Weiser River to its west can be explored by roads that trace their banks. The same cannot be said of the Salmon (except for its upper course), or of the Snake through Hells Canyon.

While there is some road access (often via unpaved roads) to the banks of these rivers, long stretches can be visited only by raft, kayak, or jet boat. (Idaho has more miles—by far!—of navigable white water than any state.) A few trails probe the wilderness, for those who want to hike or pack in. Alternatively, dozens of landing strips throughout the mountains await wilderness adventurers cramped for time. Fortunately for all, literally scores of rafting outfitters, packers, and bush pilots are at the ready to take you there.

PAYETTE RIVER

The Payette's two main forks come from very different sources. The South Fork originates on the rocky slope of the Sawtooth Range and rushes west with a white-water roar. From its source in Upper Payette Lake, amid the pine forests north of McCall, the North Fork streams south via tranquil Cascade Reservoir. The branches join near the hamlet of Banks, and proceed westerly along the edge of the Treasure Valley to join the Snake at the town of Payette.

McCall is a logical point to begin an exploration of the Payette Basin. The mile-high mountain resort town, just over 100 miles north of Boise, is a year-round gateway to fishing the Payette lakes, skiing at nearby Brundage Mountain, and hiking and horseback riding the trails of adjacent Payette National Forest. The town claims nearly 3,000 permanent residents, but the population swells several-fold on holiday weekends.

McCall's principal summer drawing card is ★**Payette Lake,** a deep-blue mountain lake famous among anglers for its mackinaw, or lake trout. Clutching the verdant peninsula of **Ponderosa State Park** (Lick Creek Rd., McCall; 208/634–2164) like a lobster's claw, the six-mile-long lake is popular with boaters, water-skiers, and trout fishermen. Forests of pine, fir, and western larch cloak the promontory at the edge of town, making it an attraction in any season. More than 150 campsites, open mid-May to mid-October, are kept full by water sports lovers and wildlife-watchers peering at beavers and eagles, deer, and even an occasional black bear. In winter the park roads are paradise for cross-country skiers. Ponderosa State Park has a second (day-use) unit at the north end of Payette Lake, with a sandy beach and a meandering stream popular with canoeists.

In winter McCall's high point (literally and figuratively) is Brundage Mountain and its **Brundage Mountain Resort** (Brundage Mountain Rd., McCall; 208/634–4151), 8 miles north of town. McCall is in the heart of a winter snow belt—an average 150 inches a year—and Brundage is blessed with an abundance of the light, dry snow that skiers like to call "champagne powder": about 300 inches a year at its upper elevations. Six chairlifts serve the 7,640-foot summit. A majority of its runs are intermediate "cruisers," but experts love its tree skiing and overnight snowcat trips with accommodations in Mongolian-style yurts. Beginners have eight runs, served by the Bear and Easy Street chairs. In summer Brundage's ski runs become trails for mountain bikers. Brundage may not be well-known outside of the Pacific Northwest, but it's no secret to the residents of southwestern Idaho, especially those who like to avoid the crowds of Sun Valley and Bogus Basin.

The beautiful four-season **Tamarack Resort,** 20 miles south of McCall on the west shore of Lake Cascade, opened in 2004. At its heart is the Tamarack Village Plaza, incorporating the original Lodge at Osprey Meadows. The luxurious Fairmont Tamarack, being developed by former world tennis stars Andre Agassi and Steffi Graf, is scheduled for a 2010 opening. The resort has shops and restaurants (with more under construction), more than 650 vacation homes, an 18-hole

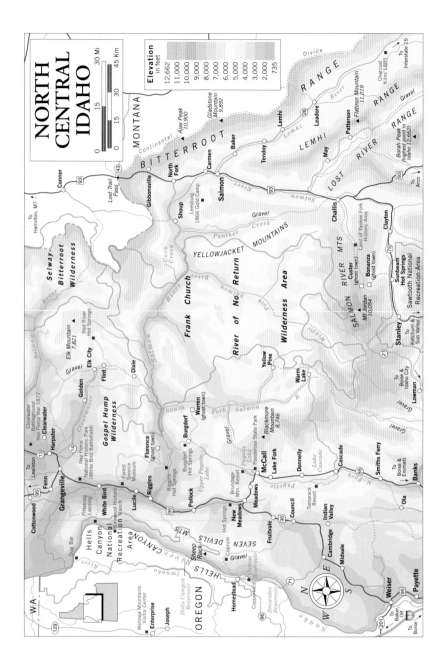

NORTH CENTRAL IDAHO

Elevation
in feet

12,662
11,000
10,000
9,000
8,000
7,000
6,000
5,000
4,000
3,000
2,000
735

30 Mi
45 Km
0   15   30

MONTANA

BITTERROOT   **RANGE**

Continental   Divide

Ajax Peak 10,900
Gladstone Mountain 9,892

Lemhi
Leadore
Patterson
Flatiron Mountain 11,019

LEMHI   **RANGE**

Baker
Carmen
Tendoy
May

Borah Peak (highest point in Idaho 12,662)

LOST RIVER RANGE

Conner
To Hamilton, MT
Lost Trail Pass

North Fork
Gibbonsville

Shoup
Leesburg 1866 Gold Camp

Salmon

Challis

Clayton

To Arco

Panther Creek
Gravel Creek

Selway-Bitterroot Wilderness

Corn Creek

YELLOWJACKET   **MOUNTAINS**

Frank Church

River of No Return

Wilderness Area

Custer (ghost town)
Bonanza (ghost town)
Mt Jordan 10,054

SALMON RIVER MTS

Land of Yankee Fork Historic Area

Sunbeam Hot Springs

Stanley

Sawtooth National Recreation Area

To Ketchum & Sun Valley

Elk Mountain 7,821
Red River Hot Springs

Elk City
Flint
Dixie

Golden
Gravel

Gospel Hump Wilderness

Warren (ghost town)

Yellow Pine

Warm Lake

Blackmore Mountain 8,746

To Boise & Idaho City

Lowman
Gravel

Clearwater Battlefield (Nez Perce War 1877)

Harpster
To Lewiston
Fenn

Florence (ghost town)

Burgdorf
Burgdorf Hot Springs

Ponderosa State Park

Cascade

Smiths Ferry

Banks

To Boise & Emmett

Cottonwood
Grangeville

Nez Perce National Historic Park (White Bird Battlefield)

Forest Service Museum

Riggins
Riggins Hot Springs

McCall
Lake Fork

Donnelly

Payette
Lake Cascade

N Fork

White Bird
Pittsburg Landing
Kirkwood Historic Ranch

Lucile
Pollock

Brundage Mtn. Resort
Meadows

Dug Bar

Hells Canyon National Recreation Area

New Meadows
Hot Springs

Fruitvale

Council

Tamarack Resort

Indian Valley

Sheep Rock
Cuprum
Gravel

SEVEN DEVILS MTS

HELLS CANYON

Cambridge

Midvale

Wallowa Mountains Visitor Center

Enterprise

Joseph

OREGON

Homestead

Coppersfield

Brownlee Reservoir

Hells Canyon Reservoir

Oxbow Reservoir

Weiser

Payette

To Baker, OR

To Boise

Charcoal Kilns 1885
To Interstate 15

W A

N
E
S
W

Robert Trent Jones, Jr., golf course, and an 840-acre ski resort with four chairlifts and additional surface lifts. Sometimes compared to Utah's Deer Valley, it has a higher summit than Brundage (7,700 feet) and a greater vertical drop (2,800 feet). *311 Village Dr., Tamarack; 208/325–1000.*

McCall itself, meanwhile, celebrates the snowy season with the **McCall Winter Carnival,** one of the leading festivals of its type in the country. Launched in the mid-1960s, this event—which runs for 10 days in late January and early February—is best known for its elaborate, user-friendly ice sculptures. Kids *and* adults are encouraged to play on them. As many as 10,000 people a day visit McCall during its carnival.

The little town that supports all this activity once depended upon lumber for its economic wherewithal. When the final Boise Cascade mill closed in 1977, McCall was glad that a tourism infrastructure was already in place—since the 1920s, vacation homes have lined the Payette Lake shore. Although the homeowners and other short-term visitors are mainly Boise-area residents, they have contributed to the growth of McCall's rambling downtown by supporting its galleries, gift shops, restaurants, and motels. It was in diminutive McCall that

Snow sculpture at the McCall Winter Carnival.

teacher-astronaut Barbara Morgan taught for 22 years; Morgan became the first teacher to travel to space since Christa McAuliffe, completing NASA's STS-118 mission in August 2007.

McCall has been used to out-of-towners for some time now. The 1938 Spencer Tracy movie *Northwest Passage* was filmed at Payette Lake; hundreds of Idahoans (including many Native Americans) were hired as extras. During shooting, Tracy, Robert Young, Walter Brennan, and other cast members stayed at a beautiful inn on the lakefront; it's now the **Northwest Passage Bed & Breakfast** (201 Rio Vista Blvd.; 208/634–5349) one of several B&Bs in McCall.

McCall visitors can also stop in at the U.S. Forest Service smoke-jumpers' base on Mission Street, an institution here for more than half a century, and at the state fish hatchery on Mather Road, where chinook salmon are spawned.

Stop by the Payette National Forest office in McCall to pick up an audio cassette to guide you on backcountry roads, then head north from McCall on the paved road that runs 16 miles up the North Fork Payette River to **Upper Payette Lake,** an opaline gem. The road then turns to gravel as it crests 6,434-foot

Secesh Summit and descends to **Burgdorf Hot Springs,** 14 miles farther. This settlement was developed as a spa in 1865 by German immigrant Fred Burgdorf, who ran a 20-room resort hotel here for 58 years. Today Burgdorf's hot-springs pools remain open year-round, but the only lodging is a national forest campground.

Warren, 18 miles east of Burgdorf in the Salmon River Mountains, doesn't have a lot to look at today, either. Today it's an outpost for hunters and anglers; 125 years ago it was a

"China Polly" Nathoy Bemis on her wedding day. (Idaho State Historical Society)

CHINESE GIRL IN IDAHO

Thousand Pieces of Gold is a biographical novel describing the life of Lalu Nathoy, later known as Polly Bemis, a native of northern China. By the time she was 18 years old, Lalu had been sold four times: by her father to a bandit for two bags of soybeans; to a Shanghai brothel; to a slave merchant of immigrants in America; and to Hong King, a saloon keeper in Lewiston, Idaho, who kept prostitutes for miners.

[San Francisco] On the auction block, Lalu closed her eyes against her own nakedness and the men who milled around, poking, prodding, and pinching. . . . A woman's harsh voice ordered her to dress and Lalu knew she had not been purchased for a wife.

[Portland, Oregon] Dimly, she heard a young, handsome Chinese man greet them, felt him take her from the woman and place her on a mule.

He had a packstring of ten mules, eight loaded with supplies. . . . He was Jim, he said. A packer Lalu's master, Hong King, had commissioned to fetch his slave.

Nine days travel through thickly wooded trails brought them to Lewiston, a strange town made up of tents, makeshift houses of canvas stretched across wood frames, and buildings so new Lalu could smell the rawness of the wood.

There are sixteen hundred men in Warrens, twelve hundred Chinese, four hundred or so whites. And there are eleven women. Three are wives, two are widows, and half dozen are hurdy gurdy girls. But they're all white. You'll be the only Chinese woman, an attraction that will bring men, Chinese and white, from miles around.

Lalu's life fell into a strictly circumscribed routine revolving between the saloon and Hong King's shack. Though she slept in her own room behind the saloon, Hong King refused her permission to talk to anyone except customers from whom he could profit.

—Ruthanne Lum McCunn, *Thousand Pieces of Gold*, 1981, describing the 1880s

The North Fork of the Payette River is an outstanding place to kayak.

gold-rush boomtown, a county seat, and the home of a governor. It was also the home of "China Polly" Bemis, one of the state's best-known backcountry characters, thanks to the publication of a novel based on her life, *Thousand Pieces of Gold,* by Ruthanne Lum McCunn.

Born into poverty in China in 1852, sold into slavery by her parents during a famine, Polly was smuggled into the United States in the 1870s. She was working as a dance-hall girl in a Warren saloon in the early 1880s when she met professional gambler Charlie Bemis. When Charlie was shot and critically wounded by a vengeful Nez Percé he'd badly beaten at the poker table, Polly nursed him back to health, winning his heart in the process. Charlie bought a small ranch deep in the Salmon River canyon about 15 miles north of Warren, and the two lived in this isolated homestead for almost 50 years, supporting themselves by goldsmithing and raising their own food. Polly outlived Charlie by two years and died in 1933.

Ice fishing on Lake Cascade.

NORTH FORK OF THE PAYETTE

From Payette Lake, the North Fork of the Payette River runs south 65 miles to its confluence with the South Fork, passing first through Lake Cascade (known as Cascade Reservoir prior to the development of Tamarack). The final 20-mile drop to Banks is regarded as one of the most challenging white-water kayaking runs in the world.

Route 55 follows the river to Banks and beyond, passing through several hamlets with interesting stories along the way. **Lake Fork,** for instance, was founded around the turn of the 20th century by immigrants from Finland, and residents still point with pride to the Finnish Evangelical Lutheran Church (1917) on a hilltop east of the village. Near Donnelly is the townsite of Roseberry, whose assortment of abandoned late-19th-century buildings—a general store, church, schoolhouse, and several houses—comprise the **Valley County Museum.** The old McCall City Hall was relocated here in 1978 and now contains historical displays of its own.

Lake Cascade, with 110 miles of shoreline, was created in 1948 by a Bureau of Reclamation dam on the North Fork. Today the lake is a mecca for camping (600 sites), boating (24 launches), and fishing (trout, salmon, whitefish, and perch; ice-fishing in winter). Near the dam and the lake's southeastern shore is the town of Cascade, whose economic mainstay is clearly signaled by the cluster of sporting-goods stores and outdoorsmen's cafes along the highway. There's also a big Boise Cascade sawmill.

East of Cascade, a paved Boise National Forest road runs 25 miles to Warm Lake, well known among anglers for its good trout fishing. Campgrounds and lodges with restaurants provide hospitality for the fishing crowd. Also worth investigating are an Idaho Fish and Game Department salmon trap and a national forest interpretive site, both on the South Fork of the Salmon River. Gravel roads continue north, south, and east to defunct mining villages like Yellow Pine and Edwardsburg, right to the edge of the Frank Church–River of No Return Wilderness Area.

SOUTH FORK OF THE PAYETTE

After its descent from the Sawtooth Range to the old gold-mining districts around Idaho City, the South Fork of the Payette traces a course through **Garden Valley.** Rugged rapids, not to mention a 40-foot waterfall that demands a portage, make the South Fork canyon one of the most popular streams for white-water rafting in the United States. Natural hot springs along the riverbanks not only add to the enjoyment for rafters picnicking or overnighting beside the South Fork; they also heat greenhouses to give this valley a year-round growing season. In the min-ing-boom era of the 1860s and 1870s, Garden Valley earned its name from the produce it provided the upland gold and silver towns. Two streams popular with anglers are the Deadwood River entering the South Fork of the Payette about three miles west of Lowman, and the Middle Fork of the Payette which connects with the South Fork in Garden Valley near Crouch.

The North and South forks of the Payette join at **Banks,** whose buildings one can count on a single hand. It's got a store, a restaurant, and headquarters for rafting outfitters. There are more white-water companies south of Banks, where the Payette's rapids are gentler, more conducive to family adventure, than those above. Hundreds of rafters may be spotted on this river any weekend day between May and September. **Cascade Raft and Kayak** (7050 Rte. 55, Horseshoe Bend; 208/793–2221) has been offering white-water trips on the Payette—its North Fork, South Fork, and main river below the confluence of the forks—since 1985, and ranks at or near the top among outfitters on this river. It also operates the Cascade Kayak School, for aspiring paddlers.

At the mill town of Horseshoe Bend, the Payette executes a 270-degree westward arc and flows toward Black Canyon Reservoir and the town of **Emmett.** Route 52 parallels the river along this route. As you approach Emmett and the Treasure Valley, you may cross an avenue with the curious name of Frozen Dog Road. Around the turn of the 20th century, a Kansas City writer named William Hunter claimed in a series of humorous newspaper columns that he had been the editor of a fictional Idaho newspaper, *The Howling Wolf.* (In fact, he had briefly ranched along the Payette.) His columns, later compiled in book form, were called "Tales of the Frozen Dog."

WEISER RIVER

The Weiser rises in the highlands west of Cascade Reservoir and the Payette River, carving a small but pretty valley between there and the uplands that overlook Hells Canyon. When it was settled in the 1870s and 1880s, this was considered marvelous fruit-growing country. Apple and cherry orchards still speckle the countryside, although cattle, dairy, and hay are now more important to the economy.

Even before the arrival of white settlers, the Weiser Valley was a gathering place for Shoshones, Nez Percé, and Umatillas from Oregon, who came for the wild berries, fish, and game. Thus when a town was built here, it was given the name of Council.

Idaho's most notorious outlaw of the early 20th century grew up on a ranch along Cottonwood Creek, just south of Council. Hugh Whitney, then 22, and his older brother Charlie left in 1910 to work as herders in western Wyoming. When they were fired because of Hugh's propensity for using his pistol and rifle to round up the sheep, the younger Whitney beat the foreman to death. Arrested for manslaughter, he escaped while awaiting trial.

The Whitneys lay low for a year, but in 1911 Hugh and another friend held up a southern Montana saloon where they had lost all their money gambling the previous night. With the law on their tails, Hugh shot and killed a conductor and wounded a sheriff's deputy during a train robbery attempt. Then, heading south by horseback through eastern Idaho, Hugh was rejoined by Charlie. The Whitney brothers robbed a bank across the border in Wyoming... and disappeared.

Forty-one years later, an old Montana rancher named Charlie Whitney, now a respected bank director and school board member, went to visit his friend the governor to confess his sordid past. After the 1911 bank robbery, he said, he and

Hugh had labored in the Midwest, served in France during World War I under assumed names, and bought a ranch near Glasgow, Montana. Hugh had married, moved to Saskatchewan, and confessed his identity on his deathbed a year earlier. Charlie now followed suit. Wyoming granted him a full pardon, and he returned to his ranch, where he died in 1955.

SNAKE RIVER

The Idaho-Oregon border region of the Snake River can be divided into two, roughly equal portions. The southern half, flowing northward from the Treasure Valley, is comprised of a series of long, serpentine reservoirs. The northern half is dramatic Hells Canyon.

THREE RESERVOIRS

The Snake River reservoirs—from south to north, Brownlee, Oxbow, and Hells Canyon—have been controversial since long before the Idaho Power Company began dam construction in 1955. Built without fish ladders or other facilities to allow spawning salmon to return to their places of origin, the dams became death traps for adult salmon bound upstream, while juveniles were unable to power themselves back downstream through the many miles of slackwater in the reservoirs. Salmon runs that once exceeded 10,000 chinook every fall just ceased to exist. But the reservoirs created a new fishery, much beloved by area anglers, of trout, bass, crappie, and giant catfish.

Huge white sturgeon also once migrated up and down the Snake and Columbia rivers to the Pacific Ocean. The dams have also limited their mobility, but these primordial creatures persist in deep pools of the free-flowing Snake, including Hells Canyon. The fossil record dates this milky-gray, cartilaginous fish back to Cretaceous times, 100 million years ago. Bottom feeders whose size and life expectancy boggles the mind, they are now protected by the Idaho Fish and Game Department. Fishing for them is catch-and-release only.

Brownlee Dam, 29 miles from Cambridge, is a rock-fill dam with an impermeable clay core. Completed in 1959, it created 57-mile-long Brownlee Reservoir, where numerous summer homes have been built despite the relative desolation of its landscape. Downriver, Oxbow Dam is a 205-foot barrier that backs up 10-mile-long Oxbow Reservoir, and 320-foot-tall Hells Canyon Dam (1968) creates a reservoir 20 miles long.

The Snake River near the Salmon River confluence just above Hells Canyon.

Route 71 crosses into Oregon along the west shore of Oxbow Reservoir, with a spur road (the **Snake River Road**) that returns to Idaho and follows the east bank of Hells Canyon Reservoir. Idaho Power operates year-round recreational parks on each of the three reservoirs as well as at **Copperfield,** just below the Oxbow Dam in Oregon.

Only two buildings still stand from a town that in 1910 was known as "Gomorrah on the Snake." Like an Alaskan pipeline town of the 1970s, Copperfield grew to a population of about 1,000 during construction work on a hydropower plant for Oregon's Iron Dyke copper mine. Its streets were lined with saloons, brothels, and gambling halls.

In 1913 the sheriff snubbed a direct order from Oregon Governor Oswald West to clean up the town. So on January 1, 1914, West sent his private secretary—a prim, proper, 5-foot-3-inch, 104-pound dynamo named Fern Hobbs—to Copperfield to deliver a formal proclamation of martial law. Backed by a half-dozen National Guardsmen, and with worldwide press attention focused (the governor didn't shy from positive publicity), Hobbs saw that every den of iniquity in town was closed and that all alcohol and games of chance were confiscated and removed from town. The women of easy virtue left on their own, and there was little left of Copperfield by 1915.

HELLS CANYON

The paved Snake River Road enters ★ **Hells Canyon National Recreation Area** on the Idaho side of Hells Canyon Reservoir below Oxbow Dam. Established by Congress and signed into law by President Gerald Ford in 1976, the recreation area, much of it roadless wilderness, surrounds a canyon that is deeper by half (and narrower by a mile) than the far-more-famous Grand Canyon of the Colorado River in Arizona. At 8,043 feet deep—from the 9,393-foot peak of He Devil Mountain in Idaho's Seven Devils Range to the surface of the Snake near Hells Canyon Dam—this colorful chasm has no peer in North America.

The national recreation area has its headquarters in Oregon at the **Wallowa Mountains Visitor Center** (88401 Rte. 82, Enterprise, OR; 541/426–5546), where there are extensive exhibits. The **Idaho Office** (Rte. 95, Riggins; 208/628–3916) focuses on the Seven Devils Mountains section of the park (see below). The **Snake River Office** (2535 Riverside Dr., Clarkston, WA.; 509/758–0616) has the most complete information on white-water rafting and jet boating, two of the most popular activities here.

Just below Hells Canyon Dam, at the mouth of Hells Canyon Creek on the Oregon side of the river, is the put-in point for river trips (April–October) through the wilderness canyon. (Drive Route 71 northwest from Cambridge, Idaho, crossing the Snake River three times to reach the launch point.) Once they start out on this "national wild and scenic river," whitewater rafters, kayakers, and drift boaters have only three places where they can take out: Pittsburg Landing, Idaho, at 32 miles downstream; Dug Bar, Oregon, at 51 miles; or Grande Ronde, Washington, at 78 miles. The canyon has only two major (Class IV) rapids on the river: Wild Sheep Rapid at 6 miles, and Granite Creek Rapid at 8 miles from the dam. Beyond them, a river trip through Hells Canyon is a relatively easy float.

Jet-boat excursions begin well downriver at Clarkston, Washington. But back-packers can pick up the **Snake River National Recreation Trail** at Granite Creek (below Hells Canyon Dam) and follow it 28 miles to **Pittsburg Landing** (17 miles southwest of White Bird via gravel Deer Creek Rd.). En route, there are numerous late 19th-century mining sites as well as prehistoric native petroglyphs.

There are primitive campsites along the riverbanks en route, plus a rare few wilderness lodges that have stood in Hells Canyon since homesteading days. The most important of these is the **Kirkwood Historic Ranch,** 6 miles upstream from Pittsburg Landing and an overnight camping stop for many jet-boaters traveling into the canyon from Clarkston. Built in the 1930s, this homestead has a small museum of Hells Canyon history.

Petroglyphs testify that Pittsburg Landing itself was a Native American camp for hundreds of years before white settlers arrived. (Rock etchings within Hells Canyon indicate habitation as long ago as 8,000 years.) About 60 people lived at the Landing in the 1930s, when it was part of the Circle C Ranch; the ranch was purchased in 1975 for inclusion in the national recreation area. Pittsburg Landing is the only point in Hells Canyon between the dam and Lewiston—a distance of about 100 miles—that is accessible from Idaho; drivers must negotiate a 17-mile gravel road from Route 95 at White Bird.

SEVEN DEVILS MOUNTAINS

It is not only from within the canyon that one can grasp its magnitude and its majesty. While you can gaze upward with awe from the depths of the gorge, your panoramas are limited. To truly see Hells Canyon you have to see it from the heights of the Seven Devils Mountains in the heart of the Hells Canyon Wilderness.

A view of Seven Devils from Heaven's Gate Lookout in the Hells Canyon Wilderness.

Nez Percé legend holds that Coyote, the progenitor of their race, dug Hells Canyon in a single day to protect the people of the Wallowa Mountains from the evil Seven Devils. Modern visitors regard their mountain namesakes as breathtaking.

The most dependable road access is via the unpaved 28-mile Hornet Creek Road northwest of Council, although adventurous four-wheel drivers might risk the steep, 8-mile Kleinschmidt Grade from Hells Canyon Reservoir. The backcountry byways join near Cuprum, a bustling copper-mining settlement at the turn of the 20th century, now a wide place in the road. In dry weather, passenger cars can proceed another 13 miles north to 6,847-foot **Sheep Rock,** a National Natural Landmark, from which views across Hells Canyon are at their most sensational.

Motor vehicles can travel as far as Black Lake, 54 miles from Council, or the Heaven's Gate Lookout, 17 miles from Riggins, both via Payette National Forest roads. Cars cannot proceed across the boundaries of the wilderness area. Some 32

Looking down into Hells Canyon
from Dry Diggins Lookout.

small lakes, which speckle the region around these rugged 8,000- to 9,000-foot peaks, are best seen by backpackers and horseback riders.

Papoose Cave, more than a mile long and an estimated 945 feet deep, is one of the 10 deepest caverns in the United States, and the most extensive limestone cave system in Idaho. Found on the Seven Devils' northeastern flank, this chamber is strictly for experienced spelunkers, as it requires technical knowledge and equipment.

SALMON RIVER

From its multiple sources in the Sawtooth Range to its confluence with the Snake at the lower end of Hells Canyon, the Salmon River drains 14,000 square miles of central Idaho, more than a sixth of the state's land.

Weaving through the middle of Idaho in every direction—east from Stanley's alpine peaks, north through pine forests surrounding the town of Salmon, west to the arid gorge country of Riggins, then north again before plunging west and south into the Snake—the Salmon zigzags through the second-deepest canyon in the country, some 6,000 feet below its canyon rim. For the lower half of its course, it marks the rift between the northern Idaho Panhandle and the rest of the state, and between the Pacific and Mountain time zones.

Pictographs thousands of years old still adorn some of the Salmon canyon's rocks. Explorer William Clark investigated the Salmon as a possible westward passage in 1805, but gave up on it and turned back. Trappers, prospectors, and settlers began successfully floating the river later in the century, but each voyage required them to build new wooden scows with heavy oars. This was, after all, the "River of No Return," a label firmly attached by the 1954 Marilyn Monroe–Robert Mitchum movie of the same name. It wasn't until after World War II that anyone succeeded in taking a surplus military raft back upriver. Times have changed, though: now jet boats and small planes make the trip up and down the Salmon with ease.

Unfortunately, for the namesake salmon the journey is more arduous. Because the 420-mile Salmon is one of the longest undammed rivers in the lower 48 states, the fish are theoretically able to return up the river from the Pacific Ocean to their spawning grounds. But practically speaking, even though eight dams on the Columbia and lower Snake rivers in Washington and Oregon have been equipped with fish ladders, the salmon's once-prolific numbers have been reduced to a trickle. Considerably more bountiful are steelhead, an ocean-going rainbow

RAFTING ON THE SALMON RIVER

The country has changed little since Lewis and Clark passed nearby. Up over the mountains looming above us on the south, it is another hundred and fifty miles to civilization. We float through the heart of a land—the size of the state of Connecticut—that is virgin wilderness. At least for a while.

You feel it. There is a wonderfully frightening sense of isolation. Looking downstream, I see ridge after high ridge receding into the distance, mountains that rise four, five thousand feet above us. Green, forested slopes, all unbroken. Around every bend a clear sparkling side stream tumbles down to join the Salmon and from every one of them you can dip a cup of cold, pure water....

The days on the river become a delirium of blazing sun, rocky walls, white and wild water, streams, forests, flowers, wilderness. I'll be back, I say. But I don't know for sure. I keep hoping above hope that nothing will change. But it will. And so will I. Someday I may not even need wilderness or a wild river. But somebody else will. Nice to think that it costs only a little love and care to pass on such treasures to another generation.

—Boyd Norton, *Snake Wilderness*, 1972

trout that thrills anglers with its size and strength when it runs the Salmon and other Idaho rivers each autumn.

UPPER SALMON (MAIN FORK)

Fed by the snows of the Sawtooth and White Cloud mountains, the main Salmon flows fast and free down from Galena Summit, through Stanley (see page 139) before turning east. In 1909 a mining company built a small concrete dam just below **Sunbeam Hot Springs** (Rte. 75, Stanley; 208/838–2211), 13 miles downriver from Stanley, to generate electricity for a nearby stamp mill. Two years later the mine was sold and the dam abandoned. It was finally dynamited in 1934—so that we can say in truth that the river is once again unfettered by any dam.

The Sunbeam Hot Springs are submerged during the Salmon's spring runoff, but at other times these non-commercial riverside springs are divided off from the

The historic Yankee Fork Gold Dredge, a reminder of gold mining days.

river by rock walls. They vary in size and temperature. An old bathhouse, now a changing room, stands above them beside the river.

After soaking a bit in the hot springs, turn north up graveled Yankee Fork Road, otherwise called the Custer Motorway. In 1990 the Idaho State Parks system designated this 36-mile backcountry route through the Salmon River Mountains as the main artery of the **Land of the Yankee Fork Historic Area** (Custer Motorway and Rte. 93, Challis; 208/879–5244). Contained within Challis National Forest, the Yankee Fork of the Salmon River attracted droves of placer gold miners between about 1872 and 1911. Its most important communities were **Bonanza** and **Custer.** The road goes clear to Challis, but you will need a high-clearance, four-wheel-drive vehicle to negotiate the 26 miles beyond Custer.

One of pioneer Idaho's most poignant and tragic tales unfolded in Bonanza during the little town's boom era. It involved a young couple, Richard and Lizzie King, English immigrants who were befriended by one of Bonanza's founding fathers, hotelier Charles Franklin.

Richard King was a prospector, Lizzie the proprietor of a saloon and dance hall. When Richard died in a shootout, Charles Franklin helped Lizzie plan the funeral and soon became her intimate companion. But their marriage plans were derailed when a young man named Robert Hawthorne arrived in Bonanza and charmed Lizzie into wedding him instead, in the summer of 1880. Franklin was heartbroken, but his pain turned to grief when the newlyweds were found shot to death in their honeymoon cabin. He buried the couple next to Richard King, but refused to acknowledge Lizzie's new surname on her gravestone.

No one was ever convicted of the crime, nor was the murder weapon found. And Franklin, still in love, never got over Lizzie's death. Ten years passed, his hotel went to seed, and he became a backwoods recluse. In 1892 two prospectors found his decomposed body in his cabin, a locket photo of Lizzie King Hawthorne clenched in his hand. Franklin was buried in an unmarked grave, but the headstones of the other three principals can still be seen surrounded by a low picket fence in the Boot Hill cemetery, just west of the Bonanza ghost-town site.

Besides the graveyard and a Forest Service guard station built in 1934, there's not much left of Bonanza, which once had a population of 600. But 2 miles downstream, around the foot of Bachelor Mountain, Custer has preserved several late-19th-century buildings. Among them is a one-room schoolhouse with museum displays of items from the era: mining artifacts, household goods, weapons, even gaming tables. The general store will set you up with a shallow dish for gold panning, if you feel lucky, or direct you on a short trail to the General Custer stamp mill, through which ran $12 million of gold between 1881 and 1904.

Two generations after the demise of Custer and Bonanza, a new breed of miners staked their claim in the Yankee Fork. Having ascertained that $16 million in gold and silver could be recovered from the streambed, the Salmon River Mining Company in 1940 erected a 988-ton, diesel-powered dredge at the mouth of Jordan Creek, not far downriver from the Bonanza site. As it turned out, the **Yankee Fork Gold Dredge** (Custer Motorway; no phone) produced only one million dollars by the time it exhausted its accessible ground in 1952. Today, for nine weeks from July 1 to Labor Day, guides will describe how the assembly-line dredge scooped gravel from the river bank, separated out the gold and discharged the tailings. The rest of the year, the environmental monster is an ugly reminder of days of not-so-yore.

The interpretive center for the Land of the Yankee Fork Historic Area is just south of the town of **Challis,** near the junction of Route 75 and U.S. 93. Just over 1,000 people live today in Challis, founded in 1878 as a supply center for area silver and gold miners. Today its economy is more dependent upon cattle ranching. Behind the Yankee Fork interpretive center looms a 60-foot cliff used by Shoshone Indians from the 13th to 19th centuries as a *pishkun,* or "buffalo jump." Bison were driven up to the precipice until they plunged over the edge to their deaths. All parts of the beast were used by the tribe for food, clothing, tools, and shelter. The site is listed on the National Register of Historic Places.

The hour's drive north from Challis to Salmon is rather uneventful, except for the endless views of a pristine stream flowing through evergreen forests; national forest campgrounds; clusters of summer homes near Cabin and Rye Grass creeks; and a possible detour to the Pahsimeroi River Hatchery. If you look carefully, however, you might see part of the herd of some 200 wild horses that run free on Bureau of Land Management land in the Pahsimeroi Valley. (Wild horses are available for adoption at a cost of $125 per animal, maximum four per year, with a promise of proper animal maintenance.)

The town of **Salmon,** largest in this part of Idaho with 3,300 residents, was well known to trappers and traders at least a generation before Leesburg was founded. Located where the northward-flowing Lemhi River joins the Salmon, the site was visited by Lewis and Clark when their Shoshone guide, Sacagawea, identified the Lemhi as the river near which she had been born. In the 1830s, mountain men like Jim Bridger, Joe Meek, and Kit Carson made winter camps at the confluence. Their stories are recounted at **Lemhi County Historical Museum** (210 Main St.,

Salmon; 208/756–3342). The museum will also tell you about the development of white-water transportation in the region. Today Salmon bills itself as "the white-water capital of the world."

Well, that may be a publicity tag given by self-serving outfitters. But it is true that Salmon's economy is built at least as much on outdoor recreation—rafting, fishing, hunting, and horse packing—as on the more traditional pursuits of logging and cattle ranching. The town is east-central Idaho's most important gateway to the rivers, mountains, and national forests.

Salmon's **Sacajawea Interpretive, Cultural and Education Center** (200 Main St., Salmon; 208/756–1188) honors Lemhi County's most famous historical figure, Shoshone native Sacagawea, in a visitor center, an amphitheater, and a one-mile interpretive trail. Elsewhere in this small town, a historic Episcopal church and Odd Fellows hall attract passing attention, as do several riverside bed-and-breakfast inns. The 21st-century sensibility is decidedly green; a new generation of urban refugees raise and sell their own herbs and vegetables, and gather at vegan-friendly Loryhl's Kitchen to discuss the issues of the day.

A couple of pistol-packing Challis girls. (Idaho State Historical Society)

HUNTING IN GRIZZLY COUNTRY

How much underwear should you take on a two-week hunt? One pair is sufficient. Hunters never change any of their clothes during a hunt, no matter how long they're out. If you are hunting in grizzly country, however, you may want to take a backup set of underwear, just in case. (Should you startle a sow griz with cubs, your first set of underwear may get badly shredded. That is the only reason I mention it.)

If this is your first outfitted hunt, and you have just bought a brand-new pair of cowboy boots, you may be tempted to beat up the boots so that they look well used. This can be dangerous to your health. The outfitter will look at your boots and then tell one of his wranglers, "Put Mr. Jones there on Nightmare and see if he can't get that horse tamed down a bit." Yeah, right. In truth, outfitters would never name a horse Nightmare. Their horses are all named Old Joe, Old Sam, Old Muff, Old Something. Horse names are interchangeable. It really doesn't matter what the horse is named, because horses are too dumb to know their names anyway. Wranglers use a generic name for all horses, as in "Whoa, you bleeping bleep of a bleep, whoa!

—Patrick F. McManus, *The Good Samaritan Strikes Again*, 1992

Sacagawea's **Lemhi River,** which runs more than 50 miles from the flank of the Lemhi Range, joins the main Salmon River at Salmon. The village site where Chief Cameahwait, Sacagawea's long-lost brother, welcomed the Lewis and Clark expedition in August 1805 lies on Kenny Creek, about 14 miles up Route 28 from U.S. 93. Lewis said the Indians "perfectly convinced me that we were on the waters of the Pacific Ocean" when they fed him salmon. A gravel road retraces Lewis and Clark's descent from 7,373-foot Lemhi Pass on the Continental Divide to the small town of **Tendoy,** on Route 28. The 11-mile road to the Montana state line is not well maintained, but it once served as a stage route.

Tendoy is named for a longtime chief of the Lemhi band of Shoshones whose moderate diplomacy earned the respect of both his people and the U.S. Government. During his lifetime Chief Tendoy (1834–1907) experienced

Ed Chaney and his two companions during a hunt for chukar, a partridgelike game bird.

everything from early white settlement to the coming of the motorcar. He opposed the relocation of his tribe to a reservation (it did not take place until after his death), but he kept his tribe out of destructive wars while practicing civil disobedience that would have made Thoreau proud. His hillside grave is two miles northeast of the village of Tendoy on Agency Creek, but it is on private land and cannot be visited.

The earliest Mormon settlement in Idaho—predating Franklin by five years —was established at Lemhi in May 1855. Twenty-seven missionaries of the Church of Jesus Christ of Latter-day Saints settled among the natives and built a mud fort they named for a Nephite king in the Book of Mormon. In its infancy, Lemhi had two dozen cabins. By the time Brigham Young himself visited in 1857, the missionaries had baptized more than 100 Shoshones. Young sent 58 more pioneers from Salt Lake City to bolster the settlement. The following year, however, President James Buchanan sent 2,500 troops to the region in anticipation of a rumored Mormon secession from the Union. The Shoshones, seeing an opportunity to recapture their tribal lands, raided Fort Lemhi, stole its 200 cattle, and killed two defenders. The rest of the bastion promptly pulled up stakes and abandoned the valley, never to return.

MIDDLE SALMON (MAIN FORK)

From the town of Salmon it's 21 miles to the village of North Fork, where the short **North Fork of the Salmon River** joins the main Salmon River after flowing from Lost Trail Pass on the Montana border. The 7,014-foot pass over the Bitterroot Range is just 25 miles uphill from the confluence. At North Fork the main Salmon River turns sharply west. A 32-mile road, just over half of it paved, follows the stream to Corn Creek, the favored put-in point for most rafters attempting the six-day, 79-mile run to Vinegar Creek.

Where the road ends, the vast **Frank Church–River of No Return Wilderness** begins. Larger than any other federally designated wilderness in the lower 48 states, larger even than Yellowstone National Park, this primitive region encompasses 3,678 square miles of six national forests, including much of the Salmon River and its entire Middle Fork. It honors environmental champion Frank Church, a four-term Idaho Democratic senator (1956–80) whose progressive legislation preserved more wilderness in Idaho than in any American state after Alaska and California.

Below Corn Creek, the Salmon runs past a handful of remote guest-ranch resorts, including Mackay Bar and the Shepp Ranch, accessible mainly by private plane, and the mouth of the South Fork, whose plethora of Class IV and V rapids mark it as one of the most challenging white-water streams for kayakers and rafters in North America.

Riggins Hot Springs, which bubble up beside the river 11 miles before Riggins, were considered medicinal by Nez Percé in the centuries before the white man's arrival. Later, miners used the geothermal waters to treat aches and pains. The hot springs have been privately owned since 1975, and are now a part of the Lodge at Riggins Hot Springs. *Salmon River Rd., 9 miles east of Riggins, 208/628–3785.*

The springs are accessible by road, traveling east from Riggins. They are also a turnoff point for Allison Creek Road to the site of Florence, one of Idaho's earliest and richest gold towns after the precious mineral was discovered in 1861. By the following summer more than 10,000 prospectors had established residence on the Florence Basin. The ground yielded $50,000 a day in that first full year; by the time the earth had lost its profitability, some $10 million in gold had been hauled away. By the end of the 19th century, however, Florence was already a ghost town. There is nothing to see on the site today.

LOWER SALMON (MAIN FORK)

The outfitting center of **Riggins** sits on the bank of the Salmon River where it is joined by the Little Salmon, flowing north from the New Meadows area. Named for a turn-of-the-century ferry operator and his son, a civil engineer, it is best known for its May rodeo—with a parade that shuts down Idaho's lifeline, U.S. 95—and its plethora of river guides. The town of 450 people, about halfway between Boise and Lewiston, is also headquarters for the Hells Canyon National Recreation Area.

Thirty miles north of Riggins the now-wide Salmon skirts **White Bird Hill,** site of the first battle of the 1877 Nez Percé War (see page 49), and enters its final stretch through the desolate Doumecq and Joseph Plains. This 43-mile stretch is characterized by sparse grazing land, abandoned homesteads, and little else.

MIDDLE FORK OF THE SALMON

Cutting a northward course through the heart of the Frank Church Wilderness is the Middle Fork of the Salmon River, rated by experts as one of the world's top-

(following page) The Salmon River courses through some of America's most rugged backcountry in the River of No Return Wilderness Area.

Running Tappan Falls on the Middle Fork in the River of No Return Wilderness.

10 white-water rivers. Narrower and steeper than the main Salmon, the Middle Fork demands a higher degree of rafting skill than its big brother. Rafters put in at Boundary Creek, at the end of a 23-mile Boise National Forest road off Route 21, north of Stanley. The next hundred miles to the confluence of the main Salmon pours them over a hundred rapids, many of them rated Class III and higher. They pass a handful of airstrips, Forest Service guard stations, and private ranches, but not another road. Despite the remoteness and permit restrictions, 10,000 people float the Middle Fork every year; the numbers have included the former president and first lady, Jimmy and Rosalyn Carter.

Typical of the Middle Fork are its lovely, white-sand beaches. Keep an eye out here for deer, elk, black bears, and bighorn sheep that come to the river to drink. From some of these beaches, short trails lead into gorges where archaeologists have discovered artifacts and rock paintings 8,000 years old.

Run from May to September, the Middle Fork offers plenty of challenge even to experienced rafters. There's Hells Half Mile; Velvet Falls, a deceptive hole that spans most of the river; Powerhouse Rapids, a Class IV churner; and Weber Rapids, another Class IV where the first recorded drowning in a professionally guided group occurred.

But rafters sometimes have trouble focusing on the river, with myriad other attractions such as hot springs like those at Loon Creek, which fill a log-lined pool, and Sunflower, whose springs cascade down rocks like a shower. The Middle Fork area also has hikes, to spots like Veil Falls, a sacred Native American site (well marked by ancient pictographs) with a marvelous view, as well as pioneer homesteads and gold-camp ruins. And the scenery is no less fascinating: rock columns rise to 7,000 feet above the river, and exposed granite cliffs remind many adventurers of Yosemite.

LOCAL FAVORITE PLACES TO EAT

Banks Store and Café. 7864 Rte. 55, Banks; 208/793–2617. $-$$

A standby for Payette River rafters, this café is an Idaho landmark, serving up omelets, hamburgers, and pasta dishes.

Bertram's Salmon Valley Brewery. 101 S. Andrews St., Salmon; 208/756–3391. $$

The menu at this brewpub—opened in 1998 in the century-old Redwine Building by Zimbabwean immigrants Nick and Helen Bertram—ranges from traditional pub fare like fish-and-chips and rib-eye to pasta and sushi. Try a Mt. Borah Brown Ale or Sacajawea's Stout.

Bistro 45 Wine Bar & Cafe. 1101 N. 3rd St., McCall; 208/634–4515. $-$$

Wine lovers flock to this casual spot for light dishes like salads, open-face panini sandwiches, and bowls of mussels and clams. International wines are offered by the bottle and glass, with a special emphasis on West Coast reds.

McCall Brewing Co. 807 N. Third St., McCall; 208/634–3309. $$

Handcrafted ales and stouts attract thirsty skiers and anglers to this brewpub. The menu includes aged prime rib, marinated sirloin steaks, and beer-cheese soup. Rooftop dining in summer provides views of Payette Lake.

The Mill Steaks & Spirits. 324 N. 3rd St., McCall; 208/634–7683. $$-$$$

A popular, rustic steak-house log cabin, the Mill claims the country's largest assemblage of beer taps amid its antique Western decor. The surf and turf choices include lamb chops and Alaskan king crab legs.

Seven Devils Steak House. Main St., Riggins; 208/628–3351. $-$$

Rafters and hikers appreciate the hefty cuts of beef served up at this very casual local favorite, which also offers great homemade soups and sandwiches. The building dates from the 1800s, and in the adjoining bar names of past patrons are written on the ceiling and walls.

Shady Nook. U.S. 93 N, Salmon; 208/756–4182. $$

This riverside steak-and-seafood house, established in the late 1940s, is decorated with big-game trophies, wildlife art and ranch antiques. It's best known for its charbroiled steaks, but the pan-fried Idaho trout is also excellent.

Y-Inn Cafe. 1200 N. Main St., Challis; 208/879–4426. $

Apple dumplings are a specialty at this log-cabin restaurant with friendly service and tasty burgers, open for three squares a day.

LOCAL FAVORITE PLACES TO STAY

Best Western Salmon Rapids Lodge. 110 S. Main St., Riggins; 208/628–2743 or 877/957–2743. $$$

Nestled in a canyon overlooking the confluence of the Little Salmon and Salmon rivers, this favorite accommodation of rafters and fishermen is built of pine logs and river rock. River-view and canyon-view rooms have lodge-style furnishings; there's an indoor pool and outdoor hot tub.

Greyhouse Inn Bed and Breakfast. Milepost 293, U.S. 93, 12 miles south of Salmon; 208/756–3968 or 800/348–8097. $$

Children are welcome at this country inn, built in 1894. There are four rooms in the main house, an additional carriage house, and four outlying cabins.

Hotel McCall. 1101 N. Third St., McCall; 208/634–8105. $$–$$$

This early-1900s lakefront hotel was renovated and expanded in 2007. The 12-room inn is now a charming B&B served by the hotel's original clocks and McCall's first and only elevator.

Lodge at Osprey Meadows. 311 Village Dr., Tamarack; 208/325–1000 or 866/649–6903. $$$

The first of the luxurious Tamarack Resort's accommodations, this multistory lodge overlooks an 18-hole golf course and has a pool, spa, fitness center, cross-country skiing center, and fine-dining restaurant. Rooms, many with sweeping greens views, are classically alpine-elegant.

Northwest Passage Bed & Breakfast. 201 Rio Vista, McCall; 208/634–5349. $$

The cast and crew of the 1938 movie *Northwest Passage* stayed in this beautiful pine-log inn during the filming of that classic. Moved from Payette Lake's Crystal Beach, it now has five wood-paneled rooms with fireplaces and Depression-era furnishings.

Syringa Lodge. 13 Gott La., Salmon; 208/756–4425 or 877/580–6482. $$

High on a bluff with a panoramic view of the Salmon River and adjacent Bitterroot Mountains, this spruce lodge occupies a 19-acre homestead site. Rooms are executed with near-perfect cozy rusticity.

Whitetail Club & Resort. 501 W. Lake St., McCall; 208/634–2244 or 800/647–6464. $$$

This posh golf resort spreads along the south shore of Payette Lake. Built in 1948 as the Shore Lodge, it recently become a boutique resort with a polished restaurant, a marina, and ski packages. Each of 77 elegant guest suites has mahogany furnishings and Italian linens.

NORTHERN IDAHO
THE PANHANDLE

The Idaho Panhandle juts up like a chimney from the state's southern hearth, stretching nearly 250 miles from the Salmon River to the Canadian border—but as little as 45 miles wide in the far north. Majestic mountains rise above forests of tall pines that shelter glistening lakes, rushing rivers, and abundant wildlife. Recreation abounds here, with miles of hiking and bicycling trails, world-class golf courses, and private lakeside and riverside retreats contributing to a booming tourism industry.

Once misleadingly branded by the activities of white-supremacist zealots, a small number of whom made their homes in this narrow corridor between Washington and Montana, the Idaho Panhandle is actually one of the more liberal parts of the state. Moscow is one of the most active university towns in the Pacific Northwest. The lakeside city of Coeur d'Alene has a thriving and open-minded artists' community, as well as the most creative dining scene north of Boise. A fervent campaign by animal-rights activists led to the closing in 1995 of a popular greyhound-racing track at Post Falls, and the nearby Coeur d'Alene Indian Reservation has launched the nation's largest (38-state) lottery.

Logging and mining have traditionally sustained the economy of northern Idaho, far more so than in the semi-arid southern part of the state. They have contributed to the emergence of a sectionalism so strong that many residents of the Panhandle refer to their region as "North Idaho," as if it were a separate state. Idaho's 10 northern counties fall in the Pacific Standard Time zone, while Boise and the rest of the state are on Mountain Standard Time. Economically and geographically, the Panhandle has a stronger link to Spokane, the metropolitan center of eastern Washington, than it does to Idaho's capital. Locally, eastern Washington and the Idaho Panhandle region are together referred to as the "Inland Empire."

NEZ PERCÉ COUNTRY

The thread that connects northern and southern Idaho is U.S. 95, which runs virtually the length of the state from the Treasure Valley to the border of British Columbia. Thirty miles after crossing the Salmon River at Riggins, it leaves the canyon with an arduous climb to the crest of White Bird Hill. The initial battle

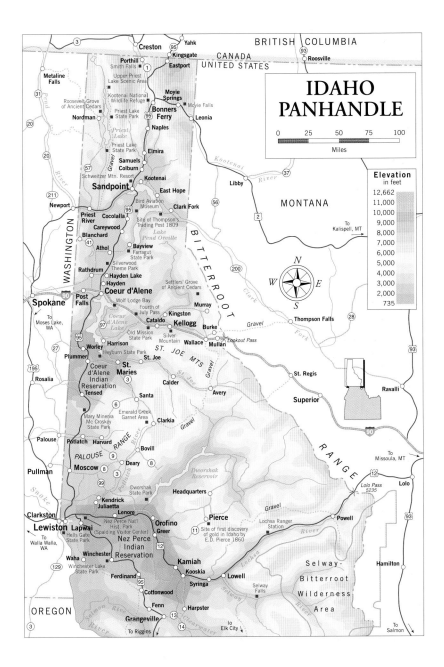

IDAHO PANHANDLE

0	25	50	75	100

Miles

Elevation
in feet

12,662	
11,000	
10,000	
9,000	
8,000	
7,000	
6,000	
5,000	
4,000	
3,000	
2,000	
735	

BRITISH COLUMBIA

CANADA
UNITED STATES

WASHINGTON

MONTANA

OREGON

Creston · Yahk
Kingsgate · Roosville
Porthill
Smith Falls · Eastport
Upper Priest
Lake Scenic Area
Metaline
Falls
Kootenai National
Wildlife Refuge
Moyie
Springs
Roosevelt Grove
of Ancient Cedars
Moyie Falls
Priest Lake
State Park
Bonners
Ferry · Leonia
Nordman
Naples
Priest
Lake
Priest Lake
State Park · Elmira
Samuels
Colburn · Kootenai
Schweitzer Mtn. Resort
Sandpoint · East Hope
Libby
Newport
Bird Aviation
Museum · Clark Fork
Priest
River · Cocolalla
Careywood
Blanchard
Site of Thompson's
Trading Post 1809
Bayview
Athol · Farragut
State Park
Silverwood
Theme Park
Rathdrum
Hayden Lake
Hayden
Coeur d'Alene
Settlers' Grove
of Ancient Cedars
Spokane
To
Moses Lake,
WA
Post
Falls
Wolf Lodge Bay
Fourth of
July Pass · Kingston · Murray
Cataldo · Kellogg
Old Mission
State Park
Silver
Mountain · Wallace · Mullan
Burke
Harrison
Heyburn State Park
Worley
Plummer · St. Joe
Coeur
d'Alene
Indian
Reservation · St.
Maries
Calder
Tensed
Santa · Avery
Rosalia
Mary Minerva
Mc Croskey
State Park
Emerald Creek
Garnet Area · Clarkia
Palouse
Potlatch · Harvard
Bovill
Pullman
Moscow · Deary
Dworshak
State Park
Dworshak
Reservoir
Headquarters
Kendrick
Juliaetta
Lenore
Clarkston
Lewiston · Lapwai
To
Walla Walla,
WA
Nez Perce Nat'l
Hist. Park
(Spalding Visitor Center)
Nez Perce
Indian
Reservation
Orofino
Greer
Pierce
Site of first discovery
of gold in Idaho by
E.D. Pierce 1860
Powell
Lochsa Ranger
Station
Waha
Winchester
Winchester Lake
State Park
Kamiah
Ferdinand
Kooskia · Lowell
Cottonwood
Syringa
Selway
Falls
Hamilton
Fenn · Harpster
Grangeville
To Riggins
To
Elk City
To
Salmon

Kootenai River

BITTERROOT

Clark Fork

Thompson Falls

St. Regis

Ravalli

Superior

RANGE

To
Missoula, MT

Lolo Pass
5235 · Lolo

Selway-
Bitterroot
Wilderness
Area

To Kalispell, MT

of the Nez Percé War was fought about halfway up the hill in June 1877, when chiefs Joseph and White Bird led their people in a crushing defeat of the U.S. cavalry. The victory was bittersweet, provoking a four-month flight toward sanctuary in Canada, which ended when they were overtaken just short of the border in Montana (*see* the History chapter). A roadside interpretive station, part of Nez Percé National Historical Park, commemorates the battle. Formerly tortuous U.S. 95 was replaced by streamlined new grade in 1975, but a portion of the old highway is now a backcountry byway with a twisting descent from the top of White Bird Hill to the sleepy village of White Bird; en route it passes numerous signs describing specific incidents of the battle.

The stark ridges of the battlefield give no hint of the striking panorama that awaits on the north side of the hill's crest. As far as the eye can see stretches the **Camas Prairie** (one of three by that name in Idaho), where the Nez Percé once harvested the prolific, starchy bulbs of the camas lily, a staple of their diet. This fertile land is now a patchwork of wheat, barley, alfalfa, pea, and rape fields framed by the Clearwater River.

Stretching from Hells Canyon to the Bitterroot Range on the Montana border, Idaho County is the state's largest—but the county seat of **Grangeville** has only 3,200 people. Timber and farming are the economic mainstays. Grangeville's greatest fame comes from the **Ray Holes Saddle Company** (213 West Main St.; 208/983–3017). Born in 1911 and raised as a wrangler, Ray Holes learned leatherwork as a teenager and spent two years in the mid-1930s apprenticed to saddle craftsmen throughout the Rockies. From 1936 to his retirement in 1972, Ray's custom riding and pack saddles with trademark flower designs earned a reputation for durability and comfort. The shop is still a family business, and the Holes name is as well known among Western horse lovers as Pendleton shirts and Tony Lama boots. There's no store here, but Holes leather products can be ordered online at www.rayholesleathercare.com.

In keeping with the horsemanship theme, Grangeville is home to Idaho's oldest rodeo, held as part of the Border Days celebration over Fourth of July weekend. At most times of the of year, however, it's a quiet town, more frequently a pit stop en route to hiking, biking, rafting, or to the Nez Percé Indian Reservation than a destination in itself.

Perhaps the most intriguing sight of the Camas Prairie is atop a hill 2.5 miles from the small town of Cottonwood. The **Monastery of St. Gertrude** was built in 1925 as a convent and priory by Benedictine sisters, the oldest of whom had immigrated from Switzerland in 1882. Built of locally quarried blue porphyry stone, the monastery's handsome, twin 97-foot towers are easily seen from the highway. An ornate chapel with a hand-carved altar and the St. Gertrude's Museum, whose collection includes a wide variety of religious and pioneer artifacts, are open to visitors. *Keuterville Rd., Cottonwood; 208/962–3224.*

Just past Cottonwood, the road enters the **Nez Percé Indian Reservation.** That the tribe has been self-governing since 1948 is somewhat paradoxical, since two-thirds of reservation lands are owned by white families who have lived here for many decades. With less than 1,400 square miles, the reservation encompasses only about 10 percent of traditional tribal lands, which extended through much of northeastern Oregon and southeastern Washington. Of the approximately 2,000 Nez Percé (Nimi'ipuu, which means simply "the people," in their own tongue) on tribal rolls today in the Northwest, 1,600 live on the reservation.

Established in 1965, ★**Nez Percé National Historical Park** comprises 38 sites in four states, 29 of them in Idaho and the remainder in Oregon, Washington, and Montana. The Spalding Visitor Center, on a ridge overlooking the Clearwater River on U.S. 95 near the tribal headquarters village of Lapwai, contains a fine collection of Nimi'ipuu artifacts—including beautiful feathered bonnets, a rare 150-year-old buffalo-hide tepee, colorful accoutrements worn by Nez Percé horses, and traditional salmon-fishing traps and spears, as well as multimedia presentations on the history and culture of the Nez Percé. *U.S. 95, 11 miles east of Lewiston; 208/843–2261.*

The visitor center is named for Henry Spalding, an irascible Presbyterian who established a mission near here in 1836, then abandoned it in 1847 after the Whitman Massacre in neighboring Washington. Nothing remains of the mission. Still visible a mile south of modern Lapwai are the parade ground and officers' quarters of old Fort Lapwai, which was maintained by the U.S. Army from 1862 to 1884, and played a key role in the Nez Percé War (*see* the History chapter). Spalding is buried in a small graveyard near the visitor center.

One mission does remain from that era. About a dozen miles south of Lapwai, Mission Creek Road branches to the south off U.S. 95 and leads 3.5 miles to the restored **St. Joseph's Mission,** the first Catholic mission to the Nez Percé, built at Chief Slickpoo's village in 1874. An orphanage school operated here from 1902 to 1968. The church is open to the public as part of Nez Percé National Historical Park. Not far distant is **Winchester Lake State Park** (Winchester Rd., Winchester; 208/924–7563), a popular year-round recreation area for fishing, cross-country skiing, and camping that is five miles in circumference.

A lush old-growth forest of red cedar in Clearwater National Forest. Idaho's wettest region, the area receives over 50 inches of rain a year in some places.

Two important trails pass through the national historic park and the Nez Percé reservation: the Nez Percé and Lewis and Clark national historical trails. The Lewis and Clark trail recalls the explorers' journey along the Clearwater River in 1805 and 1806. The Nez Percé Trail, which runs from Oregon through Idaho, Wyoming, and Montana, traces the route taken by Chief Joseph and 800 followers in their epic 1877 flight of nearly 1,500 miles with the U.S. cavalry hot on their heels. It links many of the sites of the national historical park.

The Nez Percé Indian Reservation embraces many of the towns of north-central Idaho, even those whose populations are not primarily Native American: places like the Clearwater River towns of Orofino, Kamiah, and Kooskia. These communities are accessed via U.S. 95, downhill from the visitor center and across the river. Here it merges with U.S. 12, which follows the Clearwater and its tributaries upstream all the way to Lolo Pass on the Montana border. This route parallels the Lewis and Clark Trail. Downstream 8 miles is Lewiston, the Panhandle's second-largest city.

LEWIS AND CLARK COUNTRY

The banks of the Clearwater, Idaho's largest river after the Snake and Salmon, have been inhabited for thousands of years. Near the village of Lenore, 26 miles from Lewiston, archaeological digs have revealed a community of hunters and gatherers who lived in pit houses—primitive, covered holes in the ground—about 9,000 years ago. Other excavations indicate continuous occupation in the millennia since.

The town of Orofino is nestled in the Clearwater River Canyon.

Explorers Meriwether Lewis and William Clark and their party traveled the lower Clearwater in five cedar canoes they built in the early fall of 1805. A historical marker today commemorates the site about 12 miles east of modern Lenore.

The largest town on the Clearwater is **Orofino,** nestled where Orofino Creek empties into the Clearwater about 40 miles upstream from Lewiston. About 3,250 people live in this logging community. The town is notable for the lovely Dining On The Edge restaurant, one of the finest restaurants in the entire Clearwater River valley. The 1.8-million-acre Clearwater National Forest has its headquarters on U.S. 12 just south of town. Former Idaho Governor and U.S. Secretary of the Interior Cecil Andrus worked as a logger in Orofino before launching his political career. Orofino, however, takes its name not from timber but from upcountry mining camps: *oro* is the Spanish word for gold.

Orofino Creek yielded Idaho's first discovery of the precious mineral in August 1860. The man who discovered it was one of the busiest characters in the state's history, Elias D. Pierce (1823–97).

Pierce was 15 when he left his native Ireland for Virginia. He studied and practiced law, fought in the Mexican War in 1846 (earning the rank of second

This prospectors' chow house in Thunder Mountain features a rather pricey and limited menu. (Idaho State Historical Society)

lieutenant), got engaged in Indiana in 1847, then left his fiancée waiting when he took a wagon train to the California goldfields in 1848. By 1852 he had become a successful trader, traveling up the Columbia River from Portland to trade goods for Nez Percé horses. Between 1853 and 1856 he worked as a canal engineer in northern California, where he was the first man to climb Mt. Shasta, and served as a state representative. Returning to the Northwest, he ranched near Walla Walla, where he heard stories of gold on Nez Percé lands in 1860.

About 30 prospectors followed Pierce to Orofino Creek. When the stream yielded gold dust, the party built cabins and wintered by the creek, staking their claims and laying out the townsite of Pierce City. When the snow melted in the spring of 1861, several thousand hopeful miners descended on Orofino Creek like locusts. The boom was short-lived, however, and was important mainly for inspiring other, more successful prospecting in the Idaho mountains. The Orofino gold played out within about six years, yielding $3.5 million.

Elias Pierce himself left in 1865 to become a partner in a stage line between Boise and Sacramento. When word came from Indiana that his fiancée, whom he had not seen in some two decades, was being courted by another, he raced back to the Midwest and married her. After a last prospecting trip to California, he retired with his wife and eked out a living on a veteran's pension. The town of **Pierce,** however, has survived as a logging center on the edge of Clearwater National

Forest. About 750 people live in the town today. Pierce's two-story log court-house, built in 1862, is the state's oldest government building and is maintained by the Idaho Historical Society.

Orofino is also notable as the gateway to **Dworshak State Park** with its namesake reservoir and popular campground and beach. At a height of 717 feet, Dworshak Dam is the tallest dam of its kind (straight axis, concrete gravity) in the Western Hemisphere, and the third-highest dam of any kind in the United States. Films and guided tours are offered at a visitor center six miles west of Orofino. *Freeman Creek Rd., off County Rd. P1, Clearwater; 208/476–5994*

U.S. 12 continues southeast from Orofino, up the pretty Clearwater Valley another 23 miles to Kamiah and 30 to Kooskia, before it turns sharply east. When Lewis and Clark trod this land during their cross-country return from Fort Clatsop, at the mouth of the Columbia, in 1806, they bivouacked for four weeks (May 14–June 10) at a site now called **Long Camp,** a little over a mile north of Kamiah on the east side of the Clearwater River, opposite Route 12.

Kamiah is a fine example of modern economic adaptation. A single-industry community, it was on its way to becoming a ghost town after a large lumber mill shut down in the early 1980s. Merchants then banded together to give their downtown business district a facelift to attract tourism. Today nearly every building along the three-block main street has a late-19th-century Western facade, including the city hall, library, and fire station. A town of 1,200 people, Kamiah has some quaint shops and restaurants as well as a festival calendar that includes two Nez Percé celebrations: the Mat'alyma Root Festival in May and Chief Lookingglass Days in August.

Kamiah is still within the bounds of the Nez Percé reservation. The natives will tell you, however, that they were not the first ones here: coyote and other wild creatures preceded them. Tribal myth holds that Coyote came to the Clearwater when he learned that a huge Monster was eating his fellow animals. Armed with knives, firewood, flint, and steel, he allowed himself to be swallowed by the Monster, whereupon he built a fire by the fiend's heart and began slicing away at that organ until the Monster died. As the animals that had been devoured now raced from its mouth and other cavities, Coyote dismembered the Monster and threw its body parts in all directions, creating a tribe wherever the parts landed. When Fox pointed out that there still were no people in the Clearwater and Salmon River country, Coyote squeezed the blood from the Monster's heart, its drops begetting the Nez Percé. Today the **Heart of the Monster Site,** two miles southeast of Kamiah on U.S. 12, preserves this Nez Percé creation myth and is

BEARS AND THE BEHOLDER

Black bears, such as the one pictured here, are far more common than the elusive grizzly.

In 1806, explorers Lewis and Clark, having crossed the continent to the Pacific Ocean, returned east through present-day Idaho, traversing the state from an area near Lewiston to Lolo Pass and on to Montana. Their description of the Shoshone they encountered and their notation of a hunt, is markedly different from that described by Theodore Roosevelt some 80 years later.

As Seen by Lewis and Clark

As soon as we had encamped, Tunnachemootoolt and Hohastilpilp, with about twelve of their nation, came to the opposite side and began to sing, this being the usual token of friendship on similar occasions. We sent the canoe for them, and the two chiefs came over with several of the party, among whom were the two young men who had given us the two horses in behalf of the nation. After smoking some time, Hohastilpilp presented to captain Lewis an elegant gray gelding, which he had brought for the purpose....

[Our] hunters killed some pheasants, two squirrels, and a male and a female bear, the first of which was large and fat, and of a bay colour; the second meagre, grisly, and of smaller size.

—*Meriwether Lewis, circa 1806, describing the area between modern Lewiston and Lolo Pass in the Bitterroots*

As Seen by Theodore Roosevelt

As the beast sprang out of the hollow he poised for a second on the edge of the bank to recover his balance, giving me a beautiful shot, as he stood sidewise to me; the bullet struck between the eye and ear, and he fell as if hit with a pole axe.

Immediately the Indian began jumping about the body, uttering wild yells, his usually impassive face lighted up with excitement, while the hunter and I stood at rest, leaning on our rifles and laughing. It was a strange scene, the dead bear lying in the shade of the giant hemlocks, while the fantastic-looking savage danced round him with shrill whoops, and the tall frontiersman looked quietly on.

Then we supped on sugarless tea, frying-pan bread, and quantities of bear meat, fried or roasted—and how very good it tasted only those know who have gone through much hardship and some little hunger, and have worked violently for several days without flesh food. After eating our fill we stretched ourselves around the fire; the leaping sheets of flame lighted the tree trunks round about, causing them to start out against the cavernous blackness beyond and reddened the interlacing branches that formed a canopy overhead. The Indian sat on his haunches, gazing steadily and silently into the pile of blazing logs, while the white hunter and I talked together.

—**Theodore Roosevelt,** *"Hunting in the Selkirks," 1893, Kootenai River, Northern Idaho*

Black bears, such as the one pictured here, are far more common than the elusive grizzly.

an integral part of Nez Percé National Historical Park. Locals still point out the stone mound beneath which Monster's heart and liver are buried.

Kooskia, another lumber town, nestles between the Middle Fork and South Fork rivers where they join to form the main Clearwater River. U.S. 12 follows the Middle Fork 22 miles east to tiny Lowell, then continues up the Lochsa River another 65 miles to Powell before climbing to Lolo Pass. The highway more or less parallels the Lolo Trail, the rugged route Lewis and Clark followed and on which Chief Joseph's Nez Percé fled in 1877. An old Nez Percé path linking the camas beds of the Clearwater Valley with the buffalo plains of Montana, the Lolo Trail is now a primitive dirt byway (Forest Road 500) paralleling U.S. 12 some three to 10 miles to the north. Don't tackle this route without a good four-wheel-drive vehicle and two days to travel its 90 miles.

It's best to stay on U.S. 12 to **Lolo Pass.** The important east-west highway connecting Missoula and Lewiston was completed only in 1962. Points of natural interest are everywhere; those made by human hand are few and far between. The Lochsa Ranger Station, 24 miles upstream from Lowell, has a fine small U.S. Forest Service museum. The **DeVoto Memorial Grove** of western red cedars honors conservationist Bernard DeVoto, a former *Harpers* and *Saturday Review* editor who won both a Pulitzer Prize and a National Book Award for his works on the history of the U.S. West. The Lolo Pass Visitor Center, at 5,233 feet on the Idaho-Montana border, has exhibits describing the journey of Lewis and Clark across the Bitterroots, as well as on local natural history.

The Lochsa River, which U.S. 12 follows nearly to its source, and the Selway River, which joins the Lochsa at Lowell to form the Middle Fork of the Clearwater, are both classified as "wild and scenic rivers," and are considered two of the most challenging in the state for white-water rafters and kayakers. Both have their headwaters in the **Selway-Bitterroot Wilderness Area,** a rugged, nearly impenetrable, but spectacularly beautiful region of forested mountains, steep gorges, and alpine lakes on the west slope of the Bitterroot Range.

The wilderness area has its headquarters at **Elk City,** an old gold-mining (and now a logging) town of 450 people on the South Fork of the Clearwater, some 65 miles southeast of Kooskia via Route 14. In the 1870s Elk City was perhaps the largest Chinese community in Idaho, with Asian miners outnumbering whites by about 1,500 to 12. But physical abuse and legal discrimination (U.S. law forbade aliens from owning mining land after 1887) forced the Chinese to leave their claims or suffer deportation.

SILCOTT'S FERRY, CLEARWATER RIVER, LEWISTON, IDAHO.

Before bridges were built in Idaho, hand-operated ferries made river crossings possible. (Bancroft Library, U.C. Berkeley)

LEWISTON

Largely a blue-collar city, Lewiston, with a population of 31,000, boasts Idaho's largest wood-products mill, owned by the giant Potlatch Corporation (two-hour tours are conducted at 1 PM daily); but it's also home to small Lewis-Clark State College. A pair of bridges cross the Snake to Lewiston's smaller twin city of Clarkston, Washington.

At 740 feet above sea level, the confluence of the Snake and Clearwater is the lowest point in Idaho. A 16-mile bike trail connects a series of parks at the nexus of the two rivers, popular with water-skiers and windsurfers. Lewiston's geography has blessed it with the state's longest growing season (200 days), and enabled it to nurture hundreds of different species of trees, planted by urban foresters to enhance its natural beauty.

Established in 1861 after the Pierce gold rush, Lewiston started out as a wild and woolly tent town that quickly grew to 10,000 people, and just as quickly dwindled to fewer than 400 when southern Idaho mining strikes superseded those in the Clearwater basin. The young city was designated Idaho's capital in 1863, but territorial administration moved to Boise the following year. The boomtown survived, however, as a hub for steamboat and stagecoach traffic, and later for the Union Pacific railroad.

Most of the buildings in Lewiston's **Downtown Historic District,** a recipient of thoughtful urban renewal, date from the early 20th century. In particular, **Morgans' Alley** is an architecturally delightful shopping arcade with mainly small boutiques, linking four brick buildings with arches and passageways. The Nez Percé County Historical Society has a museum in the **Luna House** (306 Third St., at C St.; 208/743–3531), built in art-deco style of the 1930s.

Lewiston's primary tourist appeal is its proximity to the lower end of Hells Canyon National Recreation Area (*see* the North-Central chapter), which starts about 30 miles south of Lewiston. Eight separate jet-boat operators run day-long and overnight excursions into the canyon. Find information at the National Park Service office on the west bank of the Snake about two-and-a-half miles south of Clarkston. **Hells Gate State Park** (Snake River Ave.; 208/799–5015), 4 miles south of Lewiston along the Snake's east shore, is the most popular departure point for jet-boat trips. In addition to its marina, the park also offers camping, fishing, hiking, and equestrian trails: you can rent mounts at the stable.

For dramatic views of Lewiston and its two rivers, forgo U.S. 95 for the old **Spiral Highway,** which climbs to the top of Lewiston Hill on the north side of

Genesee Valley Lutheran Church (above) was established in Latah County in 1878.

This 300-foot-high rail trestle, built in 1908, bridges Lawyer Canyon north of Ferdinand.

Idaho pea pickers during the Great Depression of the 1930s. (Farm Security Administration, Library of Congress)

the Clearwater. The 1917 road, a marvel of early highway engineering, climbs 2,000 feet in 9.5 miles, with 64 curves in a nearly continuous four percent grade.

MOSCOW

Even by the Spiral Highway, Moscow is barely a 45-minute drive north of Lewiston. Moscow (pronounced *moss*-koh, not *moss*-cow) sits at the heart of the rolling Palouse Hills, a unique and marvelously productive agricultural district that extends well into Washington. Up to 75 bushels per acre of soft white winter wheat are harvested in the Moscow area—the highest rate in the world. About 500 million pounds of dry peas and lentils—90 percent of the U.S. total—come each year from the Palouse.

It follows that the land-grant **University of Idaho** (UI; Third and Line Sts., Moscow; 208/885–6111)—the state's first college when it was chartered in 1889—places a priority on agricultural sciences, as well as forestry, mining, and engineering. The university enrolls about 12,500 students, many of whom share curricula (as well as social activities and athletic rivalries) with Washington State University, 10 miles across the state line in Pullman. Visitor highlights of the

UI campus include the **Kibbie Dome,** a 17,500-seat indoor stadium, and the **Shadduck Arboretum,** which displays more than 200 species of plants. Every February the UI campus hosts the four-day **Lionel Hampton–Chevron Jazz Festival,** which attracts many top jazz musicians from around the United States.

Some folks say Moscow was named for a Pennsylvania village. Others claim the town's first (1875) postmaster was such a pessimist, he compared the woes of isolation in Idaho to those of Ivan the Terrible's Russia. Be that as it may, the town has grown as an educational center, and as a hub for the district's farmers, to its modern population of more than 20,000. Main Street is a pedestrian-friendly strip of galleries and bookstores, small restaurants, and student-oriented bars and coffeehouses. The elegant **McConnell Mansion** (110 S. Adams St., 208/882–1004), open to the public, is still furnished as it was when built in 1886 by William McConnell, Idaho's first senator and third governor. At the edge of town on the Washington state line, the **Appaloosa Horse Club Museum and Heritage Center** (Rte. 8 W; 208/882–5578) honors the spotted pony so important to Nez Percé culture, and offers trail rides to visitors.

Despite its agrarian setting, Moscow offers easy access to several locations of decidedly more "backwoods" flavor. East of the college town, for instance, Routes 8 and 3 run 49 miles to Clarkia and the **Emerald Creek Garnet Area.** If you've got your heart set on finding the Gem State's state gem, the star garnet, this is where you'll have to look. (The only other place that yields this stone is in India, where the public isn't invited to dig.) Exceedingly high pressure and temperatures are required to form garnets; the four- or six-ray star effect, known as asterism, is caused by inclusions of titanium dioxide in the crystal. Most deposits are in strata just above bedrock, so you should expect to dig. Come equipped with a shovel, a bucket, a mesh screen, and rubber boots. Digging permits are issued at the site by Idaho Panhandle National Forests from Memorial Day to Labor Day only. *National Forest Rd. 447, 8 miles off Rte. 3, then a 0.5-mile walk, Clarkia; 208/245–2531.*

COEUR D'ALENE COUNTRY

The White Pine Scenic Route extends 50 miles from the turn-of-the-20th-century company town of Potlatch, on the Palouse River, to St. Maries, on the St. Joe River. The route passes one of the largest stands of old-growth western white pine in North America. One pine that took seed in the late 16th century—the time of the Spanish conquistadors—stands at the Forest Service's **Giant White Pine Campground** (Rte. 6; 208/245–2531) on Mannering Creek, just south of the

A typical farm in
the Palouse Hills
outside Moscow.

Logging and mining have been the economic mainstays of the Coeur D'Alene region since the mid-19th century. White pines have been cleared away to construct a flume for a placer mine near Murray in this photo from the 1880s. (Idaho State Historical Society)

Latah-Benewah county line; it measures six feet across and nearly 200 feet high. Trees like this one are rare, however. They were largely logged out in the late 1800s and early 1900s.

Nine miles north of the Potlatch junction, U.S. 95 crosses a saddle with a sign indicating westward-leading **Skyline Drive.** This unpaved, winding, 23-mile road leads through 5,300-acre **Mary Minerva McCroskey State Park** (Skyline Dr., Plummer; 208/686–1308), occupying a wooded ridge that is notable principally for its lack of development and its fine views across the Palouse Country. No signs announce the park, a favorite of hikers and cross-country skiers. It was a gift to the state by pharmacist Virgil McCroskey (1877–1970), who personally bought each parcel of land in the park, threaded them together with the road, and named it in honor of his pioneer mother.

Descending from McCroskey Park, U.S. 95 enters the **Coeur d'Alene Indian Reservation** (850 A St., Plummer; 208/686–1800), which encompasses about 108 square miles, including the southern half of Coeur d'Alene Lake. The Coeur d'Alene (pronounced *core* duh-*lane*) tribe didn't make a friendly impression on French-Canadian fur traders, who passed through here in the early 19th century in the wake of the Lewis and Clark expedition. Because the natives were too shrewd to swap valuable furs for cheap trinkets, the traders decided they must have "hearts of awls"—*les coeurs d'alènes.*

Today this tribe of 3,000 has lost none of its shrewdness. From its tribal offices at Worley, where a bingo parlor and a July festival have long drawn visitors, the tribe has launched a National Indian Lottery, offering players in 36 states one of the largest jackpots in the country.

Built on timber, **St. Maries** is the quintessential Idaho logging town. Its first sawmill was constructed in 1889 to process logs "driven" (floated) down the St. Joe and St. Maries rivers. Lake transportation was supplemented by rail when an extension line reached here in 1909. St. Maries was then a raucous community where loggers played as hard as they worked, cavorting in riverfront saloons and floating brothels.

Today most folks drive through St. Maries (pop. 2,600) without a second thought. But if you detour to the hilltop Woodlawn Cemetery, you may spend a sober moment at Fire Fighters' Circle, where 57 gravestones are set in a ring. Beneath each granite slab lies a man who died trying to stop the spread of the Great Idaho Fire of 1910. On both sides of the Bitterroot Range, beginning in July, hot continental winds fanned several hundred smaller blazes into a single giant inferno that raged from the Salmon River north into Canada. Many small

Tugboats are used to move logs on the St. Joe River near St. Maries.

One of the worst fire disasters in U.S. history took place in August of 1910. Half the town of Wallace was burned along with three million acres of timberland. More than 80 people, mostly firefighters, lost their lives. (Barnard-Stockbridge Collection, Univ. of Idaho Library)

towns were wiped off the map as their panicked residents fled. By the time the conflagration burned itself out at the end of August, more than 4,600 square miles in 21 national forests had been razed. Besides the loss of life, the blackened terrain invited severe erosion and infestations of harmful insects.

The U.S. Forest Service was only five years old at the time of the Great Idaho Fire, and was woefully unprepared—in terms of both manpower and equipment—to take on a blaze of this extent. Soon thereafter Congress authorized deficit funding and established rules for federal-state cooperation in firefighting. One of the few objections was raised by Idaho's Senator Weldon Heyburn, who called the fire "divine providence to get the land ready for homesteaders."

It is supreme irony that Idaho's oldest state park was named for Senator Heyburn, who vehemently opposed the national forest system and considered state parks "a subject of embarrassment." **Heyburn State Park** preserves the delta of the St. Joe River, where it enters Coeur d'Alene Lake between natural silt

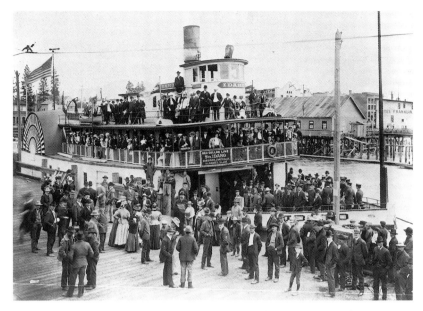

The steamboat *Idaho* at dock in Coeur D'Alene in 1907. (Idaho State Historical Society)

levees, pinching off four other lakes, now known as Benewah, Chatcolet, Hidden, and Round lakes. The lower 4 miles of the St. Joe are indeed a river within a lake. The state park, created in 1908, offers camping, fishing, and other activities, and includes a lodge, a restaurant, and summer homes. To get there, drive 12 miles southeast of Worley. *Rte. 5, St. Maries; 208/686–1308.*

National Geographic once included ★ **Coeur d'Alene Lake,** a glacial product of the Ice Age, in a list of the earth's five most beautiful lakes. Nestled in pine forest at about 2,200 feet elevation, the narrow, 23-mile-long lake is home to more osprey than any other location in the western United States; these fish hawks know good trout habitat. The tributary St. Joe River is one of the highest navigable streams in the country; indeed, lake steamers once ran upriver as far as St. Joe City, 12 miles above the town of St. Maries, itself eight miles from the head of the lake. Today cruise boats from Coeur d'Alene visit several times weekly in summer.

The modern town of **Coeur d'Alene** is at the north end of Coeur d'Alene Lake, where U.S. 95 crosses east-west I–90, a half-hour's drive east of Spokane. A rapidly growing city of 36,000, it is noted as a recreational hub and a center for artists and small-businesspeople, who have turned its main street, Sherman Avenue,

A float plane (above) is one way to view the beauty of Coeur d'Alene Lake.

into a charming strip of restaurants, galleries, and other small shops. There's no better time to visit than on the second Friday of each month, when galleries stay open late and serve wine and snacks during regular art walks. The first weekend of August, Art on the Green adds a downtown street fair.

Rising from the lakefront at the heart of the city, the **Coeur d'Alene Resort** dominates the town's tourist trade. Its 18-hole golf course is one of the most beautiful in the country, with a mobile signature hole (the 14th) anchored off-shore. A floating boardwalk, claimed to be the world's longest at 3,300 feet, sur-rounds the marina that fronts the 18-story, 338-room hotel. Regular lake cruises begin immediately west of the resort at Independence Point. Because of speedboat and other activities, including jet skiing and parasailing, the lake is not as widely embraced by anglers as other lakes in northern Idaho. *115 S. Second St., Coeur d'Alene; 208/765-4000*

Sherman Avenue was named for General William Tecumseh Sherman, the Civil War hero. In 1877, in the wake of Little Bighorn and the Nez Percé War, Sherman passed through this region scouting strategic sites to build forts to control the "Indian problem." Congress subsequently approved a 999-acre site where the Spokane River flows from Coeur d'Alene Lake, and Fort Sherman

A quieter option is to just sit by the lakeside and watch the sunset.
The Coeur d'Alene Resort on the Lake is visible in the background.

(1878–1900) was born. Part of the site is now occupied by City Park and the two-year **North Idaho College,** where the original powderhouse survives as the small Fort Sherman Museum. The former officers' quarters and chapel have been incorporated into the college. The **Museum of North Idaho** (115 Northwest Blvd.; 208/664–3448), on the edge of the original fort grounds near downtown, has extensive historical exhibits on logging, mining, steamboat travel, and the traditional culture of Panhandle tribes. It's beside City Park, which has a sandy beach (patrolled by lifeguards all summer) and expansive lawns for picnicking.

The southernmost promontory of Coeur d'Alene city is **Tubbs Hill,** a 150-acre park that environmental advocates have succeeded in keeping out of the hands of condominium developers. A 3.5-mile loop trail circles the hill, surrounded by water on three sides.

Coeur d'Alene's popularity as a visitor destination is indicated by the number of bed-and-breakfast homes in and near the city: 28 at last count (more than five times as many as Boise). The very first of them, the **Greenbriar Inn** (315 Wallace St.; 208/667–9660), is worth looking at even if you're not staying. Listed on the National Register of Historic Places, the Colonial Revival–style home, built of brick in 1908, is furnished with period antiques.

The town of **Post Falls,** seven miles west of Coeur d'Alene toward Spokane, dates from 1871, when German immigrant Frederick Post purchased a homestead site from Coeur d'Alene chief Seltice and sealed the contract with a signed pictograph painted on a granite face. This "deed" is now the focus of Treaty Rock Park. Post built a sawmill beside the picturesque Spokane River waterfall that now bears his name; today a huge Louisiana-Pacific lumber mill stands just upstream, and the waterfall—a hydroelectric generator since 1906—can be viewed from Falls Park.

The two parks are linked by a segment of the Trail of the Coeur d'Alenes known as Centennial Trail; this paved path (for nonmotorized travel) runs 73 miles from Spokane to the Silver Valley, 20 miles east of Coeur d'Alene. With much of it built on old rail sidings, it has become very popular among bicyclists, including many who train for triathlon competitions. Part of its gentle grade cuts across rivers and lakes on 36 bridges and trestles.

Wolf Lodge Bay, known for its winter gathering of bald eagles that feed on spawning kokanee salmon, is Coeur d'Alene Lake's most northeasterly reach. It is also a departure point for half-day drives around the **Lake Coeur d'Alene National Scenic Byway.** The 75-mile loop meanders down the lake's lovely eastern shoreline on Route 97, turns north on Route 3 past a chain of nine small lakes, and returns 12 miles to Wolf Lodge Bay via I–90 over Fourth of July Pass. These marshy lakes comprise a wonderful wetland habitat for mammals and birds, including the largest nesting population of wood ducks in the Pacific Northwest.

Fourth of July Pass, four miles east of Wolf Lodge Bay, got its name from Captain John Mullan, who in the pre–Civil War years directed a corps of Army engineers in building a 624-mile road from Fort Benton, Montana, on the Missouri River, to Walla Walla, Washington, near the Columbia. The party celebrated July 4, 1861, on this 3,081-foot saddle, and marked the date with an inscription still visible on a giant white-pine stump. Modern Interstate 90 parallels the Mullan Road across the Idaho Panhandle.

In the heart of the triangle sketched by the Lake Coeur d'Alene Byway—almost equidistant from I–90 and Routes 97 and 3—is one of Idaho's most delightful guest ranches. The staff at **Hidden Creek Ranch,** reached off East Blue Lake Road from Harrison, teach Native American culture and environmental sensitivity along with the more common horseback riding and wrangling.

SILVER VALLEY

East of Fourth of July Pass, I–90 enters the Silver Valley. Its scenery is surprisingly reminiscent of the Appalachian valleys of West Virginia, with high, rolling, darkly wooded mountains and canyon-bottom mining towns. But instead of coal, silver is king. More than one billion troy ounces of silver, as well as mass quantities of lead and zinc, have been extracted from the rocks of the Coeur d'Alene River valley since an 1882 gold rush first attracted miners here.

Before the miners, however, there were missionaries. A legacy of that pioneer era is the Mission of the Sacred Heart, preserved within **Old Mission State Park** (Off I–90 at Cataldo; 208/682–3814) near the township of Cataldo, 24 miles east of Coeur d'Alene. Idaho's oldest building was constructed on a hilltop between 1850 and 1853. It was designed by Jesuit Father Antonio Ravalli under the stewardship of the noted missionary Father Pierre De Smet, and built by a band of Coeur d'Alene tribesmen. Ninety feet by 40 feet, the pew-less, Greek Revival–style church still hosts services on special days, most important of which is a Feast of the Assumption pilgrimage by Coeur d'Alene Indians and subsequent pageant every August 15. A visitor center near the parking area provides a walking guide to the mission (and its original artwork), the adjacent parish house, and the cemetery. (The town of **Cataldo** was named after Father Joseph Cataldo, missionary to the Coeur d'Alenes in the mid-1860s.)

Cataldo Mission of the Sacred Heart, constructed in 1848,
is the oldest building in Idaho.

The Cataldo Mission still hosts occasional services.

Just past the Kingston-Enaville junction, the mining presence in the valley becomes blatantly obvious in the barren slopes, long subject to poisonous sulfur-dioxide emissions. It wasn't until the 1970s that the Environmental Protection Agency began enforcing strict anti-pollution measures here.

Pinehurst and Smelterville are gateways to **Kellogg,** home of the giant Bunker Hill Company. Legend has it that in 1885 a carpenter and gold prospector named Noah Kellogg, searching for his straying jackass, found the animal standing on an outcrop of a lead-and-silver lode in Milo Gulch, just south of present-day Kellogg. By 1899 conditions at the Bunker Hill and Sullivan Mining and Concentration Company were so oppressive that miners responded with violent riots. The company (which renamed itself in 1956) survived better than the unions; in the face of economic recession in the early 1980s, however, company layoffs reduced the Bunker Hill Company mine, smelter, and refinery operations to a shadow of what they had once been. Many of the old company buildings have been adapted to new uses. The Staff House, for instance, contains the **Shoshone County Mining and Smelting Museum** (820 McKinley Ave.; 208/786–4141), while another structure has been converted to a youth hostel.

Kellogg's saving grace is **Silver Mountain.** The ski-and-snowboard area has boomed since 1990, when the world's longest single-stage gondola—at 3.1 miles—began operating from just off I–90 to the upper slopes of 6,300-foot Kellogg Peak. The varied terrain suits all ability levels, and the facility has a tubing park. In keeping with its focus on recreation, the town has developed a Tyrolean atmosphere, and resort business is booming. There are new lodgings and restaurants, and condominium sales have skyrocketed in the 21st century. In summer the gondola serves sightseers, mountain bikers (this mountain is a favorite biking destination in north Idaho), and music lovers. A summer concert series brings popular jazz, rock, and blues performers to an open-air amphitheater near the gondola's upper terminal. *610 Bunker Ave., Kellogg; 208/783–1111*

Wallace's most famous one-time resident, Lana Turner, poses for this portrait with her mother in 1924. (Barnard-Stockbridge Collection, Univ. of Idaho Library)

I–90 continues through the small towns of Osburn and Silverton to ★**Wallace,** easily the most fascinating of the Silver Valley mining towns. The entire core of this town of 1,000 people has been designated a National Historic District, deservedly so for its many well-preserved, late-19th-century buildings. Wallace was incorporated in 1888, burned virtually to the ground in 1890, and was immediately rebuilt; today the main streets remain lined with brick buildings from the 1890s, as well as Victorian- and Queen Anne–style private homes.

The most impressive structure in town is the **Northern Pacific Depot Railroad Museum** (219 Sixth St.; 208/752–0111), whose chateau architecture rivals that of renowned Canadian Pacific hotels like The Empress in Victoria and the Banff Springs Hotel, on a smaller scale, of course. Built in 1891 as an elegant train station, the museum (whose collection details the district's rail history) was moved to its present location in 1986 to make room for the I–90 freeway. Until the elevated

DIRTY CLOTHES RIVER

Mullan, 6 m. (3,245 alt., 2,291 pop.), is not, as mining towns go, wholly without its prepossessing aspect. Founded in 1884 between two silver-lead mines and shaken since by strike after strike, it has managed to evade in some degree the complete and pitiless homeliness that usually falls like a blight on towns in such regions.... On the right, as the highway leaves the west end of town, is the river, but it is not the lucid stream of a mile ago. It has been diverted to the mines here, impregnated with poison, and turned free. It now looks like a river of lye, or, worse, it looks as if all the dirty clothes in the world had just been washed in it.

—*Idaho, A Guide in Word and Picture (by Vardis Fisher for the WPA)*, 1937

freeway section was completed, Wallace had the only stoplight on the interstate between Seattle and Boston. When the last pylon was set in place and traffic began to move past the city in 1988, coinciding with its 100th anniversary, something near and dear left Wallace: its ladies of easy virtue. Wallace was the last community in the United States, outside of Nevada, to permit bordellos to operate. In 1988 the federal government closed the final four. Today the **Oasis Rooms Bordello Museum** (605 Cedar St.; 208/753–0801) offers tours of one of those brothels, the furnishings of its cribs intact.

Visitors interested in silver-mining history can visit the **Wallace District Mining Museum** (511 Bank St.; 208/556–1592) to view artifacts and photographs. But for the real enthusiast, a tour of the **Sierra Silver Mine** (420 Fifth St.; 208/752–5151) is essential. After buying a ticket at the mine's downtown office, visitors board a trolley that takes them to the mine entrance, where they are fitted with hard hats. From there, they are led on an hour-long, 1,000-foot descent of a U-shaped tunnel, while a guide describes mining techniques and history. Wear sturdy walking shoes. Tours run daily in summer.

From Wallace, I–90 leads 14 miles east through Mullan, another small mining town, to the Montana border at 4,725-foot **Lookout Pass.** There's a small downhill and cross-country ski area here, and plenty of summer mountain-biking terrain. This is also a very popular venue for snowmobilers, who come from

An abandoned mine near the historic mining town of Bayhorse in Custer County.

three states and Canada in the winter.

Silver Valley adventurers might prefer to take backroads north from Wallace to a whole handful of small, off-the-beaten-track mining towns. The main street of **Burke,** which runs through a constricted gorge seven miles up Canyon Creek, once had a hotel whose residents had to close their window shutters or lose them when trains steamed past (earning it a mention in *Ripley's Believe It or Not*).

Murray, 24 miles north of Wallace over Dobson Pass on Prichard Creek, was the home of Maggie "Molly B'Damn" Hall, a good-hearted Irish saloonkeeper who favored gentlemen who sprinkled her bath with gold dust. When she died of pneumonia at the age of 35 in 1881, the entire town closed down for a day of mourning.

Several century-old buildings survive in Murray, still home to about 100 people. Also in Murray is the Sprag Pole Museum, Steak, and Rib House, which combines a 10,000-square-foot mining museum with an excellent restaurant. From Murray the dramatically beautiful Coeur d'Alene River Road crosses Thompson Pass and descends to Thompson Falls, Montana.

Star garnets, which are found only in Idaho and India, may still be unearthed by visitors to the Emerald Creek Garnet Area in Idaho Panhandle National Forest.

NORTHERN PANHANDLE

A few miles north of the city of Coeur d'Alene, a turnoff from U.S. 95 leads east two miles to **Hayden Lake,** secluded in dense woods and dotted by many gorgeous estates. A cute, eponymous lakeside village has upscale shops and fine restaurants. Due east of town is a public boat launch at Honeysuckle Beach. On the lake's southern shores, the Clark House—Idaho's priciest mansion when it was built for F. Lewis Clark in 1910—now provides luxury accommodations.

For more than 25 years, beautiful Hayden Lake was better known for the ugliness of the late Rev. Richard Butler's neo-Nazi Aryan National stronghold than as a quiet summer treat for big-city refugees. The group surrendered its 20-acre holdings in the wake of a lawsuit in 2000, and the property was burned to the ground and turned into a nameless "peace park" the following year. Today it is also used by North Idaho College for botany and ecology courses.

About 15 miles north of Hayden, **Silverwood Theme Park** focuses on transport, with barnstorming (stunt-flying) shows each evening at 6 (weather permitting), biplane and glider rides throughout the day, and an interesting aircraft museum. The park also has a train that runs nonstop around a 3.2-mile track, a

Lake Pend Oreille near Memaloose Point.

LABOR UNREST IN THE MINES

Labor unrest festered in the Coeur d'Alene district. Newly unionized hard-rock miners were frustrated when mine owners—already faced with falling silver prices and rising rail rates—responded to their demands for higher pay by cutting wages, firing union members, and hiring armed guards to protect scab laborers.

Tensions climaxed on July 11, 1892, when a gun battle and dynamite blast at the Frisco mine in Gem, near Wallace, left six dead and 25 injured. State and federal troops, who arrived with a martial law declaration, rounded up 300 miners and suspected union sympathizers and detained them in prison camps ("bullpens") for two months. Eventually, two dozen union leaders were tried and jailed in Boise.

Ironically, jail time only increased the union's strength, as its leaders devoted their captive hours to creating the Western Federation of Miners. Upon their release, they were able to convince most Coeur d'Alene district mine owners to increase their wages to union scale: $3.50 per 10-hour day.

The single largest business, the Bunker Hill and Sullivan Company, refused. On April 29, 1899, several hundred miners seized a train, loaded it with explosives, and headed for the Bunker Hill complex at Wardner, near Kellogg. Company personnel fled as angry workers aboard the "Dynamite Express" set off 3,000 pounds of dynamite and reduced the mine's concentrator and outbuildings to rubble.

Gov. Frank Steunenberg, a former printers' union member who had been elected to office with union backing, could not sanction this "Second Battle of Bunker Hill," as the miners were calling it. He requested federal troops, 800 of whom were in the valley within four days. Virtually the entire adult male population of the Coeur d'Alene area, more than 1,000 men, was herded into bullpens to be charged with conspiracy, arson, and murder. Some were held for nearly two years without trial. Thirteen were ultimately tried; 10 were convicted, fined, and imprisoned for 22 months. Martial law lasted until 1901, during which time all union miners were replaced with scabs or out-of-state immigrants. The power of the miners' union had been decimated.

But the story wasn't over yet. In late 1905, Steunenberg, now retired from public life, was assassinated when a bomb exploded at his home in Caldwell. A suspect, Harry Orchard, soon confessed to the crime and was sentenced to life in prison. In plea bargaining to avoid the gallows, Orchard (who also confessed to 17 other murders) claimed to have

Striking miners of Wallace drilling with wooden guns while incarcerated in the "bullpen" in Kellogg, 1899. (Barnard-Stockbridge Collection, Univ. of Idaho Library)

been hired by vengeful top officials of the Western Federation of Miners.

In one of the most bizarre cases in American legal history, Idaho officials sent a Pinkerton Agency detective to Denver, where, with full support of the governor of Colorado, he kidnapped union leaders William "Big Bill" Haywood and Charles Moyer, and advisor George Pettibone. The three were extradited on a special train back to Boise, where they were locked in the state penitentiary. The audacity of the action drew loud howls from civil libertarians and labor leaders and put the case in the national spotlight. The U.S. Supreme Court ruled that although the means of apprehension was illegal, the three men had no legal recourse now that they were in the custody of the state of Idaho.

The case stayed in the headlines when the first trial opened in Boise in the spring of 1907. Haywood, the most politically powerful of the accused, was defended by famed Chicago attorney Clarence Darrow and prosecuted by Idaho's newly elected U.S. senator, William E. Borah. After nearly two months of courtroom drama, it took a jury 20 hours to reach a verdict: "not guilty." Haywood was acquitted largely because the state could not produce a credible witness to corroborate Orchard's charge of union conspiracy. Pettibone was subsequently acquitted and Moyer released without trial.

Borah rode his trial prosecution to national prominence. The progressive and independent Republican senator was a fixture on Capitol Hill until his death in 1940.

LAKE. PEND D'OR E.ILLE, N.P.R.R.CROSSING LAKE,KOOTENAI CO.IDAHO.   ELLIOTT, 421 MONT.ST.

The Northern Pacific Railroad crosses Lake Pend Oreille near Sandpoint in this print from the 1880s. (Bancroft Library, U.C. Berkeley)

Victorian main street, 20 carnival rides, and the Boulder Beach Bay water park. *27843 U.S. 95 N; 208/683–3400.*

Just north of Silverwood, Route 54 heads east seven miles to **Farragut State Park** (State Hwy 54, 5 miles east of U.S. 95; 208/683–2425) at the southern tip of **Lake Pend Oreille** (pronounced "pond or-*ray*"). Not only is this lake huge in dimension, but its 1,200-foot depth is so extreme that the U.S. Navy operates a top-secret acoustic testing facility for sonar-controlled submarines from the little town of **Bayview,** just north of Farragut. (Bayview is otherwise known mainly to anglers, who use it as a base for pursuing Pend Oreille's trophy-size trout and northern pike.)

During World War II the Navy had a major inland training base where Farragut State Park now stands. The park, created in 1946 when the base was decommissioned, later became famous as a venue for national and world Scout jamborees. The visitor center displays memorabilia recalling both incarnations. Farragut Park has three miles of lakeshore and offers camping, boating, and year-round sports activities.

Dawn over rugged Idaho terrain.

The unique **Bird Aviation Museum and Invention Center** opened on a 300-acre lakeside estate near Sagle in 2007. Home to vintage aircraft, cars, motorcycles, and other machines, all in mint condition, it is owned and operated by Dr. Forrest Bird, inventor of the medical ventilator, and his wife, Dr. Pamela Bird; free tours are given by appointment. The center also has an invention camp for kids. *Bird Ranch Rd., 12 miles east of U.S. 95; 208/263–2549.*

The hub of most activity on Lake Pend Oreille is **Sandpoint,** situated at the north end of two-mile Long Bridge, which crosses the Pend Oreille River where it empties the lake. A town of about 7,000, Sandpoint is a small but thriving community of artists, excellent restaurants, and numerous outdoor attractions. The Cedar Street Bridge, a covered public market that extends over Sand Creek, has two solar-heated stories of arts-and-crafts galleries, boutiques, gift shops, and cafés. Be sure to visit the **Bonner County Historical Museum** (905 Ontario St.; 208/263–2344), which displays artifacts of the Kutenai and Kalispel tribes and of the early pioneers of the northern Panhandle.

The single biggest tourist draw in Sandpoint—with the obvious exception of the lake itself—is **Schweitzer Mountain Resort.** Idaho's second-largest ski area (after Sun Valley) dates from the mid 1960s, but only in recent years, with the construction of a luxurious overnight lodge and condominiums, has it become a destination resort. With Sandpoint served by Amtrak trains, skiers and snowboarders from east or west can disembark and be shuttled just 11 miles to this resort at the southern tip of the Selkirk Range. An average of 300 inches of snow falls every winter on Schweitzer's 2,900 acres of terrain. Eight chairlifts carry skiers up the mountain. Its 6,400-foot summit affords spectacular panoramic views across Lake Pend Oreille. There are superb expert chutes on South Ridge and the Outback Bowl, but plenty of intermediate terrain as well. Thirty-two adjacent kilometers are groomed for cross-country skiing. *Schweitzer Mountain Rd.; 208/263–9555*

In summer you can rent mountain bikes at Schweitzer. What's more, the resort is one of three local staging points (the other two are by the lake) of the annual Festival at Sandpoint. The musical event, held from mid-July through Labor Day, attracts noted performers in many popular musical genres.

East of Sandpoint, Route 200 skirts the northeastern shore of Lake Pend Oreille en route to Montana, 34 miles southeast. About halfway to the state line, the Hope Peninsula extends into the lake. It was here, in 1809, that Welsh explorer David Thompson (1770–1857), in the employ of the Hudson's Bay Company, established the first white settlement in Idaho.

North of Sandpoint, U.S. 95 continues 60 miles to the U.S.-Canada border at Kingsgate, British Columbia, en route passing through **Bonners Ferry.** Five miles from this lumber town is the **Kootenai National Wildlife Refuge** (District Rd., Bonners Ferry; 208/267–3888), a 2,774-acre wetland sanctuary for migratory birds (including the unusual tundra swan) and large mammals, sometimes including moose and black bears. Ten miles east of Bonners Ferry are **Moyie Falls,** a cascade made more impressive by its location near the Big Moyie Canyon Bridge, a quarter-mile-long span suspended 600 feet above the Moyie River.

Many of the 1,600 residents of Priest River, a town some 23 miles west of Sandpoint, are descended from Italian immigrants who came to Idaho in the 1890s as rail workers. Priest River is a junction for travelers to **Priest Lake,** the least developed—and consequently the most unspoiled—of Idaho's large lakes. But it would be untrue to call the lake undiscovered. Back in the 1920s a remarkable silent-screen actress named Nell Shipman, escaping the fervor that was

Myrtle Creek Falls near the Kootenai National Wildlife Refuge, not far from the Canadian border.

LOCAL FAVORITE PLACES TO EAT

Anytime Tavern and Grill. 1350 Main St., Lewiston; 208/746–6230. $
A true hole-in-the-wall with only four tables and a half-dozen barstools, along with a beer garden, this decades-old downtown institution is open 24 hours daily. Breakfast, including the Garbage Time omelet, is always available, and if you're really hungry you can get a two-pound hamburger.

Beverly's. The Coeur d'Alene Resort, 115 S. Second St., Coeur d'Alene; 208/765–4000. $$$
Virtually every table has a good view here, either of the lake or the display kitchen. The cooking leans to Asian fusion, with dishes like Korean short ribs and Vietnamese caramel chicken.

Capone's Pub & Grill. 751 N. Fourth St., Coeur d'Alene; 208/667–4843. $–$$
Named not for Al but for owners Tom and Teresa Capone, this sports bar has more than 40 beers on tap and a menu of soups, salads, and burgers. More than 300 antique baseball mitts hang on the walls and above the bar.

The Cedars Floating Restaurant. U.S. 95, ¼-mile south of Coeur d'Alene; 208/664–2922. $$$
Resting on floats where the Spokane River exits Lake Coeur d'Alene, this circular restaurant is approached by a footbridge or a boat dock. Diners enjoy entrées like cedar-planked salmon, pistachio halibut, or filet mignon with an apricot horseradish sauce.

Dining on the Edge. 625 Main St., Orofino; 208/476–7805. $$–$$$
Overlooking the Clearwater River, this handsome restaurant specializes in slow-roasted prime rib, marinated in herbs, and served with a half-pound of king crab legs. Large windows enable you to watch riparian wildlife.

The Historic Jameson Restaurant & Saloon. 304 Sixth St., Wallace; 208/556–6000. $$
Housed in an 1890 pool hall and brothel fully restored for the filming of *Heaven's Gate* in 1989, Jameson's has elegant Victorian decor that includes an elaborate mahogany back bar. On the menu: 32-ounce steaks, Cajun-blackened fish, and chicken dishes, pasta plates, and burgers.

Hudson's Hamburgers. 207 E. Sherman Ave., Coeur d'Alene; 208/664–5444. $
Started as a main street lunch tent in 1907, this local institution is now run by the founder's great-grandson, and the burgers are more popular than ever. The the menu is strictly classic: hamburgers, cheeseburgers, ham-and-egg sandwiches, coffee, and sodas.

Hydra. 115 S. Lake St., Sandpoint; 208/263–7123. $$–$$$
Established in 1975 in a wood-frame house beside Lake Pend Oreille, casual Hydra has a classy steak-and-seafood menu ranging from classic beef to such departures as grilled Arctic cod, lobster fettucine, and veal liver-and-onions. Local artists provide cut-glass windows and wildlife art prints.

Ivano's. 102 S. First Ave., Sandpoint; 208/263–0211. $$–$$$
Northern Italian immigrant Ivano Lippi realized a personal dream when he opened this popular restaurant in 1984. With dishes like veal Reggiano, chicken Medici, and a calamari steak, Ivano's also has seasonal outdoor dining on a garden deck and a casual wine-and-martini bar.

Macullen's. 1516 Main St., Lewiston; 208/746–3438. $$$
There's a bit of an Irish vibe at this restaurant with fine dining and a relaxed atmosphere in the low-lit basement of the late-19th-century Bollinger Plaza building. The menu is eclectic, ranging from garlicky escargots to a melt-in-your mouth Porterhouse steak to a roast duck in Asian chile sauce.

Sand Creek Grill. 105 S. First Ave., Sandpoint; 208/255–2821. $$
Perched beside Sand Creek with outdoor seating behind a century-old building, the Grill adds French-Asian flair to Northwest cuisine and decor. Inside, sit on silk cushions amid candlelit surroundings and enjoy such dishes as wild Bangkok boar, macadamia-crusted mahimahi, or chipotle-glazed Kobe meatloaf.

Veranda Restaurant. 12 Emerson La., Kellogg; 208/783–2625. $$–$$$
A lovely Victorian home decorated with European antiques, the Veranda has 12 tables for dining on an enclosed veranda. The menu is a mix of steaks, seafood, salads, and Italian cuisine. Don't miss the grilled swordfish salad or the almond-pesto salmon.

Wolf Lodge Inn. 11741 E. Frontage Rd., off I–90 Exit 22, Coeur d'Alene; 208/664–6665. $$.
This venerable steak house serves Rocky Mountain oysters (also known as fried bull testicles), beef charbroiled over tamarack wood, and not a whole lot else. It has several dining rooms in a barnlike roadhouse.

LOCAL FAVORITE PLACES TO STAY

Best Western University Inn. 1516 Pullman Rd., Moscow; 208/882–0550. $$
Just inside the Washington state line near the west end of the University of Idaho campus, this fine hotel has 173 rooms, an indoor swimming pool, and two excellent restaurants. It's the choice of virtually every college sports team that comes to play at UI.

The Clark House on Hayden Lake. 5250 E. Hayden Lake Rd., Hayden Lake; 208/772–3470. $$$
This luxury mansion, built in 1910, was masterfully restored in 1989–90 and is now a B&B and corporate retreat. Most of the 10 rooms have feather beds and lake views, some have fireplaces. There's a minimum two-night stay summer weekends. Gourmet six-course dinners are served each night.

★ **Coeur d'Alene Resort.** 115 S. Second St., Coeur d'Alene; 208/765–4000. $$$
Easily the Panhandle's number-one resort, this 18-story, 338-room lakeside hotel has a large marina, three restaurants, and a golf course whose 14th hole floats on Coeur d'Alene Lake. Rooms are contemporary and streamlined; some have fireplaces, balconies, and panoramic lake views.

The Greenbriar Inn. 315 Wallace St., Coeur d'Alene; 208/667–9660. $$$
Northern Idaho's first bed-and-breakfast is now a luxury accommodation with a restaurant, bar, and cooking classes. The Colonial Revival–style 1908 brick house is on the National Register of Historic Places.

Tinseltown even then, built a lakefront lodge and lived there from 1923 to 1926 with a 30-member production crew while filming five movies that she wrote and starred in herself. Barges and, in winter, dogsleds were used to bring provisions to the lodge. The site of Shipman's lodge is at the northern end of the 25-mile-long lake, within the Lionhead unit of **Priest Lake State Park** (Coolin Rd. 0.5 mile east of Rte. 57; 208/443–2200).

Perhaps the most pristine location in a pristine corner of the state is the **Roosevelt Grove of Ancient Cedars,** in the Granite Creek area north of the

Morning Star Lodge. 602 Bunker Ave., Kellogg; 208/783–0202. $$–$$$
This condominium resort property at the foot of Silver Mountain has a variety of lodging options, from studios with walk-out balconies to family suites with lofts and rooftop hot tubs. Ski and Stay packages are a good deal and include a free breakfast.

Red Lion Hotel Lewiston. 621 21st St., Lewiston; 208/799–1000. $$–$$$
Built on a hillside above the Clearwater River Bridge, this 182-room hotel contains a full athletic club with indoor and outdoor swimming pools, a restaurant, lounge, and the city's only microbrewery-pub, M.J. Barleyhopper's. It is easily Lewiston's best lodging option.

Selkirk Lodge at Schweitzer Mountain. 10000 Schweitzer Mountain Rd., Sandpoint; 208/265–0257. $$$
Beneath the steep gabled roof of this elegant hotel in the heart of Schweitzer Mountain Village, 11 miles from Sandpoint, are 82 rooms with alpine lodge decor. From the heated pool and three surrounding hot tubs, you can watch skiers make their last runs of the day. The Chimney Rock Grill has been honored for its fine food and wine list.

Wallace Inn. 100 Front St., Wallace; 208/752–1252. $$
This upscale motel has better-than-average rooms, a restaurant, lounge, pool, and hot tub. But the real attraction is that it's decently priced, a short walk from the historic downtown district, and close to many activities in the great outdoors of the Silver Valley.

village of Nordman. A protected area within the Idaho Panhandle National Forests since 1943, this old-growth area includes several trees whose age has been estimated at more than 2,000 years. Visitors speak of a soothing, almost spiritual feeling when they enter this ancient sanctuary. To get there, follow signs near Nordman off Route 57.

PRACTICAL INFORMATION

Note: Compass American Guides makes every effort to ensure the accuracy of its information; however, as conditions and prices change frequently, we recommend that readers also contact the local visitors bureaus for the most up-to-date information (*see* Visitor Information, below).

BUSINESS HOURS

Government and business hours (including post offices and banks) in Idaho typically are between 8 to 10 AM and 5 to 6 PM weekdays. Some major branches of banks and post offices may be open 10 to 2 on Saturday. Boutique stores and pharmacies are generally open 10 to 6 Monday to Saturday. Malls typically stay open until 9 PM Monday to Saturday, and are open 11 to 6 Sunday as well. Hours of sightseeing attractions vary, but many are open 10 to 5 Tuesday to Saturday and noon to 5 Sunday. Most are open seven days a week during summer.

Restaurants usually start serving dinner around 5:30. Many do not stay open much past 9, except in Boise and Sun Valley, where 10 may be the norm. Restaurants with lounges often open earlier for happy hour, and serve lighter meals past midnight.

CLIMATE

Between Memorial Day and Labor Day you can generally expect mild days, cool nights, and brief afternoon rainstorms anywhere north of the Snake River Plain. The mountains attract sudden thunderstorms; above timberline, even in July and August, freezing temperatures are common and surprise blizzards are not unheard of. The southern desert and lava lands, on the other hand, can be unmercifully hot and dry in summer, with midday temperatures of at least 90 degrees Fahrenheit, often over 100.

By the end of September, cooler temperatures have begun to turn the mountainside aspens yellow, red, and orange, making this a beautiful time of year to travel in much of the state. Light snows may begin to fall in October, the first heavy falls around the first of November. Ski season normally begins around Thanksgiving and runs through March, although cool springs can extend the snowy season well into April.

BEST TIMES TO VISIT

Many Idahoans consider spring their least favorite season. Snowmelt brings occasional avalanches and plenty of mud to the slopes, and cold winds keep the emerging vegetation brown. This is a good time to visit southern Idaho's Snake River Plain, before summer's heat sets in, but other areas of Idaho are best avoided at this time.

The best time to visit southern Idaho is the spring (April–June) or fall (September–October), between the dry desert heat of midsummer—when daytime temperatures may stay above 90 degrees for six straight weeks or longer—and the cold, snowy weather of the winter. The mountains, on the other hand, are most appealing in summer and winter. In summer, alpine hiking, horseback riding, and river rafting can be enjoyed; in winter, downhill and cross-country skiing.

In the Panhandle, where temperatures are milder than in the south, summer is an ideal time to visit—if you don't mind fighting crowds on the lakes.

TEMPS (F°)	AVG. JAN.		AVG. APRIL		AVG. JULY		AVG. OCT.		RECORD	
	HIGH	LOW	HIGH	LOW	HIGH	LOW	HIGH	LOW	HIGH	LOW
Boise	37	23	60	38	91	59	65	39	111	-25
Pocatello	32	15	58	30	89	54	63	35	105	-31
Sandpoint	32	19	50	32	83	48	61	35	104	-35
Sun Valley	31	1	52	22	83	38	61	23	96	-46

PRECIPITATION (INCHES)	AVG. JAN.	AVG. APRIL	AVG. JULY	AVG. OCT.	ANNUAL RAIN SNOW	
Boise	1.5	1.2	0.3	0.7	11.7	21
Pocatello	1.3	1.5	0.8	1.1	10.9	43
Sandpoint	3.8	1.9	0.7	2.5	30.6	75
Sun Valley	2.6	1.0	0.7	0.9	17.4	122

GETTING AROUND

BY AIR

Idaho is accessed by three major airports, but only one, Boise Airport (BOI), is actually in the state. Travelers to southeastern Idaho find it most convenient to fly into Salt Lake City International Airport (SLC) in Utah, which is much nearer to Pocatello (via I–15); those venturing to the Panhandle often choose to land in Spokane International Airport (GEG), Washington, less than an hour's drive west of Coeur d'Alene on I–90.

There are smaller airports serving commuter craft in Twin Falls (TWF), Pocatello (PIH), Idaho Falls (IDA), Hailey (SUN), Lewiston (LWS), and Coeur d'Alene (COE). Sun Valley travelers can fly directly into Hailey from Salt Lake City, but winter weather conditions often cause these flights to be diverted to Twin Falls or Boise.

Summer storms rake Idaho every year, especially in the mountains (above).
Fall foliage peaks during early October in the Targhee National Forest, home
to the only mature maple trees in the state.

BY CAR

The interstate highway system across southern Idaho is excellent and well maintained. I–84, which runs from Portland through Boise and Twin Falls to Salt Lake City, is the main artery. I–15, which takes travelers north from Salt Lake, through Pocatello and Idaho Falls, into Montana, extends through the southeast. The two routes are linked between Twin Falls and Pocatello by a short connector, I–86. In the northern Panhandle, I–90 runs east from Spokane, through Coeur d'Alene, into western Montana.

The north-south routes through Idaho are two-lane highways, so travel on them is not always reliable. This no doubt contributes to the sense of separation between north and south, along with the fact that they are on two different time zones, Pacific for the Panhandle, Mountain for the rest of Idaho. Mostly two-lane U.S. 95 winds its way north from Payette, on I–84 west of Boise, to the McCall area, Lewiston and Coeur d'Alene, and on to the Canadian border.

In mountainous areas, many roads lack guard rails. There's a reason for this: highway safety studies indicate fewer accidents occur where drivers are forced to exercise more caution, as on these edgy, winding routes. But beware of unpaved roads. Although many of them are wide and well graded, poor weather conditions

Spring branding time on a family ranch.

Blue camas blooming
on the Camas Prairie.

Wildflowers bloom in meadows above timberline in the Pioneer Mountains.

and heavy seasonal use can make them hazardous. Signs advise when roads are recommended for four-wheel-drive vehicles only: heed them.

In winter, mountain roads become snow-packed. Traction tires or chains are frequently required. "Studded" tires are legal in Idaho between November and April, and are a wise alternative to continually putting chains on your tires and removing them again. Also in winter, it's a good idea to travel with a shovel, blankets, and cat litter or sand (which you can spread on an icy road to help provide traction).

A couple of driving notes: Idaho is a state where you can make right turns on a red light after stopping. And it's one where you can pump your own gas. If you're looking for a gas station between 10 PM and 6 AM, your best bet is a freeway interchange.

You can get full information on statewide road conditions for Idaho at any time of year by calling 208/336–6000.

The best highway map is published annually by the State of Idaho; available free from visitor centers or from the state on request (*see* Visitor Information, below).

FESTIVALS, ANNUAL EVENTS AND RODEOS

The following listing includes leading annual festivals and rodeos in Idaho. There are many more: contact the **Idaho Travel Council,** 700 W. State St., Boise, ID 83720, 208/334–2470, for a full inventory.

JANUARY

- **Sandpoint: Winter Carnival.**
  Celebrate winter in northern Idaho with a parade, snow sculptures, Schweitzer Day, snowshoe softball, cross-country skiing, a telemark race, and more. *208/263–2161*

FEBRUARY

- **McCall: Winter Carnival.**
  An ice-sculpture contest highlights this 10-day festival that takes place the first week of February. There are also snowmobile and ski races, parades, fireworks, and an evening ball. *208/634–7631*
- **Moscow: Lionel Hampton Jazz Festival.**

Some of the world's best-known jazz musicians take part in this four-day event at the University of Idaho with competition, concerts and clinics. Last weekend in February. *208/885–6765*

MARCH

- **Pocatello: Dodge National Finals Rodeo.**
  One of the largest rodeos in the United States. Cowboys from all over the country compete in calf roping, saddle bronc, and bareback riding, steer wrestling, and bull riding. *208/233–1525*

APRIL

- **Boise: Gene Harris Jazz Festival.**
  The late Gene Harris, one of the most highly regarded jazz piano players in the world, made his lifetime home in Boise. In his memory, Boise State University launched this festival, which brings top names to Idaho's largest city. *208/426–3099*
- **Lewiston: Dogwood Festival.**
  This 10-day spring celebration features an arts-and-crafts fair, garden tours, concerts, plays, and a rodeo. *208/799–2243*
- **Riggins: Salmon River Jet Boat Races.**
  The first leg of the U.S. championship series draws entrants from as far away as New Zealand to challenge the rapids of the lower Salmon River. *208/628–3778*

MAY

- **Hagerman: Fossil Days.**
  Parade and tours of Hagerman Fossil Beds National Monument. It comes just after Western Days in nearby Twin Falls, with its chili cook-off and Old West shootout. *208/837–9131*
- **Hailey: Springfest.**
  Celebrate the onset of spring in the Sun Valley area with music, theater performances, arts and crafts, food, and more. *208/788–2700*
- **Moscow: Moscow Renaissance Fair.**
  Free concerts of medieval to modern music highlight this annual weekend show, along with period costumes (wizards, maidens, fierce dragons), jousting, and swordfights. There's also art on display and plenty of food. *208/882–1800*
- **Riggins: Rodeo.**

(top and right) Rodeos are regular summer events in towns everywhere in the state. The Oinkari Basque Dancers (above) perform at an international Basque cultural festival in Boise.

Some of Idaho's distinctive plants: lupine (top left), Indian paintbrush (top right), and hedgehog cactus (bottom).

Bitterroot (top), Western trillium (bottom left),
and long-leaved phlox (bottom right).

Wood drake duck (top left), male California quail
(top right), and chukar (bottom).

Male sage grouse (top), male mountain bluebird (bottom left),
American avocet (bottom right).

A parade kicks off this popular rodeo, held within a natural stadium framed by the steep walls of the Salmon River canyon. Locals love the cowboy breakfast, with biscuits and gravy, strong coffee, and trick roping demonstrations. *208/628–3778*

- **Wallace: Depot Days.**
Residents of the historic mining town dance in the streets during this annual fest, which has food, arts and crafts, mine tours, and old-time train rides. *208/752–0111*

JUNE

- **American Falls: Massacre Rocks Rendezvous.**
Re-creation of the 1830s meetings between mountain men and native Shoshone and Bannock tribesmen; first weekend in June at the state park. *208/548-2672*
- **Boise: River Festival.**
The year's biggest party in the state's biggest city: parades, a hot-air balloon festival, an air show, open-air concerts by national acts, and various sports events along the Boise River and its adjacent parks. *208/338–8887*
- **Burley: Idaho Regatta.**
Some 100 flat-bottom boats from all over the country compete in this Snake River speedboat festival. *208/679-4793*
- **Sandpoint: Timberfest.**
Honoring the northern Panhandle's logging industry, the timber carnival has competitions in such events as pole climbing, axe throwing, and log rolling, as well as concerts and a dance. *208/263–2161*
- **Sun Valley: Ice Show.**
Olympic medalists and champions—past shows have starred Nancy Kerrigan, Katarina Witt, Brian Boitano, and Scott Hamilton—perform at Sun Valley Resort. *208/622–2231*
- **Weiser: National Old-Time Fiddlers Contest.**
The best country fiddlers in North America compete against each other and take part in informal jam sessions during this weeklong festival. *208/549–0452*

JULY

- **Boise: Jaialdi.**
International Basque cultural festival with dancing, food, other events. Held odd-numbered years. *208/336–1540*
- **Montpelier: Oregon Trail Rendezvous Pageant.**

Experience some of the adventure and spirit reflected in pioneer diaries. Actors reenact the drama on a historic section of the Oregon Trail. *208/945–2072*

- **Nampa: Snake River Stampede and Nampa Good Old Dayz.**
  One of the most important events on the pro rodeo circuit—it's rated among the top 25 nationally—also features parades and concerts by leading country-and-western music stars. *208/466–8497*
- **Post Falls: Julyamsh Powwow.**
  Hundreds of dancers from dozens of tribes gather in the Panhandle for one of the country's largest Native American powwows. *208/773–4080*
- **Salmon: Salmon River Days.**
  Kayak and raft races on the Salmon River highlight this annual town festival, which also includes a parade and fireworks. *208/756–2100.*

AUGUST

- **Boise: Western Idaho Fair.**
  The state's largest fair features livestock and crafts exhibits, concerts by top-name entertainers, and a carnival. *208/344–7777*
- **Cataldo: Mountain Man Rendezvous and Pioneer Days.**
  Pioneer activities are re-created at Old Mission State Park. As part of the event, Coeur d'Alene tribe members attend the Coming of the Black Robes, a traditional religious ceremony honoring early missionary priests. *208/682–3814*
- **Fort Hall: Shoshone-Bannock Indian Festival.**
  Tribal members wear traditional costumes as they take part in dances, games, and time-honored arts and crafts. A highlight is the All-Indian Old Timers Rodeo. *208/238–3700*
- **Glenns Ferry: Three Island Crossing.**
  Horses, riders, and covered wagons reenact a fording of the Snake River on the Oregon Trail during this weekend-long event. There's also a parade and a barbecue. *208/366–2394*
- **Hailey: Northern Rockies Folk Festival.**
  A long weekend of outdoor concerts highlights this favorite of acoustic music lovers. There are also workshops, jam sessions, and other events. *208/788–2700*
- **Lewiston: Hot August Nights.**
  Fifties nostalgia rules the weekend in music, dancing, and a classic car cruise. *208/742–6564*
- **Rexburg: Idaho International Folk Dance Festival.**

Eight to ten days of dancing by troupes from around the world take center stage on the campus of Ricks College. *208/356–5700*

SEPTEMBER

- **Blackfoot: Eastern Idaho State Fair.**
  Enjoy a rodeo, country-and-western concerts, horse racing, a demolition derby, a tractor pull, exhibits, and a livestock show. *208/785-2483*
- **Shelley: Idaho Spud Day.**
  The potato is praised in a parade and cook-off, a yearly tradition since 1930. *208/357–7661*
- **Boise: Art in the Park.**
  A three-day juried exhibition of visual arts and accompanying music in Julia Davis Park draws an eclectic variety of creative types from all over the country. *208/345–8330*
- **Ketchum: Wagon Days.**
  A downtown procession of giant ore wagons is said to be the largest non-motorized parade in the West. Other events include concerts, a car auction, dances, and a carnival. *208/726–3423*
- **Orofino: Lumberjack Days.**
  Held together with the Clearwater County Fair, this timber-town celebration features a parade, carnival, and logging competition. *208/476-4335*

OCTOBER

- **Boise: Renaissance Faire.**
  The medieval-looking Old Idaho Penitentiary and adjacent Idaho Botanical Garden are home to this paean to the past, with plenty of music, arts, and people in odd costumes. *208/345–8330.*
- **Sandpoint: Idaho State Draft Horse and Mule Expo.**
  Horses and mules compete in numerous events ranging from driving and pulling competitions to ladies' cart races. *208/263-2161*
- **Sun Valley: Swing 'n' Dixie Jazz Jamboree.**
  More than 20 bands from around the country present four days of "trad jazz" and big-band music, along with plenty of swing and ragtime, at the Sun Valley Resort. *208/726–3423*

- **Boise: Festival of Trees.**
  The "City of Trees" celebrates Thanksgiving weekend with a display of lavishly decorated Christmas trees and holiday wreaths. *208/344–7777*
- **Preston: Idaho Festival of Lights.**
  This small town's lighting display is considered the best in the state. It's kicked off with a Veterans Day parade and continues until Christmas with parades and a big concert. *208/852–2703.*

DECEMBER

- **Sun Valley: Christmas Eve Torch Light Parade.**
  An annual Holiday Ice Show is followed by skiers carrying torches, lighting up Dollar Mountain, and a fireworks display outside the Sun Valley Lodge. *208/622–4111*

TIME

Idaho is divided between two time zones. Most of the state is within the Mountain Time Zone, but the far north—the Panhandle region, north of the Salmon River—is within the Pacific Time Zone, one hour earlier. Thus when it's noon in Boise and Pocatello, it's 11 AM in Coeur d'Alene and Lewiston.

USEFUL CONTACTS

All emergencies: 911.

GENERAL VISITOR INFORMATION

Boise Convention & Visitors Bureau. Boise Center, Front St. and Capitol Blvd., Boise; 208/344–7777 or 800/635-5240, www.boise.org.
Craters of the Moon National Monument. Rte. 20, Arco; 208/527–3257, www.nps.gov/crmo.
Hagerman Fossil Beds National Monument. 221 N. State St., Hagerman; 208/837–4793, www.nps.gov/hafo.
Idaho Falls Visitor Center. 505 Lindsay Blvd., Idaho Falls; 208/523–1010, www.idahofallschamber.com.
Idaho State Historical Museum. 610 Julia Davis Dr., Boise; 208/334-2120, www.idahohistory.net.

(top) Pack horses and trail rides in the Frank Church–River of No Return Wilderness.
(above) Rafters run Wild Sheep Rapids in Hells Canyon.

Idaho State Travel Council. 700 W. State St., Boise; 208/334–2470 or 800/847–4843 or 800/635–7820, www.visitidaho.org.

McCall Visitor Center. 102 N. Third St., McCall; 208/634–7631 or 800/260–5130, www.mccallchamber.org.

Nez Perce National Historical Park. 39063 U.S. 95, Spalding; 208/843–7001, www.nps.gov/nepe.

North Central Idaho Travel Association. 111 Main St., Ste. 120, Lewiston; 208/743–3531 or 877/364–3246, www.northcentralidaho.info.

North Idaho Tourism Alliance. 105 N. First St., Coeur d'Alene; 208/415–0105, www.visitnorthidaho.com.

Pioneer Country (Southeast Idaho) Travel Council. 430 E. Main St., Lava Hot Springs; 208/776-5221 or 888/201–1063, www.seidaho.org.

Southern Idaho Tourism. 858 Blue Lakes Blvd. N, Twin Falls; 208/733–9458 or 800/255–8946, visit southidaho.com.

Southwest Idaho Travel Association. Front St. and Capitol Blvd., Boise ; 208/344–7777 or 800/635–5240, www.swita.org.

Sun Valley/Ketchum Chamber and Visitors Bureau. 251 N. Washington St., Ketchum; 208/726–3423 or 800/634–3347, www.visitsunvalley.com.

Yellowstone/Teton Territory Travel Committee. 420 W. Fourth S, Rexburg; 208/356–5700 or 800/634-3246, www.yellowstoneteton.org.

VISITOR INFORMATION: THE OUTDOORS

Bureau of Land Management. 3948 Development Ave., Boise; 208/384–3300, www.blm.gov.

Idaho Department of Fish and Game. 600 S. Walnut St., Boise; 208/334–3700, www.fishandgame.idaho.gov.

Idaho Department of Parks and Recreation. 5657 Warm Springs Ave., Boise; 208/334–4199, www.parksandrecreation.idaho.gov.

Idaho Outfitters and Guides Association. 711 N. Fifth St., Boise; 208/342–1919 or 800/494–3246, www.ioga.org.

U.S. Forest Service. 1249 S. Vinnell Way, Boise; 208/373–4100, www.fs.fed.us.

Harvesting barley in the
shadow of the Tetons.

RECOMMENDED READING

HISTORY

Chief Joseph and the Flight of the Nez Perce: The Untold Story of an American Tragedy (2005), by Kent Nerburn. New insights on the Nez Percé War.

Fort Hall: Gateway to the Oregon Country (1963), by Frank C. Robertson. An Oregon Trail history.

Gold Camp Desperadoes (1990), by F.E. Boswell and R.S. Mather. A study of the underbelly of life in mining towns.

History of Idaho (1994), by Leonard J. Arrington. The current standard reference.

Idaho (This Land Called America) (2008), by Sheryl Peterson. A new survey of the state's history.

Idaho Entrepreneurs: Profiles in Business (1992), by Harold R. Bunderson. Includes potato king J.R. Simplot and engineer Harry Morrison.

Idaho Falls: The Untold Story of America's First Nuclear Accident (2003), by William McKeown. A recounting of a reactor explosion that took place in 1951.

The Lewis and Clark Journals: An American Epic of Discovery (2004), by Meriwether Lewis, William Clark, Members of the Corps of Discovery, and Gary E. Moulton. An abridged edition of the original three-volume, 1814 manuscript.

The Shoshoni Frontier and the Bear River Massacre (1985), by Brigham D. Madsen. A well-documented account of one of the saddest chapters in Native American history.

The Snake River: Window to the West (1991), by Tim Palmer. A cultural and economic history.

Undaunted Courage: Meriwether Lewis, Thomas Jefferson, and the Opening of the American West (1997), by Stephen E. Ambrose. The definitive history of the Lewis and Clark Expedition.

REMINISCENCES AND ESSAYS

Astoria: Or, Anecdotes of an Enterprise Beyond the Rocky Mountains (1950), by Washington Irving. Originally published in 1836. A commissioned account of early fur traders.

Fast Food Nation (2005) by Eric Schlosser. Within this muckracking investigation into fast food, Idaho potato farming (for the production of french fries) is explored in some depth.

High on the Wild with Hemingway (1968), by Lloyd Arnold. A biography of the great author as outdoorsman, with sections on his life in Ketchum. Hemingway himself never set a book in Idaho.

Idaho Snapshots (1990), by Rick Just. Vignettes about historic and contemporary Idaho.

Out West (1987), by Dayton Duncan. A modern traveler traces the route of Lewis and Clark.

Reminiscences: Incidents in the Life of a Pioneer in Oregon and Idaho (1989), by William Armistead Goulder. Originally published in 1909.

A River Went out of Eden (1992), Chana B. Cox. Eight years in the life of Salmon River homesteader Sylvan "Buckskin Billy" Hart, as written by a niece.

Thousand Pieces of Gold (1981), by Ruthanne Lum McCunn. Story of Polly Bemis, a Chinese girl sold into slavery who ended up in Idaho.

Way Out in Idaho: A Celebration of Songs and Stories (1991), by Rosalie Sorrels. Idaho's internationally renowned folk singer compiled this book of statewide tradition, including that of Native Americans and Basques.

We Sagebrush Folks (1934), by Annie Pike Greenwood. Insights into early 20th-century life on an Idaho farm.

GEOLOGY AND NATURAL HISTORY

Cadillac Desert: The American West and its Disappearing Water (1986), by Marc Reisner. The politics of water rights, still a topic of great controversy in Idaho. Reisner focused on the Colorado River but didn't ignore the Snake.

Roadside Geology of Idaho (1989), by David D. Alt and Donald W. Hyndman. An easy-to-follow survey for travelers.

The Sierra Club Guide to the Natural Areas of Idaho, Montana, and Wyoming (1988), by Jane Greverus Perry and John Perry. Detailed guide that focuses on wildlife and vegetation.

Snake Wilderness (1972), by Boyd Norton. This environmental call to action includes descriptions of the threatened wilderness in its natural and political setting.

REGIONAL FOCUS

The Henry's Fork (1991), by Charles E. Brooks. A trout fisherman's perspective.

Owyhee Trails: The West's Forgotten Corner (1973), by Mike Hanley and Ellis Lucia. A history of the three-state badlands of Idaho, Oregon and Nevada.

River of No Return (1935, reprinted in 1983), by Robert G. Bailey. Excellent early work on the Salmon River.

Secrets of the Magic Valley and Hagerman's Remarkable Horse (2002), by Todd Shallat. An account of the discovery of the world-famous fossil beds.

The Snake River Country: American Wilderness (1977), by Don Moser. Illustrated classic on Idaho's mightiest river.

Snake River of Hells Canyon (2003), by Johnny Carrey, John Carrey, and Cort Conley. A comprehensive look at the river's history and its rapids.

Snake: the Plain and Its People (1994), edited by Todd Shallat. Survey of southern Idaho's history, geology, natural history and contemporary lifestyle.

SPECIALTY GUIDEBOOKS

Flyfisher's Guide to Idaho (2002), by Ken Retallic and Rocky Barker. The ultimate guide for anglers, from novice to expert, with detailed maps.

Following the Nez Perce Trail: A Guide to the Nee-me-poo National Historic Trail with Eyewitness Accounts (2006), by Cheryl Wilfong. An essential travelogue for history buffs.

Hidden Idaho (2004), by Richard Harris. Discovering the state from highways and backroads.

Idaho for the Curious (1982), by Cort Conley. History-laden guide to Idaho, organized highway by highway. Somewhat outdated but still a good resource.

Idaho: a Guide in Word and Picture (1937), by the Federal Writer's Project. Chief editor was novelist Vardis Fisher. Offers a unique historical perspective.

Ranch Vacations (2004), by Gene Kilgore. The nations' best guest ranches.

Western Whitewater: From the Rockies to the Pacific (1994), by Jim Cassady, Bill Cross and Fryar Calhoun. Definitive volume for rafters.

FICTION AND POETRY

American Falls: Poems (1987), by Greg Keeler. Poems centered on wilderness and fishing in the West, by a Montana-based writer.

The Good Samaritan Strikes Again (1992), by Patrick G. McManus. A collection of essays and stories that have appeared in many magazines. McManus is a popular humorist who writes about nature, poking fun at the serious endeavors of hunting and fishing.

Housekeeping (2004), by Marilynne Robinson. Acclaimed novel about two sisters raised in an unconventional household in Fingerbone Lake, Idaho.

In the Wilderness: Coming of Age in Unknown Country (1996), by Kim Barnes. A Pulitzer Prize-nominated memoir about growing up in Idaho in the 1960s and '70s.

The Literature of Idaho: an Anthology (1986), by James H. Maguire.

Peace Like a River (1957), by Vardis Fisher. Perhaps Idaho's best-known novelist, Fisher was also the author of the WPA guide to Idaho.

Where the Morning Light's Still Blue: Personal Essays about Idaho (1994), edited by William Studebaker and Richard Ardinger. A collection of 35 essays and poems.

I N D E X